REPUBLICANISM IN MODERN IRELAND

Republicanism in Modern Ireland

edited by

FEARGHAL MCGARRY

* * *

UNIVERSITY COLLEGE DUBLIN PRESS

PREAS CHOLÁISTE OLLSCOILE
BHAILE ÁTHA CLIATH

First published 2003
by University College Dublin Press
Newman House, 86 St Stephen's Green
Dublin 2, Ireland
www.ucdpress.ie

ISBN 1 900621 94 0 (hardback)
1 900621 95 9 (paperback)

Cataloguing in Publication data available from the British Library

Typeset in Ireland in Plantin and Fournier
by Elaine Shiels, Bantry, Co. Cork

Text design by Lyn Davies

Index by Jane Rogers

Printed on acid-free paper in England by
MPG Books Ltd, Bodmin, Cornwall

Contents

Contents

Acknowledgements

* * *

This book originated in a conference of the same name held at the National University of Ireland, Maynooth in May 2002, which was made possible by the financial support of the Department of Modem History and the Office of Research and Graduate Studies. I am indebted to Professor Vincent Comerford, Dr Diarmaid Ferriter and Sinead McEneaney for their support in organising and running the conference. I am grateful to all who spoke at it and contributed to the discussions, in particular Professor Richard English who provided the plenary paper.

I would like to acknowledge the support of the Irish Research Council for the Humanities and Social Sciences whose Government of Ireland post-doctoral fellowship funded my research at NUI Maynooth. Dr Terence Dooley would like to acknowledge the support of the National University of Ireland which made the research and writing of his article possible. Dr Anne Dolan and Dr Brian Hanley, who hold Government of Ireland postdoctoral research fellowships, would like to acknowledge the support of the Irish Research Council for the Humanities and Social Sciences.

Finally, my thanks to Barbara Mennell, Executive Editor of UCD Press, and her team for their professionalism and support in producing this volume.

FEARGHAL McGARRY
Belfast
April 2003

Contributors to this Volume

* * *

R. VINCENT COMERFORD is Professor of Modern History at the National University of Ireland, Maynooth. His book, *Ireland*, in the series 'Inventing the Nation', is due to be published in London and New York in 2003.

ANNE DOLAN is a Government of Ireland research fellow at Trinity College, Dublin, and author of *Commemorating the Irish Civil War: History and Memory, 1923–2000* (Cambridge, 2003).

TERENCE DOOLEY is currently National University of Ireland Fellow in the Humanities, attached to the Department of Modern History, National University of Ireland, Maynooth. He is author of *The Decline of the Big House in Ireland: A Study of Irish Landed Families, 1860–1960* (Dublin, 2000).

BRIAN HANLEY is a Government of Ireland research fellow at the National University of Ireland, Maynooth. He is author of *The IRA, 1926–1936* (Dublin, 2002).

PETER HART is Chair of Irish Studies at Memorial University of Newfoundland and the author of *British Intelligence in Ireland* (Cork, 2002) and *The IRA and its Enemies* (Oxford, 1998). He is currently writing a biography of Michael Collins.

FEARGHAL MCGARRY is a lecturer in the School of History at Queen's University, Belfast. He is author of *Irish Politics and the Spanish Civil War* (Cork, 1999) and *Frank Ryan* (Dundalk, 2002). He is currently completing a biography of Eoin O'Duffy.

ANTHONY MCINTYRE is a former IRA prisoner and former member of Sinn Féin. He completed a doctoral thesis on modern Irish republicanism at Queen's University, Belfast, in 1999 and is currently a columnist for the online republican journal *The Blanket* and chairperson of the ex-prisoners group Expac.

EUGENE O'BRIEN is Head of the Department of English in Mary Immaculate College, University of Limerick. He is editor of the Contemporary Irish Writers and Filmmakers Series. His most recent books are: *Seamus Heaney: Creating Irelands of the Mind* (Dublin, 2002) and *Seamus Heaney and the Place of Writing* (Florida, 2003).

DONAL Ó DRISCEOIL lectures in History at University College Cork. His publications include *Censorship in Ireland 1939–45: Neutrality, Politics and Society* (Cork, 1996) and *Peadar O'Donnell* (Cork, 2001).

EUNAN O'HALPIN is Bank of Ireland Professor of Contemporary Irish History at Trinity College, Dublin. Amongst recent publications are *Defending Ireland: The Irish State and its Enemies since 1922* (Oxford, 1999) and (ed.) *MI5 and Ireland 1939–1945: The Official History* (Dublin, 2003). His book *British Intelligence and Ireland, 1939–1945: A Country Study* will be published by Oxford University Press in 2005.

CHAPTER I

Introduction

* * *

Fearghal McGarry

An awareness of history, and its uses, has long been a notable characteristic of modern Irish republicanism, an introspective political tradition with a marked preoccupation with the past and its own place within it. Present day republicans view the recent conflict in Northern Ireland within a tradition of armed struggle against British rule dating back to 1798. The Provisional IRA's training manual, the 'Green Book', goes further, referring to eight centuries of resistance to British oppression and explicitly stating that the organisation is fighting 'that self same war which was fought by all previous generations of Irish people'. It notes also that one of the republican movement's most important mainstays is its belief that as the direct representatives of the Dáil Éireann parliament established in 1919 'they are the legal and lawful government of the Irish Republic'.[1] Even its most outspoken critics believe that modern-day republicanism derives much of its strength from history. As John Hume observed: 'For generations our people have been reared on a notion of patriotism as fighting and dying for Ireland. The Provisional IRA are just a product of our history.'[2] The importance of history as a source of legitimacy and support is also illustrated by the role of commemoration in republican political culture. The summer pilgrimage to Wolfe Tone's grave in Bodenstown and the reading of the 1916 Proclamation outside Dublin's General Post Office every Easter remain key events in the republican calendar where important statements of policy are announced. A keen sense of history is but one of many similarities republicanism shares with its antagonist, modern Irish unionism, for which seventeenth-century sieges, eighteenth-century rebellions and the defence of a two hundred year old constitutional settlement continue to form central aspects of its political identity.

In future decades the Good Friday Agreement of 1998 will also be considered a landmark event by both political traditions, although its precise significance remains unclear at this point. For the Irish and British governments, the agreement represented an historic accommodation between both states and, more importantly, an attempted resolution of the conflict between republicanism and unionism which had fuelled three decades of conflict in Northern Ireland. Both governments assumed that 1998 would, in time, come to mark the end of physical force republicanism – or at least its marginalisation into anachronistic insignificance – some two centuries after its emergence had necessitated an earlier imperfect constitutional settlement. For the Ulster Unionist Party leader, David Trimble, the Good Friday Agreement had secured the Union (at least as long as Northern Ireland retains a unionist majority). For Sinn Féin, the agreement represented a historic compromise, albeit a merely 'transitional' one which won real influence for northern republicans pending the ultimate achievement of a united Ireland. Few observers in April 1998 predicted a smooth ride for post-Good Friday Agreement Northern Ireland but the failure to resolve decommissioning, establish an agreed police force or sustain a stable power-sharing executive some five years on was not widely envisaged. Although these issues often appear just a few choreographed moves away from resolution, the intensification of sectarianism, the decline of the political middle ground and polarisation of allegiances and the persistence of paramilitary activities remain serious obstacles in the way of peace.

But although the consequences of the Good Friday Agreement are unclear – and will remain so until the direction of the constitutional developments which will follow becomes apparent – the peace process has formed a crucial phase in the political and ideological development of the militant republican tradition of the last century. The decision to share power with unionists under devolved British rule, to decommission weapons and to end the armed campaign without securing a British commitment to a united Ireland contradict the core principles of the Provisional republican movement of the 1970s and 1980s. Together with the acknowledgement of the need for democratic consent and the accommodation of unionist concerns to achieve a united Ireland, these changes represent not so much tactical concessions as a fundamental transformation of Provisional republican ideology.[3] In the broader historical and geographical perspective of twentieth-century Irish republicanism, these changes appear less dramatic, forming part of a lengthy cycle whereby physical force republicans have periodically abandoned violent methods (which were, in any case, invariably used as armed propaganda rather than in pursuit of military victory) in exchange for actual political power. Regardless of the prevailing disillusionment with the Good Friday Agreement in republican (and, more so, unionist) circles, these changes constitute an irreversible revision of republican ideology. Within the last two decades, the characteristics which for so long defined twentieth-century militant republicanism – abstention from participation in electoral politics, refusal to acknowledge the reality of Protestant support for the Union and commitment to the use of physical force – have become increasingly anachronistic baggage willingly consigned to the past by the northern republican leadership.

Against the background of the Good Friday Agreement, and the rethinking of republican ideology which preceded it, the essays collected here examine various aspects of modern Irish republicanism in a historical context. This book originated in a conference in the National University of Ireland, Maynooth, which brought together academics from a number of disciplines and other participants from various backgrounds to consider papers on subjects ranging from Eoin MacNeill's Irish Volunteers to present-day dissident republicanism. Reflecting trends within recent academic scholarship which has developed beyond a narrow focus on political issues – be it the constitutional development of the southern state or the organisations associated with militant republicanism – the conference explored broader themes including the importance of culture, commemoration and mentalities as well as the influence of social, economic and international factors. The appeal of Irish republicanism, many of these essays would argue, is rooted in culture and identity as well as ideology and politics. It is hoped that this book reflects something of the variety of approaches and opinions on the subject evident from the conference's lively exchanges. Although a number of these essays critically assess aspects of the republican tradition and argue that republicanism should reflect its progressive ideological origins rather than its narrow nationalist past, this book is not intended to reflect any particular line of argument but rather to highlight new perspectives and explore aspects of modern republicanism which have previously received little attention.

A volume featuring analysis of republican bodies as diverse as Fianna Fáil and the Provisional IRA begs a number of questions. How much do these organisations have in common? How usefully can such disparate bodies be considered together given the vastly different social, political and economic contexts within which they have operated? The present-day Provisional IRA may regard itself as the same force which dumped arms in 1923 (an impression reinforced by popular histories presenting the organisation in this light) but the IRA of the 1930s, 1960s and 1980s mobilised distinctly different support bases in pursuit of substantially differing objectives within the radically different opportunities and constraints of their times.[4] How useful is the term republicanism as an ideological description of organisations as diverse as those considered in this book? At the heart of many of these issues lies the ideological vagueness of modern Irish republicanism, a distinctive political tradition rooted more in an incoherent blend of Fenianism, Catholic nationalism and Irish-Ireland cultural nationalism than the republican principles of the American or French revolutions. As Tom Gavin has observed, the term republicanism is generally understood in Ireland as a sort of shorthand for insurrectionist anti-British nationalism rather than any particular ideological or philosophical principles.[5] It is only in this sense, and not in any serious historical assessment of the political and social contexts within which they lived, that figures as diverse as Wolfe Tone and Patrick Pearse can be brought together in a seamless pantheon of martyrs to sustain and legitimise present day republican objectives. In reality the ideological – and actual – origins of modern Irish republicanism lie in Sinn Féin's triumph over constitutional nationalism in the years following 1916. Despite the political success of Fianna Fáil since the 1930s, it has generally been those organisations which supported physical force methods and rejected the authority of the southern state that have been regarded as holding superior claims to ownership of the republican tradition. Behind Seán Lemass's memorable admission that Fianna Fáil was a 'slightly constitutional' party was the fear of appearing a slightly republican one. Republican and constitutional politics have been popularly and instinctively understood in Ireland to occupy positions on opposing ends of the political spectrum of nationalism. The relationship between republicanism and democracy is a theme which runs through many of the essays in this volume.

An alternative defining strand of republicanism, shared by the Irish, continental and classical varieties, is the idea of active citizenship which stresses the moral duty of republicans to act in the interest of the republic. (The section of the Provisional IRA's 'Green Book' headed 'Moral Superiority' provides a concise illustration of this mindset.[6]) The not infrequent periods when republican interpretations of this duty have failed to mobilise popular enthusiasm have also contributed to republicanism's uneasy relationship with democracy. Many of these essays highlight the resulting tensions between the progressive aspects of republican ideology – a commitment to egalitarianism, anti-authoritarianism, non-sectarianism and open government – and the often exclusivist and elitist reality of the militant Irish variety. Again, one can turn to the historical origins of modern republicanism for a partial explanation of this. Since the Easter Rising, republicanism has invariably been associated with the most intransigent and uncompromising elements within nationalist politics. Until the Good Friday Agreement, militant republican organisations have repeatedly been defined and shaped by their opposition to political compromise, with the more inflexible of them generally succeeding in representing themselves as the authentic voice of republicanism.[7]

In contrast, these essays have adopted a broad definition of republicanism, inclusive of all organisations whose members have described themselves as republican. This approach is also not without problems. The term, for example, can be applied fairly indiscriminately across the entire spectrum of organisations which constituted the Irish Free State's political life. Despite naming themselves *the* republican party, Fianna Fáil's republican credentials were regarded as unimpressive by Sinn Féin legitimists and IRA militants.

All, however, were united in derision at the claims of leading figures within Fine Gael – which owed its institutional origins to pro-Treaty Sinn Féin and went on to establish the Irish Republic in 1949 – to consider themselves republicans. Even those parties which did not stand within the republican tradition – such as William Norton's Labour Party and the Communist Party of Ireland – felt it necessary to claim republican credentials in the 1930s. The very elasticity of the term would appear to limit its analytical usefulness. Twentieth-century republican organisations have been radical and conservative, bigoted and non-sectarian, left and right wing, supporters of the Soviet Union and Nazi Germany, inclusive and xenophobic, intransigent and supinely flexible. The more successful and enduring of them – such as Fianna Fáil and the IRA – have accommodated the most disparate interests and outlooks. Perhaps this too can be traced back to the emergence of Sinn Féin after the Easter Rising, a movement as adept as unionism and Redmondite nationalism at combining conflicting social and class interests. That each of the subsequent splits and schisms which constitute the institutional history of republicanism have occurred on national – and often abstract – issues has done little to alter the ideological incoherence of Irish republicanism and the political alignments of the Republic of Ireland.

The range of topics considered in the essays in this volume illustrate something of this diversity. R. V. Comerford's article traces the relationship between republicans and democracy in nineteenth-century Irish politics and offers an explanatory paradigm to account for the resilient influence of republicanism within the Irish political system. Peter Hart analyses the role played by paramilitary bodies in pushing more moderate (and representative) nationalist opinion towards violence and revolution between 1912 and 1922. Terence Dooley examines the often overlooked importance of land redistribution as a factor in the Irish revolution and its settlement. The impact of international politics and ideology on Irish republicanism is assessed in essays by Donal Ó Drisceoil and Eunan O'Halpin. Ó Drisceoil traces the ultimately limited influence of Soviet Union-inspired communism on inter-war republicanism. On the opposite end of the political spectrum, O'Halpin explores republican links with Nazi Germany through the perspective of recently released British intelligence records. Fearghal McGarry's article focuses on the range of motives underlying republican campaigns against cultural symbols of Britishness in the Irish Free State. Anne Dolan analyses the often divisive nature of republican commemoration to explore the richly textured nature of republicanism as understood and experienced by ordinary people in small towns and villages in rural Ireland. Eugene O'Brien's article provides a theoretical reading of republican texts, including the 1916 Proclamation, the Provisional IRA's 'Green Book' and recent propaganda statements by the 32 County Sovereignty Committee, in order to explore the psychological and cultural appeals of the belief system of extremist republicanism. Despite the considerable political differences between Cumann na nGaedheal, Fianna Fáil, the Official IRA and present-day Sinn Féin, Brian Hanley's article traces intriguing similarities within the discourse of these organisations when faced with difficult political compromises and criticism from more extreme quarters. Finally, Anthony McIntyre focuses on the methods of repression used within the Provisional IRA in an essay which illustrates the tensions between the progressive nature of republican discourse and the underlying realities of the internal politics of militant republicanism. McIntyre's article raises awkward questions about the corrosive double standards which have come to be applied to politics in Northern Ireland, a tendency increasingly noted by observers as diverse as unionists, dissident republicans, Tories and southern nationalists.

A number of central themes emerges from these essays: the significance of splits, schism and rivalry as a dynamic of the political culture of republicanism; the ideological incoherence, opportunism and flexibility of republican organisations; the importance of the struggle to claim political ownership of the republican tradition; the discordance between the progressive discourse of republicanism and the often intolerant nature of republican politics, activism and mentalities; the tensions between elitist violence and democratic legitimacy; and the conflict between the self-sustaining attractions of intransigent legitimism and the allure of popular support and political power. On a number of central issues such as whether to participate in political institutions previously viewed as illegitimate, the relative merits of physical force and democratic politics, and the problems of integration with political structures which fall short of expectations, republican organisations over the last century have – albeit within substantially different political contexts – been repeatedly faced by similar arguments, rhetoric and choices.

Notes

1 'The Green Book', cited in B. O'Brien, *The Long War: The IRA and Sinn Féin* (Dublin, 1999 edn), p. 401.

2 John Hume, cited in K. Toolis, *Rebel Hearts: Journeys within the IRA's Soul* (New York, 1995), p. 331.

3 See Ed Moloney, *A Secret History of the IRA* (London, 2002) for the most recent account of this process.

4 Brian Hanley, 'Change and continuity: republican thought since 1922', *The Republic* 2 (Spring/Summer 2001), pp. 92–103.

5 T. Garvin, *1922: The Birth of Irish Democracy* (Dublin, 1996), p. 11.

6 'The Green Book', cited in O'Brien, *The Long War*, p. 402.

7   One possible exception in this trend was the failure of Ruairí Ó Brádaigh's Republican Sinn Féin to make any significant inroads into Sinn Féin's support base following the 1986 split over the latter's decision to remove its ban on entering the Dáil. However, the northern leadership's strong support for the armed struggle, and dominance within the Army Council, ensured that most republicans were unlikely to have seen it as a decision taken by political moderates. There are similarities here with the inter-war IRA's low opinion of the politically intransigent but non-combatant Sinn Féin leadership of that period.

CHAPTER 2

Republicans and Democracy
in Modern Irish Politics

* * *

R. V. Comerford

The conference at which most of the papers in this volume were presented coincided with an advanced stage of the Irish general election campaign of May 2002. Insofar as the international media noticed the contest, they focused on the constituency of Kerry North where four parties were in close contention for three seats. The camera crews and commentators were rewarded with the 'shock' spectacle that made their mission worthwhile, namely the election of the Sinn Féin candidate. This was Martin Ferris, a local unemployed worker who had served some years of imprisonment on conviction for his part in a major gun running operation on behalf of the IRA in the 1980s. The impact of Ferris's election was heightened by the identity of the opponent whom he ousted, Dick Spring, whose father, Dan Spring, had represented the constituency from 1943 until succeeded by his soon to be more famous son in 1981. During a period of twenty-one years as TD for the constituency Dick Spring had become a figure of national and international stature. As leader of Labour from 1982 to 1998 he was Tánaiste for two full Dáil periods and was the strategist mainly responsible for the transformation of the presidency of Ireland, and of the image of the country, brought about by the election of Mrs Mary Robinson as president in 1990. Spring guided the party to its best ever Dáil election result in 1992 winning thirty-three seats. His subsequent agreement to join Fianna Fáil in coalition had the momentous consequence of destroying for good that particular republican party's Jacobin core-value of single-party government, which had only been dented by an arrangement with the Progressive Democrats in the period 1989–92. In a breathtaking tactical display Spring proceeded in 1994 to switch from supporting Fianna Fáil in government to an alliance with Fine Gael and Democratic Left, all the while retaining his position as Tánaiste and Minister for Foreign Affairs. He was arguably the most significant Irish politician of the

1990s and following his withdrawal to the backbenches in 1998, still only in his forties, he was accorded the status of elder statesman. His standing was epitomised by a round of golf at the famous Ballybunion course as friend and host of Bill Clinton.

The impression conveyed to the unwary TV viewer abroad of a direct contest between Ferris and Spring was, of course, misleading, since five candidates from four parties were contending for three seats, but the fact remains that the republican ex-prisoner won his seat at the expense of a patrician figure of international standing. This, however, did not mark some unprecedented development either nationally or for Kerry. Dan Spring in 1943 was an outsider working his way to a place in the political system, in his case through the trade union movement, although he was never lost for republican oratory. This essay is intended to draw attention to the extent to which, as illustrated by the case of Martin Ferris, republicanism in Ireland has proved to be a gateway to participation in the established state system, and to consider what this may illustrate about the working of democracy in the country.

Putting it another way, the intention here is to offer a contribution to the exploration of what the term republican connotes in modern Ireland. As with most other categories of political actors, the dominant discourses tend to assume that republicans are defined by adherence to a set of ideas or values, obviously in this case to be known as republicanism. This is evident from the occasional attempts to speak in general terms of the subject and also from an assessment of the unspoken assumptions of most empirical studies in the area. In Irish politico-historical studies generally, it seems fair to say, social dynamics and the push of the existential are not always given much weight, as against the claims of ideological motivation. There is, in fact, no ideal or set of ideals that defines the boundaries of Irish republicanism, past or present, much less an ideal or set of ideals that provides a self-sufficient explanation of its appeal and functions. This is not to suggest that the ideological aspect has been exhaustively explored: that is far from being the case and there is much scope for work in that vein which acknowledges its own assumptions.[1] The intention here is not to propose a replacement explanation – because there is no single explanation – but to explore another mode of explanation that may possibly provide some fresh and worthwhile perspectives.

Democracy, the other great pole of modern political aspiration and definition, connotes, like republicanism, a multitude. Depending on the range of meanings one wishes to take for each, republicanism and democracy can be compatible or not. Republicans generally insist that they are, but sometimes on the basis of decidedly limited definitions of democracy. Fearghal McGarry has cited *An Phoblacht* in 1932 castigating Eamon de Valera for having a 'false idea of democracy' because he allowed freedom of speech to the opposition.[2] Similarly, with its policy of abstention from Dáil Éireann, Sinn Féin maintained down to 1986 an attitude to the independent Irish state that rejected the right of the electorate to do wrong. The ideological basis of this stance was the theory that the rump of the pre-Treaty Dáil that continued to reject the Free State constituted the repository of national sovereignty, a function which in 1938 it had transferred, as a holy grail, to the Army Council of the IRA. For the purposes of the present exercise I am taking mutually exclusive connotations of democracy and republicanism in Ireland: democracy as non-violent, constitutional politics; and republicanism as the practice or advocacy of physical force insurgency under the banner of independence (whether the people in question do or do not have radical views about *res publica*). In the explanatory paradigm explored here, Irish republicans are excluded players threatening to disrupt a predominantly constitutional power game until such time as they decide to abide by the rules, or, alternatively, the rules are changed to admit them. Sometimes changing the rules can be slow and complicated and the outsiders may begin to play and then leave again. I am suggesting that this paradigm carries sufficient explicatory value in respect of the period from the late 1860s to the present day for it to be considered seriously.

Indeed, the first appearance of an Irish republican movement, in the 1790s, followed directly from the denial of the aspiration to admit excluded groups – especially the Roman Catholic and Presbyterian middle classes – to the political nation. The United Irishmen of the later 1790s were certainly physical force insurgents, qualifying under this and several other definitions as republicans. However, the original Society of United Irishmen was a political club formed in 1791 in a radical milieu to promote the advancement of political reform, at a time when developments in France opened up the prospect of a blissful dawn. When Britain went to war with revolutionary France in 1793 the hope of a principled new order disappeared and the United Irishmen responded by embracing conspiracy and revolution.

Daniel O'Connell, another 1790s radical, addressed the issue of exclusion in the very different circumstances of the new century and on the very different ground of the primacy of the constitution as a principle to be respected, even if some of its rules were obnoxious. His success was founded on the mobilisation of the masses to influence the deliberations of parliament (and specifically the Catholic Relief Act of 1829), an audacious innovation in the rules of constitutional politics paralleled only by the contemporary mobilisations in the United States that swept Andrew Jackson to the presidency in 1828. O'Connell incurred the deepest odium of those who equated democracy with demagoguery and saw it as the antithesis of constitutionalism, little anticipating that in a few generations the two would become synonymous in general usage. In parliament from 1829 onwards, but especially from 1835 to 1841, when he and his supporters constituted one of the factions on whose support the government of Lord Melbourne depended for a majority, O'Connell was able to act, as a successful player of the constitutional game, to promote the admission of Catholics to the spoils of power. The municipal reform act of 1840 that abolished the old corporate governments of Irish cities placed control in the hands of elected councils, thus permitting a change of control best typified by O'Connell himself becoming lord mayor of Dublin in 1841.[3]

The limitations of O'Connellite inclusion were demonstrated by the emergence of a group of middle-class intellectuals of a younger generation, the Young Irelanders as they came to be called, around the weekly *Nation*, founded in 1842. Their first problem was to achieve inclusion to the extent that their talents and dedication merited in the affairs of the movement for repeal of the union that O'Connell had launched at the beginning of the decade. Beyond that they had ambitions for the country that differed qualitatively from those of O'Connell. The hopes of the Young Irelanders were but inadequately represented by the hopeless gesture towards revolution attempted under adverse conditions and in great desperation by some of their number in July 1848.[4] This made William Smith O'Brien, John Blake Dillon and others republicans in the sense of physical force insurgents for a few days. Among the 'old fogey' element of the Young Irelanders, particularly Smith O'Brien and John Martin, one can find more definite expressions of classical republican concerns, such as resentment of standing armies, than is usual for modern Irish republicans. Both in due course refused to have anything to do with the Fenians.

Legislation on the Irish franchise in 1850 introduced a new type of voting qualification in the county constituencies that effectively extended the electorate so as to include farmers in possession of the equivalent of about fifteen acres and upwards of good land.[5] The consequence was to create a potential for popular electoral politics, something that was well in evidence in the general election of 1852 but that subsequently wilted except for occasional by-elections and some individual constituency contests at the general elections of 1855, 1859 and 1865. In the context of the United Kingdom the use of the term democracy in connection with constitutional politics becomes seriously defensible with reference to the 1860s and the campaigns of John Bright and William E. Gladstone that mobilised the nonconformist vote and created the British Liberal Party at the head of which Gladstone rose to power in the general election of 1868. Irish participation in this epiphany was sought and given, and 66 of the 105 Irish seats were won by Liberals in 1868. Indeed, one of the principal planks in Gladstone's platform in the United Kingdom as a whole was the disestablishment of the Irish state church, a commitment that he honoured with the Irish Church Act of 1869.

Simultaneously with this arrival of democracy in the United Kingdom as a whole, organised republicanism became a fixed feature of Irish life under the Fenian designation. The leadership cadres of the Irish Republican Brotherhood in Ireland and the Fenian Brotherhood in America were moved to organise in 1858 in the first instance by the conviction that an international war involving Britain was imminent, so that constitutionalism would be an irrelevance. But in any event they had already shared by 1858 in the development of a rhetoric of denunciation of parliamentary politics that focused on the political careers of John Sadleir and William Keogh who had made themselves obnoxious to some by accepting office after the general election of 1852, despite pledges to hold out for government measures which were in fact not forthcoming. Through the early and mid-1860s James Stephens employed opposition to political mobilisation as a device for maintaining his control over his followers, and for keeping them from being distracted by any alternative nationalist leadership.[6] This rhetorical posture came to form the basis of a dogmatic stance that might in subsequent decades be honoured either in the breach or in the observance.

Stephens's various bluffs having been called, he lost control of the organisation in late 1866, whereupon others attempted a rising in March 1867 that failed before gathering any worthwhile momentum. Generally relieved that the threat of revolution had not materialised, many mainstream Catholic-nationalists came within a short while to identify the now apparently innocuous Fenians as icons of nationality. Gladstone's political agents found it expedient in advance of the general election of 1868 to add amnesty for Fenian prisoners to the more conventional benefits to be expected from a Liberal victory – disestablishment, tenant right legislation and support for denominational education.

As Fenians began to regroup in 1868 they were determined to have done with the Stephens dictatorship and settled instead on government by a representative supreme council. The rigid authority exercised by Stephens was now a thing of the past and already at the general election of November 1868 in several constituencies groups of Fenians took an active part on behalf of a small number of candidates who for varying reasons attracted their support, including George Henry Moore and Richard Pigott. With an electoral system that was not corrupt but was still highly venal, those involved either as officials or agents generally expecting remuneration at every turn, a small group of highly motivated campaigners could make an impact out of all proportion to their numbers or the extent of their committed support. This is what happened with the cadres of Fenians who began to intervene in elections from 1868 onwards and made their mark at by-elections in 1869 and the early seventies, defying half-hearted expressions of disapproval by the supreme council.[7] In 1869 and early 1870 G. H. Moore made serious efforts to launch a new nationalist movement and in the process conducted negotiations with members of the Supreme Council, who were apparently quite prepared to consider adopting a supportive role.

The potential of Fenian activists was a prime consideration in the mind of Isaac Butt as he set about launching his home rule movement in May 1870. He could play to the anti-Gladstonian sentiments that they shared with the conservatives who formed the original nucleus of the Home Government Association. Butt was also able to call in a substantial personal debt of gratitude owed to him for his work in the courts on behalf of Fenian prisoners. In any event Butt secured the good will of significant Fenian interests before launching his association. Fenian cadres played a significant role in a number of the by-elections in 1871 and 1872 that established Butt's movement as an electoral success over most of the country, and led to an influx of MPs elected to support Gladstone in 1868 and now looking to what would secure their seats next time. Seeking to accommodate this new intake, mainly Catholic and moderately nationalist, in time for the next general election (which came in 1874), Butt held a conference in November 1873 at which the Home Rule League was inaugurated. Representatives attended from the IRB following an agreement that the organisation would give Butt three years in which to prove that his parliamentary movement could produce results. In the background to this development stands the new constitution adopted by the IRB in March of the same year. This acknowledged the primacy of democratic constitutionalism both de facto and de jure:

> The IRB shall await the decision of the Irish nation, as expressed by a majority of the Irish people, as to the fit hour of inaugurating a war against England, and shall, pending such an emergency, lend its support to every movement calculated to advance the cause of Irish independence consistently with the preservation of its own integrity.[8]

The IRB and individual members paid to this policy as much or as little heed as they had earlier accorded to the ban on parliamentary activity, which is to say that they invoked it when convenient and ignored it when that suited their purposes better.

By 1875 at least two members of the supreme council of the IRB, Joseph Biggar and Frank Hugh O'Donnell, were also MPs and so had sworn fealty to the queen and constitution on top of their Fenian oaths. In a celebrated instance of political gamesmanship, Biggar inaugurated a campaign of obstructionism in the Commons, finding an ally in the Home Rule member returned for Meath at a by-election in 1875, Charles Stewart Parnell. An attempt in 1876–7 to withdraw Fenians from parliamentary politics, instigated by John Devoy, then the strongman of Irish activism in America, was followed in 1878–9 by a campaign, in which Devoy was also deeply implicated, to push everyone into a united front with parliamentarians, Fenians and farmers to agitate the land question. This 'new departure', leading as it did to the land war of 1879–82, the radicalisation of the home rule party in the general election of 1880, and the rise of Parnell to a position of national leadership, is a classic instance of large scale entry of outsiders to the business of democratic politics, which are changed in the process. Partly because so many of his MPs were not from a propertied or legal background and so could not support themselves at Westminster from their own resources, as members had hitherto been expected to do, Parnell was driven to create a mechanism for funding party members, which in turn made possible a new kind of party discipline. The rules were being rewritten. Although fractured by the crisis over Parnell's leadership in 1889–91, the parliamentary party created in the 1880s through the incorporation of activists from previously unrepresented regions of the socio-economic spectrum, many of them Fenians or ex-Fenians, survived for more than thirty years, becoming in that time the epitome of constitutional propriety.

The Fenian role in political life in the later nineteenth century cannot be defined solely in terms of membership of an organisation. From the later 1860s identification with Fenianism was an option available to almost any young Irish Catholic man (and also to some Protestants), in the towns in the first instance but increasingly in every rural parish also, particularly as associational life in general began to flourish for the population at large in the later decades of the century. The Fenian oath was taken before one witness and offered a rite of passage to the sense of national fellowship. As a matter of course, the swearing was not formally recorded. As with most youthful pledge-taking, the majority of sworn Fenians seem to have returned more or less quickly to the compromises of ordinary life (many no doubt repented at their next annual or monthly sacramental confession), while a minority developed a more long-term commitment represented by affiliation to the IRB. Judgement of this can only be impressionistic, but it seems fair to say that, if all those who took the Fenian oath had joined the organisation and remained, it would have been an enormous body by the end of the century. The intangibility of the pledge issue is strikingly illustrated by the fact that Patrick Maume has been able to make a plausible case for the suggestion that Parnell was sworn in as a Fenian following his release from Kilmainham in May 1882, and that this happened in what would seem 120 years later a most improbable choice for a discreet tryst, the Library of Trinity College, Dublin.[9] If this did indeed happen, then there is every reason to surmise that Parnell may have allowed the oath to be administered to him on a number of earlier occasions by Fenians whose confidence he needed to secure. It may be of some significance in this context that there remains an element of mystery about what precisely transpired between Parnell, Davitt and Devoy in the preparation of the 'new departure'.[10] Regardless of the very particular case of Parnell, Fenian oath-taking followed by conformity to conventional norms of politics was a typical mode of political being in Ireland for forty or more years before the Great War.

Although William Butler Yeats cannot easily be cited as typical in many aspects of life, he is a prime instance of someone who in early manhood sought assurance of his place in the scheme of things Irish by taking the Fenian oath, but subsequently allowed circumstances and calculation of advantage to dictate the nature, extent and level of his patriotic commitment. Although Fenianism/republicanism flourished among the devotees of the cultural nationalism of the period from the mid-1880s onwards, such as Yeats, it was not by any means a mandatory or universal requirement for belonging to the fellowship of the revival. Nevertheless, when this generation came to provide from among its ranks a cadre of political activists, they defined themselves in the main as republicans and the republic declared at Easter 1916 became their ideological lodestar. Under the banner of Sinn Féin they routed the Irish Parliamentary Party at the general election of 1918 and this victory was widely interpreted as popular endorsement of the republican ideal.[11] Republicanism in the sense of physical force insurgency had achieved its apotheosis at Easter Week and was revived in 1919 with the Irish Volunteers, soon generally known as the IRA, embarking on a guerrilla campaign against the forces of the crown. Whether Ireland would have evolved as an independent state without the invoking of arms is an endlessly debatable question. What is certain is that the resort to armed insurgency, in 1916 and 1919–21, was what determined much of the detail of independence as it actually came to pass, including the personnel of the new regime. The guardians of democracy in the newly formed Irish Free State of 1922 were from among the republicans of a short time before.

The series of metamorphoses from republicanism to democracy in the generations up to and including the transition to independence might be less remarkable were it not for the continuation of the pattern in the generations that followed. Those who resisted the settlement of 1921–2 in the civil war of 1922–3 were assertively republican in a way not seen before in Ireland because their main pretext for opposing the new order was that it amounted to betrayal of the republic. The subsequent place of the concept of the republic in the constitutional history of the independent state is a study in itself. The 1937 constitution is widely perceived as having instituted a republic de facto, while avoiding the use of the term. Without any change in the constitution, the state was declared by an act of 1949 to be a republic. The arguments in favour of the change put forward by the Taoiseach of the day, John A. Costello, included the very practical consideration that this would help to reduce uncertainty about the effective territorial reach of certain insurance contracts.[12] In independent Ireland the republic as a form of government had ceased to be an issue of contention between political parties. But insurgent republicanism was a different matter.

Fianna Fáil attempted to nail down the magic by adopting a subtitle in the second official language: 'the republican party'. This particular gambit failed

and irredentist sentiment remained as an enduring source of emotive justification of insurgency or a stance favourable to it. Fianna Fáil succeeded in
going from foundation in 1926 to the democratic achievement of power in
1932 because it placed itself on a multi-plank platform that appealed
successfully to a range of social and economic discontents, and won the votes
of many who in 1922 had not opposed the Treaty and still in 1932 cared little
about it one way or the other. However, the party was the creation of de
Valera and of a cadre of those who like him had taken the republican side in
the civil war and had come by 1926 to the view that they lived in a polity where
democracy was the only available route to power. The accession of Fianna Fáil
to office in 1932 and the party's subsequent tending of democracy is perhaps
the most striking instance of the transformation of republicans into mainstream
players of the constitutional game, but it was to be by no means the last.

Seán MacBride (1904–88), the son of Maud Gonne and Major John
MacBride, was a republican who opposed both the establishment of the Irish
Free State and the Fianna Fáil demarche of 1926–32. Through the twenties
and thirties he filled various high-ranking roles in the IRA. Qualifying as a
barrister, he became the regular defence counsel for republican defendants in
the non-jury courts in the early forties.[13] This transition can be seen as a
marking a half-way stage on the road to participation in democratic politics.
In 1946 he founded Clann na Poblachta, a political party designed to attract
republicans and, indeed, others alienated from Fianna Fáil after that party's
decade and a half of ascendancy. In the run up to the general election of 1948
MacBride and his party brought a sense of renewal to a political system that
was beginning to look and feel jaded. While the total of ten seats it actually
achieved in 1948 disappointed expectations, Clann na Poblachta became a
key component of the inter-party government that displaced Fianna Fáil from
1948 to 1951. As Minister for External Affairs in the inter-party government
MacBride obtained access to the world stage and set out on the road that
brought him the Nobel peace prize and the Lenin peace prize in the 1970s.

Crisis in Northern Ireland produced in 1970 a split within Sinn Féin and
the IRA between advocates of the old intransigency (the Provisionals, as they
became) and a leadership that was attracted to a more nuanced (and to a
considerable extent Marxist) analysis of the world around them. The latter,
successively as Official Sinn Féin, Sinn Féin: the Workers' Party, the Workers'
Party, New Agenda, and Democratic Left became wholehearted practitioners
of electoral politics, a process that ultimately led to participation as one of
three parties in the rainbow government that held office in Dublin from 1994
to 1997. The party's leader in government was Proinsias de Rossa who gave an
impressive performance as Minister of Social Welfare. Having been interned
without trial in the period 1956–9 as a suspected IRA activist, de Rossa is the
epitome of the paradigm being investigated here. He subsequently crowned

his political career by overseeing the amalgamation of Democratic Left with the oldest democratic party in the state, the Labour Party, of which he is currently president, in addition to being one of its elected members of the European Parliament.

Democracy, as currently understood, is not a single entity but a congeries of arrangements needed to maintain consensus government in the conditions of a society in which individual rights carry substantial weight. One of these necessary arrangements is the opportunity for individuals to attain positions of influence that accord with their abilities and ambitions. The success of democracy in independent Ireland has been predicated on the relative openness of the political system to ambitious individuals without inherited advantages, and this is a success story that began long before independence. (This openness is not at all incompatible with the creation of political dynasties, although the signs are that these rarely survive beyond the second generation.) There have been various avenues of access to political power in Ireland for those born outside the ruling elites, most of them – such as the professions, trade unionism or sport – commonly occurring in the same capacity in other democracies.

Physical force insurgency, especially as a recurrent phenomenon over nearly a century and a half as in the Irish case, is a less common avenue, and it calls for some attempt at explanation. The existence of a continuing stimulus to nationalism and irredentism in the shape of British control of all or (since 1922) part of the country is not the point: one of the things to be explained is why nationalism and irredentism for so many took the form of conspiratorial commitment to insurgency, given that for most of the period in question there was no imminent crisis such as would make insurgency feasible, constantly eager though Fenian leaders were to descry such a crisis. Nationalism/irredentism took the specific form of Fenianism/republicanism for many Irishmen in the second half of the nineteenth century in a context in which societal factors favoured this.

The structural characteristics of Roman Catholicism may be a factor here. There were, of course, always some Protestant Fenians but as a social phenomenon Fenianism has to be related to the Catholic collectivity. It is suggestive, if nothing else, that at the end of the 1850s as Fenianism first took root elsewhere, among the Presbyterians of the north-east the 'great revival' of 1859 was under way. Nothing more than coincidence can be safely read into the timing but the possibly equivalent roles of republicanism among Catholics and enthusiastic religion among Protestants deserve some consideration. Following its early- and mid-nineteenth-century consolidation, the Roman Catholic Church in Ireland was a particularly monolithic institution at national and parochial levels with the parish priest cast in the role of guardian of a system of social control. De facto, the main outlet available over much of the land for the inevitable resentment bred by such social control was provided by the fellowship of those who had sworn the Fenian oath. The dissenting and fissiparous aspects of Protestantism, displayed, for example, in revivalism, and typified by the proliferation of late nineteenth-century worshipping communities and church buildings in Belfast and Dublin, provided safe-guards against clerical domination of the Roman Catholic type. Rome's post-enlightenment outlawing of oath-bound societies succeeded in Ireland to the extent of rendering the Freemasons alien and untouchable in the eyes of the Catholics at a time when in England and among Irish Protestants that body was a part of the social fabric. By contrast ecclesiastical condemnation had succeeded in making Fenian membership in Irish Catholic eyes to be an anti-clerical act but not a betrayal of the collectivity. Fenianism was one of the most universally occurring associational movements throughout the land, and among the Irish abroad. Having been apotheosised in the second decade of the twentieth century as republicanism, it retained in Ireland, in the IRA more than in Sinn Féin, both social function and revolutionary import. Indeed, it provided – from James Connolly and the Irish Citizen Army in 1916, to the Republican Congress of 1934 to the Marxist turn of the 1960s – the venue for the socialist revolutionary challenge otherwise so notably absent in twentieth-century Ireland.[14]

Looking at the twentieth century, there is some irony in the fact that, while independent Ireland developed the British constitutional/democratic inheri-tance with considerable success, 'British' Northern Ireland had a much less happy experience in this respect. Indeed, it can be argued with some conviction that the unionist resistance to Home Rule that led to partition was the most devastating blow struck against constitutional democracy in modern Ireland or Britain, the most notorious case of running off the pitch with the ball when losing in the game, involving as it did a rejection of the law as solemnly enacted by parliament. As against this, it might be argued that the proposal for Home Rule failed to meet one of the other rules of the demo-cratic game, namely that provision should be made for minorities. It was in precisely this respect that the state of Northern Ireland in its turn failed the test of democracy as the Catholic/nationalist minority, finding itself in a political set-up that it had not bargained for in the first place, was not given the oppor-tunity to look to its interests. The concomitant of this was that individual Catholics had no opportunity to climb to the heights within the political system and scarcely any better hope in any area of public service. If republicanism had survived alongside a developing democracy since the 1860s, and continued to do so in the south, it was scarcely surprising that it survived among the nationalists of Northern Ireland, albeit for much of the time as an adjunct of the movement in the south.

Physical force insurgency was by any criterion an inappropriate contribution to the movement for change in Northern Ireland that was sparked in the mid-1960s by the civil rights movement in the USA and by the general vindication of individual rights with which that decade is associated. Obvious leaders for the movement were to hand in Northern Ireland in the persons of Catholics who had achieved advanced education as a consequence of post-Second World War meritocratic reform, an elite typified by John Hume. But it was not only Catholic teachers with the ambition to make a mark on the world who saw the inappropriateness of violence: as we have seen above the majority of those in the IRA and Sinn Féin had the same conviction. This is not the place to look in detail at the emergence of the Provisional republican movement, but it is clear that it was made possible by the inability of the regime in Northern Ireland to secure democracy by responding promptly and appropriately to the civil rights case. This in turn was due not to unwillingness on the part of Terence O'Neill as prime minister of Northern Ireland, but to his inability to win the support of the unionist collectivity as a whole for change.

The problem was that the political system in Northern Ireland had failed to provide outlets for the naturally and properly ambitious not only among the Catholics but also throughout much of the Protestant population. The perceived need to maintain a secure unionist majority at Stormont provided the pretext for what was effectively one-party rule. Harry Midgely, who began his career as a trade union activist, can be cited as an example of someone from outside the unionist fold who reached cabinet rank in the government of Northern Ireland. As the leader of the Commonwealth Labour Party his inclusion in the cabinet from 1942 to 1945 served as a gesture towards wartime 'national government' but was achieved only after he had broken with the Northern Ireland Labour Party on the issue of support for partition. There were very few comparable examples: advancement more usually came through the close connections of the Orange Order. The effect of the abandonment of proportional representation in the 1920s was not only to minimise the representation of nationalists but also to inhibit diversity of political representation on the unionist side. Under the first-past-the-post electoral system the charge of 'splitting the unionist vote' was a ready-made inhibition on the emergence of challenges from within unionism. So, the ascendancy of the Ulster Unionist Party was assured. When the unionist establishment moved in the later 1960s to accommodate Catholics, it provoked the resentment of a significant sector of Protestants, who perceived that they, too, were on the outside but, as they believed, with prior rights. This opposition found its expression in the voice of fundamentalist religion and its pre-eminent leadership in the person of Rev. Ian Paisley. He had operated with great effect through the Free Presbyterian Church for several years before extending his base with the foundation of the Democratic Unionist Party in 1971. Arguably, it was the previous exclusion of Protestants, rather than of Catholics, that rendered the smooth transition to a new order impossible. The impasse permitted the slide into three decades of violence in which the Provisional IRA made most of the running for most of the time, and in which more than 3,500 died and many times that number were maimed or had their lives otherwise devastated. The denouement provides a spectacular case of the old trope of republicans coming to terms with democracy, albeit with several original twists.

Whatever else the volunteers and victims of the Provisionals may have died and been killed and maimed for, the one certain outcome of their sacrifices has been to secure a place in the political sun for an identifiable group of individual Sinn Féin leaders. This is something they have achieved not by military or electoral victory but through limited success on both fronts very effectively coordinated and exploited. Anyone thinking that ideology is irrelevant to republicanism would be disabused by reading a recent account of the breathtaking duplicity employed in order to keep rank and file – and most of the leadership – in the dark about plans for compromise through much of the 1980s and 1990s.[15] Equally, anyone trying to maintain that republicanism is essentially a matter of principles is left floundering by the demonstrated readiness to compromise in return for a share of power and thereby, apparently at least, to join in the democratic system. The pain of sacrificing these principles has been softened by a campaign of approval orchestrated by the US, British and Irish governments and others. The paradigm of the outsider gaining admission to the game has never been more strikingly realised than in the case of Martin McGuinness, one-time IRA leader in Derry excluded from the academic stream of second-level education (and so from university) through failure in the eleven plus examination, now holding the office of Minister for Education and pushing towards the elimination of the examination that caused his disappointment.[16]

The admission of McGuinness and his colleagues has involved the composition of a new version of the democracy game, with rules set out in the Good Friday Agreement of 1998. The principle of majority rule has been confined to the determination of Northern Ireland's membership of the United Kingdom. Membership of the executive is allocated roughly pro rata to numerical strength, but only to parties that identify with one 'community' or the other, unionist or nationalist: neutrals are discounted for this purpose, which constitutes a rather startling exclusion. For some the bottom line for democracy is a realistic possibility that governments can be changed by a majority of the voters at election 'throwing the rascals out' and installing a different set of people in power. The new system in Northern Ireland would seem to render that possibility rather remote.

More intriguing and more elusive are the unwritten rules of the new order. When de Valera came to power in 1932 he removed legal constraints on the IRA and courted its support for several years before turning decisively against it and enshrining in the 1937 constitution the following measure: 'The right to raise and maintain military or armed forces is vested exclusively in the Oireachtas.' (Art. 16.6.1). Those who voted for Martin Ferris in May 2002 were aware that participation of his party in government had been ruled out by the main parties in the Dáil in the spirit of this constitutional provision. However, Sinn Féin was admitted to the executive in Northern Ireland with the future of its armed wing still apparently undecided. And it remains to be seen what plans the British government has for enforcing (or the Irish or American governments or the European Union, or Amnesty International have for demanding) on both sides of the divide such basics of democracy as freedom from cruel and unusual punishment inflicted by paramilitaries under the guise of law enforcement.

In the nature of things Irish democracy, north and south, will continue to experience flux and uncertainty. It is not for the historian to speculate as to whether or not in Ireland democracy will continue to be menaced by private armies, kangaroo courts and knee-capping, but it seems fairly safe to predict that the country's historically applicable definitions of either democracy or republicanism, and possibly both, will have to change. The consequences for democracy would be imponderable if republicanism (along with loyalism) were from now on to have as its predominant connotation the meaning of 'localised mafia'. One of the indispensable elements of democracy is that the power to impose punitive justice be held only by those who are publicly accountable for their actions.

Notes

1   A possible venue for this is the recently launched journal of the Institute of Ireland: *The Republic: A Journal of Contemporary and Historical Debate*.

2   See below, p. 76.

3   3 & 4 Vict., c. 108.

4   R. Davis, *The Young Ireland Movement* (Dublin, 1987).

5   Representation of the People (Ireland) Act, 1850 (13 & 14 Vict., c. 69).

6   R. V. Comerford, *The Fenians in Context: Irish Politics and Society, 1848–82* (Dublin, 1985), pp. 67–130.

7   *Ibid.*, pp. 188–90.

8   T. W. Moody and L. Ó Broin (eds), 'The IRB supreme council, 1868–78', *Irish Historical Studies* 19, 75 (Mar. 1975), pp. 310–13.

9   P. Maume, 'Parnell and the IRB oath', *Irish Historical Studies* 29, 105 (May 1995), pp. 363–70.

10   See T. W. Moody, *Davitt and Irish Revolution, 1848–82* (Oxford, 1981), pp. 221–327.

11   M. Laffan, *The Resurrection of Ireland: The Sinn Féin Party, 1916–23* (Cambridge, 1999), pp. 243–5.

12   John A. Costello in *Dáil Éireann debates*, vol. 113, cols 394–8 (24 Nov. 1948) quoted in A. Mitchell and P. Ó Snodaigh (ed.), *Irish Political Documents, 1916–49* (Dublin, 1985), p. 247.

13   B. Hanley, *The IRA, 1926–36* (Dublin, 2002)

14   H. Patterson, *The politics of illusion: republicanism and socialism in modern Ireland* (London, 1989); R. English, *Radicals and the Republic: Socialist Republicanism in the Irish Free State, 1925–37* (Oxford, 1998).

15   E. Moloney, *A Secret History of the IRA* (London, 2002).

16   See L. Clarke and K. Johnston, *Martin McGuinness: From Guns to Government* (Edinburgh and London, 2001), p. 18.

CHAPTER 3

Paramilitary Politics and
the Irish Revolution

* * *

Peter Hart

I

Two of the biggest questions facing historians of twentieth-century Ireland are: why revolution and why violence? That is, why did Ireland's long-standing political conflict metamorphose into a direct challenge to the British state after 1912 and why did this confrontation take the form of armed rebellion after 1915? After all, the Land War of 1879–82 presented many of the same features of mass mobilisation, popular violence and official repression, leading to a crisis of state legitimacy and radical political realignment – without descending into mass homicide. On the other hand, moving forward into the twentieth century we quickly encounter numerous civil conflicts in Europe and elsewhere based on the same premises of ethnicity, nationalism and state breakdown that dwarf the Irish experience in the scale of their suffering. Seen from this perspective, the events of the Irish revolution can appear not only typical but also minor.

I would like to make use of both the chronological and the cross-national comparisons, and add a third regarding the events of the revolution itself which I will come to later. One of the factors – the key factor in my opinion – that separates 1912–22 from the 1880s, and which unites Ireland with other troubled countries, is the presence of paramilitary organisations: in particular, the Irish Volunteers (later the Irish Republican Army). As far as I know this general phenomenon has received little comparative attention but it does merit some systematic attention in the Irish case as Ireland pioneered para-militarism in twentieth-century Europe and paramilitary politics underpinned much of what took place in the fatal decade following the introduction of the third Home Rule Bill.

By 'paramilitary' I mean unofficial armed and public militias organised along military lines for the ostensible purpose of fighting one another, the police or the official army. These features distinguish them from clandestine groups such as the Irish Republican Brotherhood or the Defenders and from unmilitary but occasionally violent organisations like the Orange Order or Land League. Such militias proliferated in inter-war Europe, most notoriously in Germany and Italy, and have also appeared in Lebanon and elsewhere. In each of these cases their appearance was symptomatic of political polarisation and the absence of governmental legitimacy in the eyes of much of the population. And in each case, the end result was the breakdown of democracy and the imposition of a new state.[1] Thus, the emergence of the Ulster Volunteer Force and the Irish Volunteers says something not just about violence but also about the state of democracy in Ireland in 1913.

By 1912, Ireland participated in the United Kingdom's political system, and was governed by the same rules, but was not fully integrated in the manner of Wales and Scotland. Instead, Ireland had developed its own parties, cleavages, and power dynamics. Victorian democratisation produced two great parties, divided by ethnicity (one overwhelmingly Catholic, one Protestant), territory (the Protestant party was concentrated in the northern province of Ulster) and mutually exclusive ideologies (nationalist home rulers versus unionist defenders of the status quo). Both had allies in the British system (nationalist-Liberal; unionist-Conservative) but Irish parties did not generally seek seats in Britain, nor did British parties in Ireland after 1886. Moreover, the Irish and Unionist Parties themselves did not seriously compete with each other for votes – and rarely competed for seats – seeking rather to monopolise politics within their own ethnic constituency. Finally, neither party sought UK-wide power: their goals were purely Irish.[2]

The nationalist Irish Party emerged out of the agrarian Land War of the 1880s, with its organisation and much of its identity based on the semi-revolutionary and ultimately outlawed Land League. Many of its original cadre of activists were drawn from the secret and separatist Irish Republican Brotherhood. Although it evolved into a coalition representing many shades of opinion, and a fully (and avowedly) democratic party, the party's radical roots adopted and maintained a semi-loyal position towards the British state and refused to accord it full legitimacy.[3] That is, the party accepted the political regime as it was – was willing to achieve its goals through negotiation and legislation – but defined its role as one of permanent opposition until it could change the regime to put itself in power. Ireland was governed by a separate administration headed by a Viceroy and a Chief Secretary – a British Minister for Ireland responsible to Whitehall and Downing Street rather than to Irish representatives as such. Nationalists believed this to be an illegal and illegitimate imposition on the Irish nation, and attacked Dublin Castle and its personnel with sustained ferocity.[4] Participation in British politics was only justified by the Party's ability to fight successfully for nationalist objectives and in particular for Home Rule so that Ireland could govern itself. Only then would democracy be properly established and the state legitimised. So commitment to the system was explicitly conditional and limited according to nationalist ideology: Irish Party MPs could not accept government office for example. Compounding this denial of regime legitimacy and authority was the counter-legitimation of nationalist violence as heroic, principled and aimed at laudable ends. Rebellion might be foolish and useless, but it was understandable and its practitioners should not be harshly punished – nor should fellow nationalists ever co-operate with the authorities in defeating the rebels. Juan Linz has argued that 'ultimately, semiloyalty can be defined by a basically system-oriented party's greater affinity for extremists on its side of the political spectrum than for system parties closer to the opposite side': in this case, unionism.[5]

The opposing Unionist Party naturally took a loyal stance but only towards the state as it was then constituted. A Home Rule parliament and executive in Dublin would represent not just a change in governance but also a total victory by their ethnic rivals and a corresponding ethnocratic threat to their own status and identity. When a Liberal government backed in parliament by the Irish Party introduced the third Home Rule Bill in 1912, after removing the previous Unionist safeguard of a House of Lords veto, the loyalists moved rapidly to a corresponding semi-loyal position, openly challenging the government's right to legislate on behalf of their enemies. In an attempt to further deter the legislation, a paramilitary Ulster Volunteer Force (UVF) was formed in January 1913 with the stated aim of resisting Home Rule by force, at least in the northern province. Numbering in the tens of thousands, staffed by ex-army officers and eventually armed with thousands of rifles, the UVF was potentially a formidable force: more than a match for the Royal Irish Constabulary.[6] This was a logical move in a political system polarised between two separate constituencies and parties in which the main prize was not patronage or a turn in government but rather victory over the rival. If the nationalists won, they threatened to gain permanent control over Irish politics by virtue of their numerical advantage. Ulster (and some British) Unionists saw the government's actions as an unconstitutional betrayal and could see no democratic remedy for their plight. If the system no longer protected them from their enemies, they would do it for themselves: a common scenario for armed mobilisation by parties and communities in other countries.

The Irish Party eschewed a paramilitary counter-move in anticipation of achieving their overriding goal of self-government by parliamentary means. In a double irony, however, the party loyally relied on the British government to uphold the rule of law and the government refused to do so – refused, at least, to answer the UVF challenge except by negotiating away nationalist demands.

This did not mean that there would be no nationalist response, however, it meant only that it would not be led by the party. Nationalist politics was not confined to the electoral arena. As in most ethnically divided party systems, the real threat to party power came not from across the divide but from its own left flank, where it was vulnerable to being out-bid by more extreme nationalists. For a generation, party leaders had prevented this by agrarian activism, reiteration of the radical rhetoric of the 1880s and by maintaining their semi-loyal 'national' position positively rejecting the British claim to rule. The Liberal alliance may have been a sentimental one for some politicians and voters, but most probably saw it in purely instrumental terms: as a tactic rather than a principle. Much of the Irish nationalist vote, and of the party's ideological legitimacy, was based on this careful balancing act.[7] It could afford to temporarily lose some floating voters to the right-wing conciliationist All for Ireland League in 1910 because they had nowhere to go but back into the fold. Nationalists would never defect to unionism – but they might answer the siren song of separatism if the Party appeared not to be defending the national interest. Yet, as the Home Rule crisis deepened, and again after war was declared in Europe, John Redmond and the party leadership stuck to their strategy of passive support for the Liberal and Coalition governments. The loss of traditional aggression was well illustrated by the flaccid slogan of the party's own paramilitary force, the National Volunteers (founded in October 1914): 'Duty, not Defiance'.

However, an alternative leadership existed within the cultural and dissident nationalist sector led by Sinn Féin, the Gaelic League and the IRB, with its own press, networks, activists, and leaders. Opinion among these people ranged from apolitical semi-loyalty to outright republican disloyalty and they shared a general contempt for party politicians as well as for Dublin Castle. Here was a set of nationalist actors normally shut off from mainstream politics by the Irish Party's hegemony and by their own ideological opposition. The creation of the UVF, the Liberal government's tolerance of it, and the Irish Party's passivity in the face of both, provided an opportunity for them to enter politics in a paramilitary guise: as the Irish Volunteers, founded in November 1913. If it had been nationalists who had initiated the process of political militarisation, the British elite would have stood united against it and it would likely have been suppressed. Because paramilitarism began with Ulster Unionism, backed by the Conservative Party and much British press and public opinion, it survived and created the space and grudging official tolerance for nationalist imitators.

Thus Ireland's political structure began to change and destabilise: the Unionist Party moved one way, the Irish Party moved another, and a new player was introduced into the game. Correctly perceiving which militia posed the real threat to their position, the nationalist establishment sought to seize control of the Volunteers once the movement began to gain popularity in the spring of 1914. Redmondite appointees were imposed upon the leading committees but they failed to control the dissidents once Redmond himself declared that Volunteers should join the British army in September 1914. The organisation split, producing a new party militia – the National Volunteers – while leaving the original separatist leadership in charge of an independent anti-war minority (often dubbed the Sinn Féin Volunteers but not in fact connected to Arthur Griffith's organisation). Including the even smaller (socialist) Irish Citizen Army, this gave Ireland four paramilitary bodies.

II

In structural terms, the proliferation and persistence of armed militias made some sort of violent crisis increasingly likely. It did not mean that a republican revolution was inevitable, though, which raises the question of ideology. Paramilitaries brought guns into politics; the British government left them there; the military council of the IRB brought them into action in 1916. To leave the question there, however, and simply equate republican conspiracy with revolution would be misleading. The Irish Volunteers were a coalition of separatists. The most important group of activists did belong to the Brotherhood but non-republicans – led by Chief of Staff Eoin MacNeill – retained a great deal of power. The 'secret history' of the Easter Rising with its plots and manoeuvres is a familiar story,[8] but it was not the case that the organisation was divided simply into rebels and non-rebels or that it provided an otherwise empty vehicle for the revolutionaries' secret plans. In fact, the Volunteers shared a strong collective identity and ethos, forged before the war broke out, before the split and before the Easter Rising was planned.

For its founders and activists, the Irish Volunteers represented and embodied the nation and national honour: 'From the people the National army has sprung'; 'Ireland called the Volunteers into being'.[9] This national status entailed notions of manhood, virility, virtue and destiny. Volunteers saw themselves as a new, idealistic generation who gave the organisation its moral force. Their function was not merely political or military, but also consciousness-raising: their existence would demonstrate Ireland's true status as a nation with its own army, not least to its own citizens. For this reason, many Volunteer advocates projected a permanent role for the organisation, even beyond a Home Rule settlement. According to the founding manifesto, Irishmen had an inherent right to bear arms and to defend that right 'in the name of National Unity, of National Dignity, of national and Individual Liberty, of manly Citizenship'. Doing so would restore a flagging spirit of nationality. Otherwise: 'If we fail to take such measures . . . we become politically the most degraded population in Europe, and no longer worthy of the name of Nation.'[10] Joseph Plunkett – later one of the planners of the rebellion – wrote in February 1914 that 'With the launching of the Volunteer movement we the Irish people not only reassume our manhood, but once again voice our claim to stand among the nations of the world'.[11] In August a writer in *Irish Freedom* (an IRB journal) declared: 'a National army is the one perfect medium of national endeavour'.[12]

Such language was far from novel in the Europe of 1914 and drew also on the self-image and rhetoric of cultural nationalism. As such it carried with it the specific corollary that the Volunteers were to be non-partisan: 'The Volunteers are the people's army and the People's Army they must remain'; 'they may owe allegiance only to the Irish Nation'.[13] In 1914 the *Irish Volunteer* admonished its readers that 'Irish Volunteers have no concern in election contests. They have their own work to attend to, and it is more important than wrangling about whether this or that gentleman will have the privilege of sitting as a cypher at Westminster until the next General Election.'[14] Even after Sinn Féin was reorganised and republicanised in 1917, the army's political virtue remained intact. When the subject of the relationship was even mildly broached at that year's party convention, it met with angry rebuke from Michael Lennon: 'The Volunteers have so far been able to get along very well without much help from Sinn Fein . . . We are not going to take our orders from Sinn Fein and we don't want politicians meddling with a military organisation.'[15] When the Volunteer Executive advocated 'immediate forward action' on behalf of political prisoners in December 1918 – after Sinn Féin's election victory – the party executive left the decision with them and added that 'in no case should there be interference with the freedom of action of the Irish Volunteers'.[16] They would be neither a party militia nor a militia party. This differentiates the Volunteers/IRA not only from the other major Irish paramilitaries of its day, but also from those in other countries, such as the Nazi SA or the fascist squadristi.

Being antipolitical did not make the Volunteers antidemocratic, however. Internally, an elected hierarchy of unit officers and national executive coexisted with a more conventional chain of command headed by a headquarters staff, and the principles of election and debate survived to become key issues leading up to the civil war in 1922. Individual members were encouraged to work for Sinn Féin in elections, and many units acted as guards for speakers and polling booths. Many active Volunteers traded on their patriotic credentials to become candidates themselves, a trend that peaked in the Second Dáil elected in 1921. But the relationship with the Dáil itself was a tricky one. The IRA technically gave its allegiance to the separatist assembly via a new oath administered in 1919 but it still guarded its autonomy and went to war with no requirement for a responsible civil authority or an explicit mandate. As presented *in An tOglach* in January 1919, just after the establishment of the Dáil, the Volunteers' task was:

> to safeguard the Irish Republic to which the overwhelming majority of the Irish people give allegiance; it is theirs to interpret the national will, now rendered vocal and authoritative in Dáil Eireann. In 1916 the elected leaders of the Irish Volunteers, feeling that they were truly interpreting the wishes and ideas of the people of Ireland . . . it has now been proved that they had truly interpreted the heart of Ireland.[17]

Here is a fascinating formulation, ostensibly recognising the democratic authority of the Dáil while reserving the sovereign right to act in the name of the Republic and the nation – as in 1916. The only election referred to is that of the Volunteer leadership itself by its own members. In April 1919 newly elected President de Valera said only that his ministry was 'of course, in close association with the voluntary military forces which are the foundation of the National Army'.[18] Tom Barry recalled of Sinn Féin and the Dáil that 'these things seemed to be of little matter then . . . in the main, the young Volunteers were satisfied that they were following in the footsteps of the greatest men in all our history – the men of 1916'.[19] As *An tOglach* put it repeatedly in 1918, the Volunteers were 'the agents of the national will'.[20]

We must immediately make a key distinction in this regard. The Volunteers were ademocratic, not antidemocratic. They typically felt themselves to be above the political process, but they never sought to change or end it in the name of a fascist, communist or militarist alternative, even in the name of national emergency. They did not frame their struggle in terms of democracy but they never denied its validity either except insofar as it constrained their own actions. In any case, these were cast as a form of direct democracy:

> A few thousand Irishmen, who took the precaution of providing themselves with lethal weapons of one kind or another, have, without contesting a constituency and without sending a single man to Westminster, compelled the Westminster Parliament to admit publicly that it dares not pass any legislation which they, the armed men, did not choose to permit.[21]

When the mighty First Southern Division declared its opposition to the Treaty in December 1921, Sean Moylan (Cork Brigadier and TD) defended the action by saying: 'We didn't think it was our business as military men but we thought we had a duty as citizens of the Irish Republic . . . not with a view to dictating to politicians.'[22] No coup d'état was ever seriously contemplated: even in 1922, despite the accusations made by the pro-Treaty camp. The guerrillas wanted to fight for Ireland, perhaps even die for Ireland, but they did not want to run Ireland – as demonstrated by their almost comical reluctance to act as governors of the Cork or Munster Republic in 1922. The Volunteers believed in martyrs, not *Führers*.[23]

Absenting themselves as an organisation from politics did not mean an absence of political identity, of course. The Volunteers were ostensibly founded as a counter to the UVF and to safeguard Home Rule, but right from the start eager activists were suggesting its status as a truly national army required a grander purpose: 'Ireland called the Volunteers into being, and they must follow the inevitable path that every movement springing from the heart of the people has followed – the path of freedom.'[24] At the first convention in October 1914 (following the first split), a new policy was adopted 'to secure the abolition of the system of governing Ireland through Dublin Castle and the British military power, and the establishment of a National Government in its place'.[25] In July 1915 a manifesto entitled 'The Present Crisis' was issued which offered the following reinterpretation:

> On behalf of the Irish Volunteers, we reaffirm the original pledge 'to secure and maintain the rights and liberties common to all of the people of Ireland.' This pledge implies the attainment of a National Government, free from external political interference. It implies resistance to any partition or dismemberment of Ireland which would exclude a part of the people of Ireland from the benefits of national autonomy. It implies resistance to any scheme of compulsory military service under any authority except a free National Government. It implies resistance to any scheme of taxation which may be imposed without the consent of the people of Ireland, and which may defeat all their hopes of national prosperity and complete the economic ruin consequent on the Legislative Union.[26]

At the second national convention, in November 1915, Eoin MacNeill added that the 'real issue is the old issue between Ireland and English domination'.[27] This implicit separatism was officially confirmed at the third convention in 1917, which declared for a republic: a position defiantly reiterated at the fourth assembly in 1922.

So the Volunteers were beholden to the higher national interest alone – or, to put it another way, to themselves alone – and this was generally accepted to mean something much more than Liberal Home Rule. The principle of military autonomy widened easily to include the choice of action, its timing and goal. Action, like consciousness and honour, depended above all on guns. The rifle, in particular, was almost fetishistically central to the Volunteers' purpose and identity. Without arms, organisation was pointless and nationalists would be emasculated. With them, ordinary politics could be disregarded: 'at the moment [1914] the rifle is the only argument of patriotism'.[28] Therefore what Volunteer organisers feared most was being disarmed. Arms were their reason for being and hanging on to them was their primary aim. *Irish Volunteer* editorials harped on this point: 'Irish Volunteers without arms, and without the firm purpose to get arms and have arms, are a manifest humbug.'[29] Just weeks before the Rising, MacNeill told a meeting that 'There was one thing they were determined on, that Irish Volunteers meant armed Irish Volunteers. They were bound in honour, for the sake of their country, in order to protect her against an intolerable tyranny, to preserve their arms.'[30]

Self-defence against the government therefore headed the list of reasons to use their precious guns. In April 1916, with portents of war all about them, the Volunteer Council announced that government harassment could 'in the natural course of things, only be met by resistance and bloodshed. None of the Irish Volunteers recognise or will ever recognise the right of the Government to disarm them or to imprison their officers and men in any arbitrary fashion.'[31] MacNeill himself raised the prospect of fighting the British army and challenged them: 'Whether it is on equal terms, or two or five or twenty or forty to one, let them come against us and we will not shirk it.'[32] When the rebel conspirators forged the 'castle document' purporting to reveal an impending round-up, they knew it would galvanize their more reticent comrades. Other scenarios calling for action followed from the 1915 manifesto and from the circumstances of the war: partition, conscription and the imposition of new imperial taxes.

Interestingly (and prophetically), Arthur Griffith had cautioned against this whole mindset from the start. The Volunteers were welcomed for their 'backbone' but they were not a panacea, he warned in December 1913. Instead he urged that 'we must work through public opinion in the circumstances of Ireland rather than through force of arms'.[33] He would be making the same arguments again in 1917, 1918 and in 1921 and 1922.

Nevertheless, all of these attitudes were shared by nearly all of the Volunteer leadership, republican, revolutionary or otherwise. So was a growing sense of embattlement and danger through 1915 and the early months of 1916. Organisers were arrested, jailed and exiled to England. The government looked ever more hostile as anti-nationalist Conservatives joined the Asquith administration in 1915 and conscription was introduced in Britain in 1916. Volunteer opinions were becoming more and more militant and expectations were rising that open confrontation was just a matter of time. The Redmondites were dismissed as irrelevant or as traitors. It was the Volunteers who stood alone in defence of a nation abandoned by party and menaced by state.

III

To restate the question: did this Volunteer ideology lead inevitably to a Rising? The answer is no. General propositions may have been shared but specific conclusions were not. When it came to strategy all paramilitary commanders, unionist, nationalist, or republican, had just three basic options to choose from:

1 *Loyalty to party and/or state.* The independent or aggressive use of violence is forgone even as a threat or deterrent. This was the road taken by the National Volunteers, who followed the Redmondite party line and backed the British war effort until 1917. The same could be said of the revived Ulster Volunteers in 1920–1 when they were largely absorbed into the Ulster Special Constabulary.

2 *Deterrence.* The group adopts a defensive posture coupled with the threat of action in certain circumstances. The key to this strategy is to maintain an army-in-being, willing to defend itself and its goals in a crisis. This was the official policy of both the UVF in 1913–14 and the Irish Volunteers before and after the 1916 Rising.

3 *Insurrection.* Direct action is taken in order to achieve some political goal, to gain an advantage over opponents or to pre-empt an enemy attack. Where the defensive strategy protects the 'rights and liberties' at issue, an offensive strategy offers positive liberation in their name. The Easter Rising cabalists were model insurrectionists.

Once Irish Party loyalists chose the first option and set up the National Volunteers in 1914, the fate of the Irish Volunteers would be determined by the choice between aggression and deterrence; attack and defence. The debate was mostly surreptitious and unrecorded, but also found its way into the separatist press. A writer in *Nationality* (owned by the IRB but edited by Arthur Griffith) urged in November 1915 that: 'we have the material, the men and stuff of war, the faith and purpose and cause for revolution'.[34] In March 1916, Seán MacDermott told an audience commemorating Robert Emmet's stillborn rebellion:

> His plans were well laid, his prominent supporters well advised, and the fact that his attempt at insurrection was a failure was due to circumstances which could not have been foreseen. They would admit that it was better that Emmet should have made the attempt and failed than that he should not have attempted at all . . . the present time was opportune for preparation [to succeed where he had failed]. They had the means, and the young men of Ireland would be unworthy of their country if they did not avail of them.[35]

But deterrence was the default position. Several weeks later *The Spark* (a separatist weekly) published a contrary anonymous piece calling for prudence that concluded: 'let us see that whatever crime the Volunteers may commit, they will never be guilty of the superlative imbecility of suicide, spectacular or otherwise'.[36] It was agreed by all Volunteers that, merely by existing, they had prevented partition and conscription and preserved the future of self-government – not to mention national honour. Another common claim was that they had effected a revolution in Anglo-Irish relations and 'put an end to the old system of ruling Ireland through police (whom we outarm)'.[37] Premature action would destroy these gains by giving the government an excuse to destroy them. And, militarily, they had no hope of winning. 'Defensive warfare', as Bulmer Hobson called the official policy of irregular skirmishing, not only offered the best tactical option, it also guaranteed organisational unity and the widest mobilisation of support.[38] If the Volunteers were attacked, all would flock to the banner of self-defence. Insurrection would divide rather than unite. Eoin MacNeill synthesised these and other arguments in two powerful memoranda written in 1916 but they were never circulated or published, a possibly crucial decision in the closely matched battle for control.[39]

While all this made eminent common sense, insurrectionist arguments had their own logic which followed Volunteer ideology to its final conclusion. As MacDermott had stressed in his Dundalk speech, this was an unprecedented opportunity and the very existence of the option of rebellion (recognised by opponents as well as themselves) called forth its advocates. Use it or lose it. After all, what if the government did act first? They risked losing their weapons and freedom without having the chance to act. And if the idea of 'hedge-fighting' could work as well as the pragmatists suggested, and be combined with German aid, the Volunteers might not only survive but also prevail against a distracted Britain. MacNeill himself accepted this line of reasoning when first told of the impending German arms landing. Indeed, this very scenario was sketched in *The Spark* in March 1916 in a series of mock newspaper stories detailing the victory of 'the Provisional Government of the Irish Republic'. After a German landing in the west, 'the Sinn Fein Volunteers mysteriously disappeared from the city [Dublin], marching ostensibly in the direction of Naas' only to return again in triumph in November after a victorious summer campaign.[40] Beyond logic, the Volunteer sense of identity also favoured the bold as commitment and self-sacrifice easily trumped practical concerns as a demonstration of corporate righteousness and of national status.

These arguments took place not just between republicans and more moderate separatists but within republicanism as well so there was no clear correlation between beliefs in means and ends. The IRB was itself split between offensive and defensive factions. Nor could the insurrectionists claim to have been winning over the Volunteers. Although they did gain a few converts, they remained a distinct and necessarily duplicitous minority within the organisation as a whole. Nevertheless, the logic of the situation always favoured them in the long run. Presuming no government first attack, the insurrectionists were able to plan, prepare, organise, and strike when it suited them. This ability depended on a marked degree of official tolerance, but this was what was on offer between 1914 and 1916. Time was on their side.

IV

The Easter Rising amply confirmed the warnings of the defensive wing of the Volunteers. Only a small fraction of the total membership took part, many units stayed out of the fight altogether, and the result was a crushing defeat. Despite the military failure and the death of so many leaders, however, the Easter Rising actually strengthened the insurrectionists. Most survived, gained retrospective approval and political credibility, and were released within a year, astonishingly free to resume and recruit. Official tolerance of paramilitarism was greatly lessened – wearing uniforms and drilling became crimes to be prosecuted – but the result was mere harassment rather than thoroughgoing repression. Paramilitarism got a second chance because the government provided it, unwilling to either grant nationalist demands or keep the gunmen in jail. The Volunteers were reorganised in 1917 and 1918 (reabsorbing many members of the National Volunteers and Citizen Army along the way) and soon rivalled in scope the mass mobilisation of 1914. The clandestine third convention was held a year late and declared itself to be the army of the republic. A new journal was launched (*An tOglach*) and a new headquarters staff was appointed, consisting largely of IRB-linked Rising veterans.

In many ways, the developments of 1917–18 repeated those of 1914–15. The same framework for decision making and the same strategic debate was rehashed. The same choices had to be made – and the same choices were made. Once again, the default and majoritarian policy was one of deterrence: now focused primarily on the threat of conscription. The Volunteers would respond if the government acted first, but even then their plans called for an active defence of local communities, not an overthrow of the state: a MacNeillite rather than a Pearsian strategy, in other words. In this period the main argument lay with the advocates of Sinn Féin's traditional policy of 'passive resistance' which was denounced as worthless and dishonourable, most notoriously in Ernest Blythe's article and pamphlet 'Ruthless Warfare'.[41] Once the threat was removed in November 1918, *An tOglach* editorials began to hint of a change of policy:

The Army of Ireland was not established to resist conscription. Its function is to fight for the rights and liberties of the people of Ireland whenever and however opportunity arises. That fighting might be in the nature of an offensive as in Easter Week, 1916, or it might be of a defensive nature . . . but the Irish Volunteers should be ready whenever they are called on to stand to arms . . . [42]

Revolutionary activists began an underground campaign against the police in 1919 and the organisation was once again divided and depleted as the less militant fell away, opposed to an unprovoked and unconventional shooting war.[43] The issue was not the principle of direct action, but rather the new tactics and targets of guerrilla war. Some rebels were willing to take part in a second rising only if it was modelled on the first. Even with a much firmer command of the leadership, the insurrectionists still took over a year and much internal upheaval to make their move. As in 1915–16, time (and British policy) was ultimately on their side. The now republican army was finally able to officially renew its offensive in January 1920 with a series of raids on police barracks. The subsequent armed struggle apparently justified the insurrectionist case, leading to negotiations over the 'full national demand' in 1921.

Which brings me to my third and final comparison: between the events of 1916 and 1922. The actions of the anti-Treaty IRA in the latter year have often been equated with those of the Easter rebels, not least by themselves. Thus, the occupation and defence of the Four Courts against the Provisional Government has been seen as a kind of self-conscious replay of the last stand in the GPO. Can we equate these two events? The same constraints and drives, the same ideology, the same internal conflicts, were present in both the run-up to the Rising and the civil war. In both cases, the lines of division followed the three options that defined paramilitary strategy. And, just as 1916 was preceded and enabled by the 1914 split, so too was the civil war by division over the Treaty. In each case, the movement had recently absorbed a huge number of new fair-weather recruits (Redmondites and Trucileers respectively) who overwhelmingly backed the loyal faction: in 1921–2 this meant loyalty to the pro-Treaty majority in the Dáil and GHQ. As with the National Volunteers and the UVF before them, the pro-Treaty IRA was rapidly absorbed by the state. This left an unpopular and militant minority, who retained the lion's share of activists and arms but were themselves divided over the remaining choice of direction: insurrection or deterrence. There followed the same sort of internal tug of war as took place in 1915–16. Liam Lynch, and most of the pre-eminent First Southern Division, wanted above all to maintain army autonomy and its role as defender of the republic against British tyranny – thereby resurrecting the idea that the Volunteers should remain as the permanent national guardian of national freedom. So long as the army kept its guns, authority, and nerve, the Treaty could not be imposed and the nation could be reunited around the old cause. Civil war, or even precipitous renewal of war with Britain, would destroy everything. In other words, Liam Lynch and his allies were the new MacNeillites, with the Free Staters taking the place of the Irish Party as pro-British collaborators. This semi-loyal and defensive option was backed by a slim majority of the fourth (anti-Treaty) Army Convention and newly elected Executive.

As before, a belligerent minority lay within the anti-Treaty minority, led by Rory O'Connor and Tom Barry. Not that they wanted to attack their former comrades: that would run against the grain of Volunteer thinking, which always focused on Britain as the enemy. Rather, the offensive options considered were against Northern Ireland and the remaining British garrison in Dublin, with the aim of reuniting the army by renewing the old war (unity also being an aim of the 1916 planners). When these were brought to a vote in the IRA Executive and Convention in the spring of 1922, however, they were narrowly defeated. The strategic disagreement could not be reconciled and split the army again in June 1922, leaving the insurrectionists free to act.[44] And then, for the first time, they ran out of time. On 28 June, it was the army of the Provisional Government which acted first by laying siege to the Four Courts.

It is at this point that the 1916–1922 analogy breaks down. The rebels had not seized buildings as part of a 1916–style military plan, a site of sacrifice, or to seize power. The whole anti-Treaty IRA had done the same all over Ireland to maintain their position as a standing army and to keep the Free State at bay. Theirs was a deterrent posture, not an aggressive one: they saw the pro-Treatyites as the aggressors even before the outbreak of open war. If the latter-day insurrectionists had managed to provoke a British attack (as they almost did) then a genuine replay of the first rising might have taken place. But the vital fact was that it was the Irish government that struck first.

We can also turn the comparison around and re-evaluate the more familiar events of 1916. Much has been made of the role of republican ideology in framing and driving the Rising. Was it intended by its planners to be an inspirational 'blood sacrifice' to save Ireland's soul with little consideration for conventional military success? First of all, even though most of the Volunteers chose not to participate come Easter Monday, a thousand or so people were willing to fight that week, most of whom did not seek martyrdom. Patrick Pearse was not Charles Manson and the rebels were not members of a mystical republican cult. As much as anything, they fought for each other, their brothers, cousins, neighbours, workmates and friends. Nor should we see the conspirators as puppet-masters, stringing along the gullible (a common depiction in the aftermath of the Rising). They were intelligent and dedicated people who had chosen the separatist and Volunteer world-view as their own. In fact, most of the conspirators' ideas were widely shared within the Volunteers and IRB: the contempt for the Irish Party and compromise; the concomitant self-identification as the true representatives of the nation; the vanguardist will to act regardless of public opinion or elected politicians; the framing of the political situation as a manichean struggle with Britain; the belief that Dublin Castle was secretly planning their destruction; and their role as the upholders of national honour. Pro- and anti-insurrectionists alike also visualised a campaign in much the same way: as a series of Boer War-style encounters with themselves in the role of the native militia confounding a larger imperial army. Such a war was expected to last months, not days: Kathleen Clarke reported that the rebels thought they would be six months in the field, allowing time for German intervention and a popular uprising.[45] The possibility of a German landing was much discussed, and was felt by MacNeill and others to be reasonable justification for action. The failure of this to come off in 1916 was of course the key to the last-minute withdrawal of many units and members, not just for MacNeill, but for the commanders in Cork and Limerick as well. No one could accuse Terence and Mary MacSwiney of lacking an ideological commitment to self-sacrifice, but they accepted MacNeill's countermanding order and the logic behind it.[46]

Finally, Pearse's and Connolly's oft-quoted language of blood and martyrdom was not only – as has often been pointed out – part of the European patriotic zeitgeist, it was part of the shared Volunteer lexicon. The same phrases were used of the people killed by British soldiers in the Bachelor's Walk massacre in July 1914. *Irish Freedom* in August declared that 'the Volunteer movement was formally and effectively baptized, baptized in the blood of the Volunteers . . . The thought of arms and touch of arms have made Ireland into the thing we dreamed of. And the dawn is very near now.'[47] In October, Liam de Róiste, an armchair militant at best, wrote that it was their duty 'to carry on the old fight for Irish freedom, sanctified by the blood of the men who fought under Hugh O'Neill, Owen Roe, and Sarsfield, who struggled in '98, in 1803, in '48, in '67 for sovereign Irish independence'[48]: much the same succession claimed in the Easter Proclamation. In November 1915, another writer ('C.') evoked the same lineage and proclaimed that 'Today again is devotion to Ireland crowned with sacrifice and imprisonment. Today again has Ireland's soul been tortured with anxiety and longing, and her soil sanctified with the blood of her children.'[49] Such language was powerful, especially in a crisis, but it would not have been if it had only made sense to an inner circle of plotters. In the end, the Rising was the creation of public Volunteer ideology as much as of a secret conspiracy.

It is difficult to imagine the birth and survival of the Irish Volunteers and the IRA without the unique progression of events starting with the parliamentary struggles over the power of the House of Lords and Home Rule, leading to the creation of the UVF and its backing by the Conservative Party, the passive response of the Liberal government and their Irish Party allies, and then the sudden eruption – and equally surprising longevity – of the Great War. Without an independent nationalist militia, there would have been no rising and no subsequent 'wars'. Sinn Féin might have succeeded the Party as the nationalist front, accompanied by the same arrests and riots. Anger, frustration, mass mobilisation and new leadership might still have produced a revolutionary situation, threatening the authority of the British state. But without rifles and the catalysing impact of the Easter rebellion, guerrilla and civil war might well have been averted – as in the 1880s. Thus, the decisions made by British and Irish political elites in 1912–14 were absolutely crucial in determining the pattern of politics for the following decade.

Much of what occurred was contingent upon the calculations of leaders, caucuses and cabinets, and on the sheer unpredictable sequence of events. Nevertheless, the potential consequences were largely preset by the structure of party politics. The fundamental sectarian cleavage generated the same polarising effect on either side, squeezing out class-based or other multiethnic parties. Popular nationalism and unionism were constructed to perceive the other as a permanent threat or obstacle, antithetical not only to collective goals but also to the maintenance of ethnic identity. Rival parties of ethnic or national unity had appeared simultaneously on this basis, similarly vulnerable to extremist insurgencies, able to play on the sense of threat. After 1912, the Unionist Party managed this threat in part by building up a disciplined militia to absorb any loyalist challenge. The Irish Party chose a purely parliamentary strategy, relying on British institutions and elites to solve their problem. Unlike unionism, nationalism was institutionally divided between Irish Party organisations and a separate cluster of non- or anti-party groups. A group of these alternative activists decided to meet the threat of the UVF and the perceived anti-Home Rule conspiracy behind it, as the logic of the struggle – and soon public opinion – demanded. One side could not sit by while the other gained a clear advantage in power by acquiring arms. The same logic would work in reverse in 1920–1 when the UVF was revived in 1920 in response to the (inadequately opposed) rise of the IRA.

The Volunteers were the creature of sheer opportunity seized by ideological entrepreneurs and they too were bound by a clear set of rational choices. In strategic terms, the possibility of insurrection was not an irrational fantasy: it was built into the basic structure of events once Irish politics were (para)militarised in 1913. Even the UVF leadership contemplated a pre-emptive operation, and threatened to act independently. The joint failure of the Liberal government and the Irish Party to monopolise armed force provided the means. The presence of republican revolutionaries provided the motive, although attempted conscription or suppression would probably have had much the same result. But beyond ideology or circumstance, the very logic of the situation dictated the availability of an offensive option as a possible strategy. The same was and is true for paramilitaries everywhere who declare their role to be defensive but harbour an aspirational political agenda. In a version of the prisoner's dilemma, the actors have essentially two choices: act and risk defeat or wait and risk suppression before having the chance to act. Everything depends on the calculation of the opponent's strategy. The resulting tension between offensive and defensive strategies, along with the cyclical struggle between loyal, semi-loyal and disloyal factions, defined (and perhaps still defines) the history of the Irish Volunteers and was one of the crucial dynamics of the revolution. Another was the relationship between democracy and violence. Paramilitaries were a symptom of state and democratic failure: the fate of community and nation were at stake and the government was not trusted to defend their rights of self-government or self-preservation. Only when the new partition regimes were established did the majority of both ethnic groups transfer their trust and allegiance back to the state and its armed forces. Full democracy was restored once ethnic sovereignty or security was achieved. The introduction of paramilitary politics illustrates the difficulty – or even impossibility – of a peaceful democratic outcome to the Irish question in the early twentieth century.

Notes

1   See J. Linz, *The Breakdown of Democratic Regimes: Crisis, Breakdown, and Reequilibrium* (Baltimore, 1978), pp. 56–61.

2   For a discussion of ethnic party systems, see D. Horowitz, *Ethnic Groups in Conflict* (Berkeley, 1985), pp. 291–364.

3   For the distinction between loyal, semi-loyal and disloyal oppositions, see Linz, *Breakdown*, pp. 27–38.

4   See P. Maume, *The Long Gestation: Irish Nationalist Life 1891–1918* (Dublin, 1999).

5   Linz, *Breakdown*, p. 33.

6   See T. Bowman, 'The Ulster Volunteers 1913–14: force or farce?', *History Ireland* 10, 1 (Spring, 2002), pp. 43–7; 'The Ulster Volunteer Force and the formation of the 36th (Ulster) Division', *Irish Historical Studies* 32, 128 (Nov. 2001), pp. 498–518, for a convincingly critical assessment of the UVF's conventional military capabilities. See also A. Jackson, 'British Ireland: what if home rule had been enacted in 1912?' in N. Ferguson (ed.) *Virtual History: Alternatives and Counterfactuals* (London, 1998). C. Townshend, *Political Violence in Ireland: Government and Resistance Since 1848* (Oxford, 1983), pp. 245–55, provides an alternate view from a more political perspective.

7   See P. Bew, *Conflict and Conciliation in Ireland, 1890–1910* (Oxford, 1987) and *Ideology and the Irish Question: Ulster Unionism and Irish Nationalism, 1912–1916* (Oxford, 1994).

8   For the latest reconstruction, see M. Foy and B. Barton, *The Easter Rising* (Stroud, 1999), pp. 1–51.

9 *Irish Volunteer*, 15 Aug. 1914; 17 Oct. 1914.

10 The manifesto is reprinted in F. X. Martin (ed.), *The Irish Volunteers 1913–1915: Recollections and Documents* (Dublin, 1963), pp. 98–104.

11 *Irish Volunteer*, 7 Feb. 1914.

12 *Irish Freedom*, Aug. 1914.

13 *Irish Volunteer*, 15 Aug. 1914; 10 Oct. 1914.

14 Ibid., 12 Dec. 1914.

15 *Report of the Proceedings of the Sinn Fein Convention, 25th and 26th October, 1917* (Public Record Office, CO 904/23), p. 16.

16 Minutes of Sinn Féin standing committee, 31 Dec. 1918 (University College Dublin Archives (UCDA), Mulcahy papers, P7/D/39).

17 *An tOglach*, 31 Jan. 1919.

18 *Dail Proceedings*, 10 Apr. 1919.

19 *Irish Independent*, 8 Dec. 1970.

20 *An tOglach*, 15 Aug. 1918; 14 Sept. 1918; 31 Jan. 1919.

21 *The Spark*, 2 Apr. 1916.

22 *Private Sessions of Second Dail* (Dublin, 1922), 14 Dec. 1921.

23 Tom Garvin's *1922: The Birth of Irish Democracy* (Dublin, 1996) discusses the relationship between revolutionary thinking and democracy in Ireland.

24 *Irish Volunteer*, 17 Oct. 1914.

25 Ibid., 31 Oct. 1914.

26 Ibid., 24 July 1915.

27 *Nationality*, 13 Nov. 1915.

28 *Irish Volunteer*, 12 Sept. 1914.

29 Ibid., 1 Apr. 1916.

30 Ibid., 8 Apr. 1916.

31 *Nationality*, 1 Apr. 1916.

32 *Irish Volunteer*, 8 Apr. 1916.

33 *Sinn Féin*, 6, 20 Dec. 1913.

34 *Nationality*, 27 Nov. 1915.

35 Ibid., 18 Mar. 1916.

36 *The Spark*, 2 Apr. 1916.

37 F. X. Martin (ed), 'Eoin MacNeill on the 1916 Rising', *Irish Historical Studies* 12, 47 (1961), pp. 226–71.

38 *Irish Volunteer*, 15 Apr. 1916.

39 See Townshend, *Political Violence*, pp. 285–98.

40 *The Spark*, 19 Mar. 1916.

41 *An tOglach*, 14 Oct. 1918.

42 Ibid., 15 Nov. 1918.

43 P. Hart, *The IRA and Its Enemies: Violence and Community in Cork, 1916–1923* (Oxford, 1998), pp. 226–70.

44 The most recent account of these events is in B. Kissane, *Explaining Irish Democracy* (Dublin, 2002), pp. 115–39. See also M. Hopkinson, *Green Against Green: The Irish Civil War* (Dublin, 1988), pp. 58–76.

45 Conversation with Mrs Tom Clarke, 8 July 1963 (UCDA, Mulcahy papers, P7/D/2).

46 F. Costello, *Enduring the Most: The Life and Death of Terence MacSwiney* (Dingle, 1995), pp. 62–72.

47 *Irish Freedom*, Aug. 1914.

48 *Irish Volunteer*, 10 Oct. 1914.

49 *Nationality*, 27 Nov. 1915. Presumably the author was again referring to the Bachelor's Walk massacre.

CHAPTER 4

The 'Irregular and Bolshie situation'

Republicanism and Communism
1921–36

* * *

Donal Ó Drisceoil

British propagandists and 'die-hards' within the British establishment saw the hidden hand of Moscow at work throughout the Irish War of Independence. Had it existed, the small contingent of socialist-minded republicans would gladly have grasped it, while some writers have retrospectively argued that the contemporaneous wave of industrial militancy and rural agitation objectively invited communist leadership.[1] In reality, it was not until the eve of the Treaty of 1921 that organised communist politics became a factor, and then a peripheral one, in the Irish situation. The timing of this initial intervention was influential on its nature and a precedent was established whereby the furtherance of communist politics in Ireland was linked to the republican movement. The persistence of communist interest in the IRA arose from several factors: the belief that it was the primary (objectively and potentially) revolutionary force in Ireland; the failure of Jim Larkin to build Irish communism on a trade union base; Comintern thinking on the way forward in colonial contexts; the enduring and ambiguous legacy of James Connolly; and the fact that most of the first and second generation of Irish communists had republican backgrounds.

Connolly's son Roddy attended the Third World Congress of the Third International (or Comintern) in the summer of 1921. With Comintern backing, he led the transformation of the largely moribund Socialist Party of Ireland into the first Communist Party of Ireland (CPI) in the following October. When the Anglo-Irish Treaty was signed in December 1921, the CPI was the first organisation to come out against it, declaring in its paper, the *Workers' Republic*: 'As against any state that will foster or promote the interests of the British Empire we will fight for an Irish Republic . . . We will ally ourselves to whoever fights against the Free State for an Irish Republic.' British imperialism was seen as 'the greatest enemy to world revolution' and it was the duty of communists in the Irish context to support the republicans who rejected the Treaty, despite the socially reactionary politics of their leadership. Once the bourgeois/capitalist nationalist struggle had been won, the next stage was the fight for the workers' republic.[2] This stageist approach grew from a particular reading of James Connolly's writings and actions, as well as the application of Comintern policy.[3] The CPI, with less than two dozen members, was numerically insignificant. Its influence lay in its international dimension and the links that it forged, activist and intellectual, with some IRA volunteers at this stage. Those individuals would later attempt, in close association with the communist movement, to orientate the IRA in a socialist direction – a process that forms a central part of the story of Irish republicanism in the crucial inter-war years.

Despite the resurgence of workers' militancy during the period between the truce and outbreak of the civil war, the CPI, like the labour leadership, took a de facto 'Labour must wait' position, and concentrated its energies on influencing a republican leadership bereft of political or military ideas about the way forward. When civil war broke out at the end of June 1922, the CPI joined with the IRA 'irregulars' in clashes with the Provisional Government army in Dublin. Among those captured and incarcerated at the outset of the civil war were a number of CPI members, as well as prominent fellow travellers in the senior ranks of the IRA. In Mountjoy Jail, a group gathered around the charismatic Liam Mellows who, while not a communist, was one of the few republican leaders who felt that opposition to the Treaty required a socially radical dimension. The group, which included William Carpenter of the CPI and Peadar O'Donnell, an IRA executive member who was close to the party (and was claimed as a member on a number of occasions), held long discussions on republican policy and strategy.[4]

On the outside, the CPI abandoned its flirtation with armed action and returned to the task of attempting to influence republican policy. The party argued that the republican campaign needed to be broadened 'from a military to a military and social struggle'. By this it meant not engagement with workers' struggles, which were continuing apace, but the adoption of a political programme that would bring workers and small farmers to the republican side.[5] In early July 1922 Roddy Connolly, the party president, went to London where he collaborated with Michael Borodin of the Comintern (who later became famous for his role as adviser to the Chinese Communists) in drafting a new radical social programme, which they hoped republican leaders would adopt. The programme included nationalisation, land division, debt cancellation, an eight-hour day, free housing and social services.[6] The only senior republican to respond to the CPI proposals was Liam Mellows in Mountjoy. Copies of the *Workers' Republic* were read and discussed by Mellows and his circle. The issues of 22 and 29 July and 12 August 1922 contained details of the Connolly/Borodin programme, which Mellows combined with his own tentative ideas for a republican policy. Following a request from Ernie O'Malley, he smuggled out documents outlining his suggestions which subsequently became known as 'Notes from Mountjoy' or 'Jail Notes'.[7] A copy was captured and published in the *Irish Independent* on 21 September 1922 under red scare headlines, at a time when the government was in the process of introducing draconian new legislation. Perceptively, the paper did not accuse Mellows of adopting communist politics, but of pretending to in order to win workers as 'cannon fodder' for the republican cause. (Mellows was not suggesting recognition of workers' class interests as valid in themselves, appealing to workers' organisations or advocating a working-class leadership of the struggle.) Mellows privately dismissed attempts to brand as communist his 'hastily written outline of ideas' as 'so silly. I only referred to the "Worker" [*sic*] because it had set forth so succinctly a programme of constructive work that certainly appealed to me.'[8] The CPI hailed the Mellows document as a major breakthrough, but his ideas were otherwise ignored. The Free State officially came into existence on 6 December 1922. Two days later Mellows was among four republican prisoners unlawfully executed in Mountjoy. Government repression was taking its toll on republican resistance and it was becoming clear that the IRA military campaign was doomed. The CPI, always aware that it had hitched its wagon to a blinkered horse, now realised that it was also a losing one.

Roddy Connolly, whom many in the party blamed for the concentration on influencing republicans to the neglect of workers' struggles, attended the Fourth World Congress of the Comintern in Moscow at the end of 1922. On the national question, the Congress reiterated its policy of communist parties fighting for the most radical possible solution of bourgeois democratic revolutions, while simultaneously organising the working class to struggle for its specific class interests, thus exposing the contradictions of the bourgeois nationalist project. While the CPI could be said to have pursued the first of those tasks, it had failed in the second and was privately criticised for this at the Congress. On his return from Moscow, Connolly published a series of articles in the *Workers' Republic* on 'Past and Future Policy' in which he argued that the Free State was an advance on the previous position and that it might be possible to move from it directly to the workers' republic – in other words, to skip a stage. He called for concentration on building the organised forces of the working class and suggested that republicans should call off their armed struggle and form a new republican party or workers' republican party, take the oath and enter the Dáil. His claim that this advice was sanctioned by the Comintern caused controversy at the CPI congress in January 1923 when George Pollock, who had accompanied Connolly to Moscow, contradicted him. Connolly lost his place on the party executive and as editor of the paper amid accusations that he had been 'bought out' by the Free State and the Labour Party.[9]

Four years later, de Valera and Fianna Fáil would take the route proposed by Connolly but not as a republican party based on 'the masses' as he had suggested – rather, as a populist republican party embodying what Marxists termed a class essence, and, by extension, an ideology, that was petty bourgeois. The success of Fianna Fáil is understandably presented as evidence to support the thesis that Irish republicanism was ultimately a petty bourgeois project, and therefore an inappropriate vehicle for the advancement of proletarian interests and socialism in Ireland.[10] For socialist republicans, however, Irish republicanism was in class terms a contested terrain and could be appropriated for the proletariat and 'peasantry': this was to be achieved through class struggle rather than debate. In this framing, the workers were 'the nation'. The role of the IRA in this struggle, given its history and composition, would always be ambiguous and contradictory but the realisation by socialist republicans that it was not the appropriate vehicle through which to advance the cause of Irish socialism, particularly in the North, was arguably delayed (with politically fatal results) by the influence of the communists – whose primary interest lay ultimately with the Party and the priorities of the Soviet Union – at crucial historical junctures.

Peadar O'Donnell, who would come to personify inter-war socialist republicanism, entered the debate within the first CPI with a response to Connolly's suggested change in policy in the 3 February 1923 issue of *Workers' Republic*. His argument was basically a reiteration of previous CPI policy: continue the military struggle against the Treaty and issue a republican constitution with a radical social policy dimension. O'Donnell was a former trade union activist whose revolutionary socialist politics failed to find an organisational outlet in 1918–19; he was frustrated by the socially reactionary politics of the leadership of the independence movement, but remained within the IRA, waiting in vain for the labour movement to move into the van of the struggle following the Treaty 'sell-out'. When this did not materialise, he narrowed his horizons and devoted his energies to the subjectively classless republican struggle against the Treaty settlement – a 'stageism' that he would later reject. Connolly responded to O'Donnell in the same issue, arguing that existing republican methods entailed defeat and that the adoption of a social programme at this stage was too little, too late. The civil war moved towards its inevitable end in May 1923. The first CPI was likewise on the way out, divided, increasingly irrelevant and soon to be replaced as the Comintern affiliate in Ireland by Jim Larkin's Irish Worker League.

Larkin, who had left Ireland following the defeat of the 1913 lockout and had been active in the American communist circles, returned in April 1923 and set about regaining his leadership of the Irish labour movement. The Comintern agreed with Larkin's dismissive approach to the CPI, ordering the party to disband and join Larkin's newly formed, loosely organised League in

January 1924. Attempts to launch an official communist party around Larkin in 1925 were frustrated by the latter's egocentric behaviour. The Comintern gradually lost faith in him and began to turn towards the republican movement once again.[11] The post-civil war movement had undergone a number of important changes in the mid-1920s that facilitated closer relations with the communists in the volatile circumstances of the late 1920s and early 1930s. The IRA's decision in November 1925 to break from Sinn Féin authority, followed by the formation of Fianna Fáil by republican pragmatists in May 1926, offered opportunities for the left within the IRA, led by Peadar O'Donnell (an executive and army council member) to assume increasing prominence and influence. Of particular significance was left-wing influence over publicity/ propaganda, and thus on republican discourse, based on O'Donnell's and subsequently Frank Ryan's editorship of *An Phoblacht*.[12] Of importance also was the ascension of Moss Twomey to the position of IRA chief-of-staff in 1926. Twomey, while not belonging to the socialist republican tendency, was open to socialist ideas and not hostile to co-operation with communists when he felt it was beneficial to the republican project.

Four main tendencies have been identified in the organisation in this period. The revolutionary socialists, who wished to transform the IRA into a Connollyite citizen army and make class struggle the dynamic of republicanism, were opposed by a combination of apolitical militarists, set against any diversion from narrow militarism, and social conservatives who rejected socialism on Catholic grounds. The fourth tendency, which held the balance of power, was probably the most representative of republican thinking. Personified by Twomey, this 'middle group' was broadly sympathetic to demands for social and economic justice but regarded the achievement of national goals (unity and independence) as a necessary first step. They also saw that socialist republicanism offered its volunteers, as Patterson put it, 'a deeper rationale for refusing incorporation in constitutional politics through the blandishments of Fianna Fáil'.[13] The growing strength of de Valera's party called the IRA's raison d'être into question, while the leakage of volunteers into de Valera's party increased as it gathered momentum. O'Donnell and his associates provided the IRA with a political project that differentiated it from Fianna Fáil and fitted the radical temper of the times. The temporary success of the left in swaying this middle group facilitated the partnership with communists and led the IRA to adopt a socialist/communist programme in 1931. As we shall see, when the red scare backlash hampered its primary politico-military project, the IRA was quick to abandon socialist rhetoric, terminate its flirtation with communism and cut loose those members who wanted to develop the republican-communist nexus.

While individual republicans co-operated with short-lived communist front organisations in Ireland in the mid-1920s, it was not until 1927 that the first clear organisational linkages between republicans and the (now Stalinist) international communist movement were forged. In February, Frank Ryan and Donal O'Donoghue of the IRA attended the Comintern-organised Congress of Oppressed Nationalities in Brussels, at which a new organisation called the League Against Imperialism (LAI) was formed. The idea was that anti-imperialist/nationalist sentiment in colonial and economically 'backward' (i.e. under industrialised) countries was the best basis for building communist movements in those areas – an approach that fitted neatly with socialist republican thinking. The following year a republican-dominated Irish LAI section was established.[14] In October 1927 Mick Fitzpatrick, a senior IRA figure and member of the first CPI, attended the tenth anniversary celebrations of the Bolshevik revolution in Moscow and represented Ireland on the presidium of a newly established body that epitomised the Stalinist 'socialism in one country' approach, the Friends of Soviet Russia. He began an Irish branch in early 1928. In July 1929 another Irish section of a Comintern organisation, the Labour Defence League, was established by communist and IRA figures.[15]

The Comintern had recently abandoned its stageist approach and adopted the 'class against class' strategy. It was not yet applied in Ireland but at the second LAI congress in Germany in July 1929 Peadar O'Donnell harmonised with it, blaming (in a complete reversal of his civil war position) the 'false' stageist policy for the failure to achieve Irish freedom. His attacks on the Irish Labour Party also chimed with the new communist line that portrayed labour reformists as the enemy number one.[16] The delay in applying 'class against class' in Ireland is an example of where the Comintern deferred to Irish communists on the application of policy, a pattern highlighted by O'Connor and McLoughlin.[17] When it was applied (in the second half of 1930), it was seen to be counterproductive and was softened and adapted for Irish circumstances. However, this short episode led to the IRA creating its own communistic party which, despite being stillborn and largely rhetorical, provoked a backlash that ultimately benefited Fianna Fáil and influenced the course of republican politics at a crucial juncture.

Aside from cultivating organisational links with republicans, the Comintern's other Irish initiative in the late 1920s was to bring young Irish cadres for instruction at the Lenin School in Moscow, a key development in the 'Stalinisation' of Irish communism. Among the first group to attend between 1928 and 1930 were Seán Murray, an IRA veteran of the war of independence who had been an active communist in Britain, and Jim Larkin Jr.[18] With the help of British communists acting as Comintern emissaries, this group set about relaunching communism in Ireland in 1930 in collaboration with IRA sympathisers. Tom Bell and Bob Stewart of the CPGB/Comintern arrived in January 1930 to begin preparing the ground. One of their first actions was joining with Peadar O'Donnell in transforming the small farmers' campaign he spearheaded against the payment of land annuities into an Irish branch of the Krestintern, the Peasants' International.[19] The land annuities agitation was begun by O'Donnell in 1926. He failed to get the IRA whole-heartedly involved and by the end of the decade Fianna Fáil had taken up the issue and was beginning to reap the political benefits. Unlike O'Donnell (who pushed for abolition of the annuities which would have thrown up the question of title to land and opened up the vista of nationalisation), Fianna Fáil advocated retention of the annuities revenue in the Irish state coffers. With Comintern encouragement, O'Donnell now set about restructuring the original campaign (which had been driven by conventional nationalist/Irish historical grievance rhetoric) as well as re-articulating his anti-annuities position in the broader framework of international communist discourse. This was part of a general discursive shift in socialist republican writings in this period which reflected the ever-closer relationship with the communists. The Irish Working Farmers' Committee (IWFC), headed by O'Donnell with an exclusively republican, if not IRA, membership, was established in January 1930. It was represented at the first European Working Farmers' Congress in Berlin where O'Donnell was elected to the central committee of the European branch of the Krestintern.[20]

The economic depression was beginning to bite in rural and urban Ireland, resulting in increased non-payment of annuities and an upsurge in unemployment, unemployed workers' agitation and industrial unrest. The developing republican-communist nexus was naturally keen to take advantage of this atmosphere of growing militancy and radicalisation, particularly on the part of the IRA rank-and-file in Dublin. In March 1930 a series of meetings in Dublin designed to attract left-leaning volunteers to take up joint member-ship of the IRA and the embryonic communist party were addressed by O'Donnell of the IRA and Stewart of the Comintern. Together with Bell, Patrick Rooney of the IRA and a number of Irish communists, they formed a Preparatory Committee for the formation of a Workers' Revolutionary Party (PCWRP) which launched a new paper, *Workers' Voice*, in April. In a list of seventy-two members of the PCWRP sent by the gardaí to the Department of Justice in early June 1930, thirty are identified as active IRA men.[21] Many IRA rank-and-file, radicalised by their straitened economic circumstances, had joined the communist-led Irish National Unemployed Movement and were involved in serious clashes with the police in the early months of 1930. O'Donnell led the socialist republican efforts to draw the IRA into a united front with the embryonic WRP and the IWFC; he characterised the latter and former as complementary rural and urban wings of the same revolutionary movement. In the Easter 1930 issue of *An Phoblacht* he argued that IRA volunteers would see their role clearly if James Connolly was at the centre of organised workers, but in his absence they should become absorbed in the WRP and play the role of a workers' or citizen army. He and his allies continued to push this line at public meetings, in the pages of *An Phoblacht* and at PCWRP gatherings in the spring and early summer of 1930.

This approach was undermined when communist tactics changed and 'class against class' was belatedly, gradually and temporarily applied to Ireland. The official labour movement was the first target, followed by republicans. In mid-June the PCRWP was replaced by a reconstituted 'National Committee of the Revolutionary Workers' Party' which excluded O'Donnell and began to push the new line. In the *Workers' Voice* on 28 June an unsigned article presented the 'class against class' line on the IRA, warning volunteers against the treachery of that organisation's leadership. The new line had arrived in Ireland with the returning cadres from the Lenin School in Moscow, and was outlined in a Comintern document sent back by Jim Larkin Jr. The letter outlined the need to differentiate the communists from other radical groupings and win 'the best proletarian elements' to the official communist movement. Relations with the republican movement were to be maintained, however, as it still served as 'an avenue of approach to a section of the politically developed peasants, semi-proletarians and even certain proletarian elements'. The aim was a 'united front from below' with the IRA left, while subtly undermining its leadership and stressing the need to absorb it into the communist party.[22] O'Donnell rejected the *Workers' Voice* attack on the IRA leadership as 'sheer treachery to the working class struggle' and stressed to communists that 'the best working class fighters are in the IRA and in the magnetic field of that and the Irish Citizen Army tradition'.[23] The communists, of course, recognised this fact, but wished to win those very 'fighters' from the IRA and bring them into the communist party.

Although relations became strained, and the confrontational and sectarian communist attitude weakened the coalition, the complete breakdown that is sometimes suggested did not occur.[24] Joint membership of the IRA and embryonic communist party continued and republicans remained prominent in Comintern-linked organisations such as the IWFC, the LAI and the Friends of Soviet Russia.[25] However, the new sectarianism (which lasted until the communists realised its counterproductiveness and softened their line from January 1931) put paid to O'Donnell's hopes of a revolutionary partnership between the communist organisation and a radicalised IRA and, by November 1930, he and his allies had convinced Moss Twomey of the need for the IRA to take the initiative through the adoption of a socialist programme and the creation of a socialist organisation to complement the army. By this stage Twomey and the pragmatists were accepting the strategic advantages of presenting a socially radical face as a way of mobilising support for the IRA, especially as the communists had temporarily withdrawn from their 'partnership' and were offering a counter-attraction to discontented and radicalised volunteers/supporters and potential volunteers/supporters. The communists adopted the new title of Revolutionary Workers' Groups (RWG) in November 1930, the same month that the IRA army council appears to have accepted the need for a socialistic platform.

From late November 1930 until February 1931 *An Phoblacht* became the forum for an open debate and discussion on proposals to redefine the IRA's objectives in socially radical terms. An article by Twomey entitled 'The sovereignty of the people: Suggestions for a constitution for the Irish Republic' was the basis for contributions from all the tendencies identified earlier. Twomey, a pragmatist, trod carefully, rejecting 'references to "-isms" and class war' as 'uncalled for and misleading'; his proposals were based on 'Pearse – not Lenin' and he presented them in clear Pearsean nationalist, communalist terms. These discussions were a prelude to the February 1931 army convention's support for a new constitution for the Irish Republic and the establishment of a new political appendage, Saor Éire.[26] O'Donnell, fearing that Saor Éire would be no more than a paper organisation, stressed the need for it to be activist-driven.

A preparatory committee for the Saor Éire national congress was formed and O'Donnell, Seán MacBride and others on the army council toured the country helping to organise committees to select delegates. Despite the nominal involvement of working farmer committees, the new 'party' was dependent on IRA structures. While this mollified the conservatives who were unhappy with its radicalism, it also offered opportunities for opponents to sabotage preparations. One veteran recalled that the majority of brigade commanders were opposed to Saor Éire and utilised their authority 'to call parades, courses or classes' at the very time activities relating to the new group were occurring. This could happen because the organisational process was, in the words of one delegate, 'most undemocratic.' Meetings were held with brigade officers rather than rank-and-file volunteers, while invitations to the congress were sent only to senior officers. An IRA veteran from Kerry remembered O'Donnell coming to the county and outlining the Saor Éire plan to brigade officers: 'he made no progress towards converting them', he concluded, adding significantly that 'the Army backed Fianna Fáil at the time'.[27] De Valera's party had, in many ways, got there first: numerous Fianna Fáil cumainn were transformations of old IRA companies and much of the new party's legendary organisational strength lay in its utilisation of existing IRA structures.[28]

While the IRA left was energised by the prospect of Saor Éire, the organisation as a whole was also displaying what the Department of Justice described as a 'growing audacity and confidence'.[29] The Easter parades of 1931 were the biggest since the civil war and in June almost 10,000 people attended the annual Wolfe Tone commemoration at Bodenstown despite a government ban. They heard O'Donnell deliver a revolutionary oration, which was cited in a Department of Justice report as evidence that 'One of the principal IRA leaders has recently shown a tendency to adopt the Soviet principle formally as his model.'[30] When Saor Éire documents came into police hands in July 1931, Garda Commissioner Eoin O'Duffy's demands for increased draconian powers were given added impetus. In August an extensive memo on the 'Alliance between Irish Republican Army and Communists', in which the adoption of the Saor Éire programme was presented as marking the culmination of the process and 'the definite union' of the two groups, was presented to the government[31] and circulated to the Catholic bishops in mid-September in preparation for a joint episcopal statement to coincide with government action against the perceived subversive threat.[32]

The Saor Éire congress was held in Dublin on the weekend of 26–27 September 1931. The IRA and Cumann na mBan, the women's auxiliary, were strongly represented and formed the majority of the elected executive. The RWG were also present and one of their number, Nicholas Boran, was elected onto the executive.[33] A published manifesto included predictable attacks on Cumann na nGaedheal and Labour, but also on Fianna Fáil, the party that Saor Éire was aspiring to supplant as the political expression of republicanism. Its stated objectives were:

1   To achieve an independent revolutionary leadership for the working class and working farmers towards the overthrow in Ireland of British Imperialism and its ally, Irish Capitalism.

2   To organise and consolidate the Republic of Ireland on the basis of the possession and administration by the workers and working farmers, of the land, instruments of production, distribution and exchange.

3   To restore and foster the Irish language, culture and games.[34]

Under the shadow of imminent coercion legislation, a series of public meetings were held across the country at which O'Donnell and others shared Saor Éire platforms with Sean Murray of the RWG and Shapurji Saklatvala of the CPGB/Comintern.[35] This co-operation throws into question the claim that Saor Éire represented a counter-offensive against the threat posed by the RWG.[36] This may have been the thinking of some non-socialists in the IRA leadership, but it was clearly not the position of O'Donnell and his fellow Saor Éire architects who continued to welcome all revolutionary voices on board. The RWG criticised Saor Éire for the 'two voices' evident at the congress – the socialist voice and that of the bourgeoisie that clung to a non-class approach – and dismissed the need for a new party other than an official Communist Party of Ireland; yet they maintained their connection with this potential 'avenue of approach' to the politically developed proletariat and peasantry.[37]

The new coercion legislation was passed on 16 October 1931. Introducing it, W. T. Cosgrave, President of the Executive Council, referred to the conspiracy by republican and 'Communistic' groups to overthrow the state, and identified Saor Éire as 'a new element of danger . . . We believe that the new patriotism based on Muscovite teachings with a sugar coating of Irish extremism is completely alien to Irish tradition'. On Sunday 18 October a joint pastoral from the Irish Catholic bishops was read out in all Irish churches. It described Saor Éire as 'frankly Communistic', declared it and the IRA 'sinful and irreligious' and pronounced that no Catholic could lawfully be a member of them. The bishops called for solutions to the country's social and economic problems that were 'in accordance with the traditions of Catholic Ireland', the very solutions that Fianna Fáil was about to offer the electorate.[38] De Valera had reassured MacRory of this at a private meeting, and had reiterated his party's adherence to Catholic principles and rejection of communism during the debates on the new legislation.[39]

On 20 October a military tribunal was established and twelve organisations were banned including the IRA, Saor Éire, the RWG (incorrectly listed as the Workers' Revolutionary Party) and the IWFC. Repression began immediately with arrests, raids and searches, the proclamation of meetings and the suppression of *An Phoblacht* and *Workers' Voice*. Those in the IRA leadership who had evaded arrest were in hiding or on the run; the RWG lay low, Bell and Stewart returned to Britain and the communist bookshop in Dublin was closed down. Although the state had managed to temporarily neutralise all radical opposition by the end of 1931, the government and its supporters continued to fan the flames of the red scare, hoping that it would provide enough heat to burn off the political challenge of Fianna Fáil.[40] Cosgrave dissolved the Dáil in January 1932 and called an early general election. Cumann na nGaedheal had decided to go to the country eight months early before the economic situation deteriorated any further and to take advantage of what minister Patrick McGilligan described as 'the Irregular and Bolshie situation'.[41] While the government stressed the communist/subversive threat and Fianna Fáil's part in it, de Valera's party had been working successfully since the 1927 election to neutralise the fears of the elites in Irish society, while developing a programme (based on 'our own traditional attitude to life, a solution that is Irish and Catholic') designed to appeal to as broad a constituency as possible. IRA support was ensured by making the repeal of the new repressive laws and the release of the prisoners a central plank of its platform.[42]

Fianna Fáil took power in March 1932, complicating the challenge faced by socialist republicans and their communist allies. The political landscape had been transformed. In the short term, the communists took advantage of the newly tolerant atmosphere to reorganise and move towards the launch of a party, while the socialists in the IRA were increasingly marginalised (symbolised by the swift burial of Saor Éire) as the organisation, while not bowing to de Valera's request that it disband, took a 'wait and see' attitude to the new government. The withholding of land annuities to the British, meanwhile, sparked off the 'economic war'; its impact on cattle exports and agricultural prices, together with anxiety among large farmers about Fianna Fáil's tillage plans, provoked a radical right-wing response. The Blueshirts emerged to give a cutting edge to the concerns and interests of this class. The government now faced opposition from the radical left and a newly radical-ised right, an ideological polarisation that ultimately worked to its benefit.

Following the January 1933 election, in which Fianna Fáil consolidated its 1932 victory, much of the political heat in Ireland was generated outside parliament. The IRA stepped up recruitment, the RWG were preparing to launch a communist party and the Blueshirts became increasingly fascistic and violent. Anti-communism developed a fresh dynamic, including a series of co-ordinated attacks in Dublin which resulted in the destruction of the RWG's new headquarters and the closure of a newly established Workers' College.[43] The second Communist Party of Ireland (CPI) was eventually launched on 3–4 June 1933 in Dublin with Sean Murray as general secretary. It adopted a manifesto centred on the idea that the fight for communism would grow out of the national struggle, and that the primary task for communists was to displace Fianna Fáil and the IRA in the leadership of that struggle. Relations with the IRA reached their nadir as the army executive put an effective end to joint membership and communists at Bodenstown were attacked and had their literature seized. The CPI accused the IRA of sinking to 'the gutter of the anti-communist crusade'.[44]

The deterioration in IRA-communist relations led to the increasing isolation of the O'Donnellites.[45] Meanwhile, throughout late 1933 and early 1934, rank-and-file IRA activists, militant workers and Fianna Fáil supporters clashed violently with Blueshirts. The government banned the Blueshirts on 23 August and reactivated the military tribunal, before which both Blueshirts and IRA men were charged, thus further distancing Fianna Fáil from the IRA and strengthening its constitutional credentials. The Labour and IRA leader-ships held aloof from the street fighting against Blueshirts, both effectively lining up behind Fianna Fáil's state-centred policy. At the IRA convention of 17 March 1934 a final effort was made by O'Donnell to force the IRA into a radical political role that would offer a lead to the spontaneous anti-Blueshirt activity of the previous six months and wrest the leadership of the 'Republican masses' from 'the ball and chain formula of Fianna Fail'. His proposal for a Republican Congress was defeated, and he and his supporters left the IRA to organise such a gathering in the face of opposition from their former comrades.[46]

They allied themselves with socialists, trade unionists and Cumann na mBan activists and began organising for a congress. They received support from the CPI and its affiliates, several trade union bodies North and South and the (largely Protestant) Northern Ireland Socialist Party (NISP). The period from May to September 1934 represented the high point of the socialist republican project in Ireland. The Republican Congress initiative acted as an umbrella and an inspiration for an unprecedented wave of class agitation, organisation and struggle, and managed to briefly breach the religious divide in the North and attract organised Protestant workers to a republican banner. The IRA issued an order forbidding members to give support to Congress activities, leading to defections throughout the country, particularly in Dublin where a large proportion of the brigade went over to the Congress. At Bodenstown in June 1934 the Congress contingent was blocked by the IRA from carrying its banners.[47]

The Republican Congress finally assembled on 29–30 September 1934. There were 186 delegates present, representing Congress branches, the CPI and its 'mushroom organisations', the NISP and a number of trade unions and trades councils. There were also fraternal delegates from the international communist movement. It soon became apparent that there was a major division of opinion about the form the organisation should take and how its (agreed) ultimate objectives would be defined. Former IRA man Michael Price put forward linked policy and organisational resolutions in which a Workers' Republic would be the stated objective and Congress would form itself into a political party. To O'Donnell, this seemed to represent a complete misinterpretation of the raison d'être of the entire enterprise. He put forward two corresponding resolutions, proposing a continuation of the 'united front' approach, whereby Congress would be a 'rallying centre for mass struggles' by anti-imperialists of all parties and none, pledged to the realisation of 'the Republic', behind a working-class leadership.[48] O'Donnell argued that the adoption of the Workers' Republic slogan at this stage was premature, conceding 'the Republic' to Fianna Fáil, a party that represented the very capitalist interests that opposed its achievement. He argued that it was the type of struggle to achieve the Republic that would determine its nature, and one achieved through class struggle 'becomes a Workers' and Small Farmers' Republic because the organs of struggle become the organs of government'. As with Saor Éire, O'Donnell's concern was with action not words. The supporters of the Workers' Republic slogan argued on the basis of its clarity in appealing to the working class, north and south. O'Donnell won the day by a narrow majority and the united front approach was adopted, prompting the withdrawal of Michael Price and Nora Connolly O'Brien of the organising bureau along with almost half the delegates, while over half the claimed membership of around 8,000 subsequently left.[49]

Accusations that Congress was now little more than a communist front arose from the crucial support given to O'Donnell's resolution by the CPI delegates and those of its associate organisations. CPI leader Sean Murray had spoken strongly against Price's resolution. While Price had said that you could not get rid of British imperialism until you smash capitalism, Murray argued that 'you cannot smash Capitalism until you get rid of British Imperialism'. Murray presented James Connolly's 1916 actions as an example not only of stageism but also of the 'united front' approach. George Gilmore pointed out later that both Murray and Price were ignoring the core Connollyite concept of 'the oneness of the struggle for working-class emancipation and for national independence'. O'Donnell's contributions were not explicitly stageist, and he stressed Connollyite 'oneness' in his call for the organs of struggle to become the organs of government. Despite this, his closeness to Murray was doubtless a key influence on him; indeed, Gilmore privately wrote that the Congress idea was the brainchild of Murray and O'Donnell together.[50]

Clearly, the CPI would have had good reason to oppose a new party on self-protective grounds, while the bonds between the communists and the O'Donnellites may have influenced the latter to resist the 'Workers' Republic' formula and the possibility of a new party. The united front would (theoretically) allow the CPI to maintain a 'leading' role as a party and to continue the strategy of detaching republicans from petty bourgeois leaders. The communist argument prior to Rathmines had been that the Congress should not define ultimate long-term objectives but build maximum unity around immediate issues such as opposition to fascism and repression. When faced with the two alternatives, they supported the O'Donnell line which had the added advantage of being in line with the shift in international communist policy occurring at this time. The 'class against class' approach had backfired disastrously and the Soviet Union was now beginning to seek allies in the West against Hitler. This involved diluting the emphasis previously given to the leading role of the Communist Party in any given struggle and the adoption of a Popular Front alliance with any party that would oppose Hitler. Although the CPI line in Rathmines appears in retrospect to fit the Popular Front approach neatly, it was not so clear-cut at the time. Murray and the CPI were in fact heavily criticised by the Comintern's Anglo-American Secretariat (within whose remit Irish affairs fell) for their support of the O'Donnell resolution, a position that had the effect of not merely diluting the Party's leading role, but of 'liquidating' its identity.[51]

The end product of Rathmines was a severely depleted Congress and much bitterness. Its calls for unity had fallen on mostly deaf ears in the main-stream labour and republican movements, and over half of those who answered the original call now abandoned it. The communists and their republican allies had decided yet again to work within the confines of republicanism, now dominated by an integrationist party with state power, and to offer, as Dunphy has argued, a challenge to that party's growing hegemony not at its weakest point (class) but its strongest (nation).[52] What remained of the Republican Congress forged ahead in its efforts to create a broader 'united front'. Despite occasional co-operation around campaigns such as that against the Unemployment Assistance Act in late 1934 and in support of the Dublin tram strike in early 1935, the IRA, the Labour Party and the mainstream trade union movement rejected a united front with the communist pariah (anti-communism was still alive and (literally) kicking).[53] Communist policy itself soon shifted when the new Popular Front strategy was endorsed at the final Comintern congress in July-August 1935. Communists were now to seek alliances with left- and right-wing social democrats, and even bourgeois parties, so long as they were 'progressive' (i.e. opposed to fascism). In Irish terms, this meant, as well as supporting reformist labour, a move to 'drag behind the policy of de Valera' as Murray put it in his speech to the congress.[54] As hopes of class unity in the North, inspired by the non-sectarian Outdoor Relief riots of 1932, went up in smoke with the sectarian riots of the summer of 1935, relations between Fianna Fáil and the IRA in the south continued to deteriorate. The constitutional pursuit of republican goals was slowly yielding results, which, together with 'a judicious combination of jobbery and coercion',[55] reduced the IRA to insignificance. In June it was declared illegal, Twomey was sentenced to three years' imprisonment and the leadership went into hiding; *An Phoblacht* was suppressed in early July, while the *Workers' Voice* had folded in June. In the Dublin Corporation elections at the end of July, Congress candidates Gilmore and Ryan performed pitiably while the CPI withdrew its candidates in favour of the Labour Party.

The outbreak of the Spanish Civil War sparked a resurgence of communist/ socialist republican co-operation as, with the support of an assortment of independent republicans, socialists and liberals, the left battled vainly to counter the red scare-mongering pro-Franco campaign in Ireland and provide some 200 volunteers for the international brigades.[56] Spain was the last hurrah of inter-war communist/republican co-operation. By the end of the 1930s the Comintern had outlived its usefulness for the Soviet Union, while Irish republicanism had bifurcated into the integrationist (southern) state-centred reformism of a dominant Fianna Fáil and the militarism of an IRA rump – leaving socialist republicanism in historical limbo. Despite, and partly because of, the efforts of the communists and their fellow travellers in the IRA, Irish politics, North and South, continued to be dominated by its respective non-class based cleavages. The failure of the Irish left in all its numerous guises to offer a socialist response to the Treaty and partition created poor foundations on which to build a left-wing alternative to the dominant orders that characterised the two states that emerged in the 1920s.

The inability of republicanism to offer a way forward for Stalinist communism – never mind a route to Irish socialism – in the inter-war years did not deter later attempts to revive socialist republicanism in a different context. The communist-republican link re-emerged in the 1960s when communists from the Connolly Association, the Irish émigré offshoot of the CPGB, were influential on the new leadership of the republican movement in its attempt to revive and reformulate the O'Donnellite project.[57] The Irish communist movement, whose centre of gravity had shifted North since the Second World War, concentrated its efforts there on trade unionism and reformist politics, exerting its final important influence through the civil rights movement. Following the split in the IRA/Sinn Féin, those who had drawn their inspiration from the inter-war socialist republicans achieved brief, limited political success in the South, while the North endured a quarter century of armed conflict during which socialist politics failed to make an impact. It was resurgent (non-socialist) republicanism, in the shape of Sinn Féin, that emerged from the ashes as a major political beneficiary, echoing the success of Fianna Fáil in the earlier period.

Notes

1   For an example of British propaganda about Ireland, see R. Dawson, *Red Terror and Green* (London, 1920); on the 'die-hards', see P. Canning, *British Policy Towards Ireland 1921–1941* (Oxford, 1985), pp. 17–20; on the need for a communist party, see, for example, M. Milotte, *Communism in Modern Ireland: The Pursuit of the Workers' Republic since 1916* (Dublin, 1984); C. Kostick, *Revolution in Ireland: Popular Militancy, 1917 to 1923* (London, 1996); K. Allen, *The Politics of James Connolly* (London, 1990) and T. Crean, 'From Petrograd to Bruree' in D. Fitzpatrick (ed.), *Revolution? Ireland 1917–1923* (Dublin, 1990). The contacts between Sinn Féin/Dáil Éireann and Soviet Russia in this period had no political significance, in the sense of influencing the nature or conduct of the Irish struggle, while the bolshevist rhetoric of the labour leadership was largely empty.

2   *Workers' Republic*, 17 Dec., 12 Nov. 1921.

3   Irish orthodox communists generally regard Connolly's 1916 actions as evidence of a stageist approach (see, for example, C. D. Greaves, *The Life and Times of James Connolly* (London, 1961), p. 344); this interpretation is challenged by others (see, for example, Milotte, *Communism*, p. 24 and Allen, *Connolly*, p. 171).

4   P. O'Donnell, *The Gates Flew Open* (Cork, 1966 edn), pp. 14–17; C. D. Greaves, *Liam Mellows and the Irish Revolution* (London, 1971), p. 362. On the question of O'Donnell's possible membership of the CPI, see *Workers' Republic*, 25 November 1922 and 25 August 1923. O'Donnell's denials are contained in an interview with D. R. O'Connor-Lysaght, 23 February 1983 (copy in the Irish Labour History Museum and Archive, Dublin).

5   *Workers' Republic*, 22, 29 July 1922.

6   *Workers' Republic*, 22, 29 July, 12 August 1922; Milotte, *Communism*, pp. 59–61; 'Roddy Connolly – 60 years of political activity', *The Irish Times*, 27 Aug. 1976.

7   M. Hopkinson, *Green Against Green: The Irish Civil War* (Dublin, 1988), p. 186.

8   *Irish Independent*, 21 Sept. 1922; Greaves, *Mellows*, pp. 363–77.

9   *Workers' Republic*, 23 Dec. 1922–3 Feb. 1923; Milotte, *Communism*, pp. 63–5.

10   For variations on this theme, see R. Dunphy, *The Making of Fianna Fáil Power in Ireland 1923–1948* (Oxford, 1994); R. English, *Radicals and the Republic: Socialist Republicanism in the Irish Free State 1925–1937* (Oxford, 1994); H. Patterson, *The Politics of Illusion: A Political History of the IRA* (London, 1997); Millote, *Communism*; and Allen, *Connolly*.

11   See E. O'Connor, 'James Larkin in the United States, 1914–23', *Journal of Contemporary History* 37, 2 (2002), and 'Jim Larkin and the Communist Internationals, 1923–9', *Irish Historical Studies* 31, 123 (1999).

12   Peadar O'Donnell edited *An Phoblacht* from 1926 to 1929, Frank Ryan from 1929 to 1933.

13   See J. P. McHugh, 'Voices of the Rearguard: A Study of *An Phoblacht*: Irish Republican Thought in the Post-Revolutionary Era, 1923–37', MA thesis, UCD, 1983, pp. 494–7; Patterson, *Illusion*, p. 53.

14   J. Callaghan, 'The Communists and the colonies: anti-imperialism between the wars', in G. Andrews, N. Fishman and K. Morgan (eds), *Opening the Books: Essays on the Social and Cultural History of British Communism* (London, 1995), pp. 7–18; 'Notes on Communism in Saorstat Éireann' (National Archives of Ireland (NA), Department of Justice (DJ), 1936, Box 4/202).

15   NA, DJ 8/682; Milotte, *Communism*, pp. 93, 102–3; C. Foley, *Legion of the Rearguard: The IRA and the Modern Irish State* (London, 1992), p. 81; O'Connor, 'Larkin and the Internationals', p. 367; *An Phoblacht*, 13 July 1929.

16   Garda report on LAI Congress, Frankfurt-on-Main, 16 Sept. 1929 (NA, DJ 8/682).

17   E. O'Connor, 'Reds and the green: problems of the history and historiography of communism in Ireland', *Science and Society* 61, 1 (1997), p. 114; B. McLaughlin and E. O'Connor, 'Sources on Ireland and the Communist International, 1920–1943' *Saothar* 21 (1996), p. 107.

18   See B. McLaughlin, 'Proletarian academics or party functionaries? Irish Communists at the International Lenin School, Moscow, 1927–1937', *Saothar* 22 (1997), pp. 63–79.

19   On the land annuities issue and campaign, see D. Ó Drisceoil, *Peadar O'Donnell* (Cork, 2001), pp. 44–50.

20   See ibid., pp. 57–60.

21   Department of Justice, 'Notes on Communism', pp. 14–15; Department of Justice memo, 19 Mar. 1930; 'Revolutionary Organisations' memo, 4 Apr. 1930, Department of Taoiseach (DT S5074A-B); 'Workers' Revolutionary Party', Garda report to Justice, 13 June (NA, DJ 8/691).

22   Text of letter contained in Department of Justice, 'Notes on Communism', Appendix III.

23   *An Phoblacht*, 9 July 1930.

24   See, for example, Milotte, *Communism*, p. 100.

25   See reports in *An Phoblacht*, 14 June and 9 July, 1930, and Garda report on LAI meeting, Mansion House, Dublin, 25 Sept. 1930 (NA, DJ 8/682).

26   *An Phoblacht*, 29 Nov. 1930–28 Mar. 1931; see also, J. Hammill, 'Saor Éire and the IRA: an exercise in deception?', *Saothar* 20 (1995), pp. 57–60, and English, *Radicals*, pp. 124–6.

27 *An Phoblacht*, July-Sept. 1931; Hammill, 'Saor Éire', p. 58; J. Bowyer Bell, *The Secret Army: The IRA* (Dublin 1997), p. 82; U. MacEoin (ed.), *Survivors* (Dublin, 1980), p. 6 and *The IRA in the Twilight Years* (Dublin, 1997), p. 620.

28 Dunphy, *Fianna Fáil*, pp. 74–5.

29 Department of Justice, 'Report on the present position', Aug. 1931 (NA, DT S5864B); *An Phoblacht*, 11 Apr. 1931.

30 *An Phoblacht*, 27 June 1931; P. O'Donnell, *There Will Be Another Day* (Dublin, 1963), pp. 121–6; Department of Justice, ibid.

31 Report submitted to the government by D/J on 'Alliance between Irish Republican Army and Communists', 1931 (NA, DT S5864A).

32 P. Murray, *Oracles of God: The Roman Catholic Church and Irish Politics, 1922–37* (Dublin, 2000), pp. 320–1; Cosgrave to MacRory, 11 Sept. 1931 (NA, DT S5864B).

33 *An Phoblacht*, 3 Oct. 1931; Bowyer Bell, *Secret Army*, pp. 87, 96.

34 Saor Éire 'Constitution and Rules' (NA, DT S5864B); 'Saor Éire . . . Three resolutions adopted by First National Congress', National Library of Ireland.

35 *An Phoblacht*, 17 October 1931; *Dáil Debates*, vol. 40, col. 113, 14 Oct. 1931.

36 Hammill, 'Saor Eire', p. 62; Milotte, *Communism*, pp. 100 and 107.

37 Anon., *Communist Party of Ireland: Outline History* (Dublin, n.d.), p. 11.

38 Summary of opening statement by the Cosgrave in the Dáil, 14 Oct. 1931, and text of the joint pastoral (NA, DT S2267); *Dáil Debates*, vol. 40, cols 104–13, 14 Oct. 1931.

39 D. Keogh, 'De Valera, the Catholic Church and the "Red Scare", 1931–1932', in J. P. O'Carroll and J. A. Murphy (eds), *De Valera and his Times* (Cork, 1986), pp. 140–2.

40 M. Banta, 'The Red Scare in the Irish Free State', unpublished MA thesis, UCD, 1982, p. 45.

41 McGilligan to Joe Walshe, 18 Sept. 1931, McGilligan papers (University College Dublin Archives (UCDA)), cited in R. Fanning, *Independent Ireland* (Dublin, 1983), p. 105.

42 Keogh, 'Red Scare', pp. 144–57; Dunphy, *Fianna Fáil*, pp. 142–4; Patterson, *Illusion*, p. 61.

43 P. Greely, *The Gralton Affair* (Dublin, 1986), pp. 43–66; 'Anti-communist demonstrations 1933' (NA, DJ 8/711).

44 Milotte, *Communism*, pp. 141–3; *An Phoblacht*, 17 June 1933; *Irish Workers' Voice*, 24 June 1933; S. Bowler, 'Sean Murray, 1898–1961, and the pursuit of Stalinism in one country', *Saothar* 18 (1993), pp. 44–5.

45 See Ó Drisceoil, *O'Donnell*, p. 81.

46 Minutes of the General Army Convention, 17 Mar. 1934 (UCDA, Seán MacEntee papers, P67/525); P. O'Donnell, 'The Irish struggle to-day', *Left Review*, 2 Apr. 1936, p. 299.

47 On Congress activities, see *Republican Congress*, May-Sept. 1934; G. Gilmore, *The Irish Republican Congress* (Cork, 1978 edn); P. Byrne, *The Irish Republican Congress Revisited* (London, 1998 edn); 'Notes on the Republican Congress Movement', 1936 (NA, DJ, Box 4/202); Ó Drisceoil, *O'Donnell*, pp. 84–90.

48 *Republican Congress*, 6, 13 Oct. 1934; Gilmore, *Congress*, pp. 45–51; Byrne, *Revisited*, pp. 30–2; O'Donnell, 'Irish struggle', p. 299; Hogan, *Could Ireland*, p. 129.

49 *Republican Congress*, 6 Oct. 1934.

50 Gilmore, *Congress*, p. 54; Gilmore to Coughlan, quoted in English, *Radicals*, p. 221.

51 McLaughlin, *Proletarian Academics*, p. 73

52 Dunphy, *Fianna Fáil*, p. 188

53 See Ó Drisceoil, pp. 90–4.

54 Milotte, *Communism*, pp. 159–60; Bowler, 'Sean Murray', p. 47.

55 *United Ireland*, 2 Nov. 1935.

56 See F. McGarry, *Irish Politics and the Spanish Civil War* (Cork, 1999), *passim*.

57 See Milotte, *Communism*, pp. 265–7 and Patterson, *Illusion*, pp. 96–121.

CHAPTER 5

'Too Damned Tolerant'

Republicans and Imperialism in the Irish Free State

* * *

Fearghal McGarry

On 3 January 1922 a Sinn Féin official (posing as secretary of the Irish Free State's Decoration Committee) wrote to several of Dublin's largest businesses appealing for oversized Union Jacks in anticipation of a pro-Treaty victory in the vote on the Anglo-Irish Treaty. He explained that it was intended to raise the Union Jack over the Dáil 'as soon as the result of the discussion is known. We would be grateful if you would give the bearer your largest flag. We will, of course, return it to you as soon as the one which we have ordered arrives.'[1] This unconvincing hoax was duly denounced in the Dáil by an indignant W. T. Cosgrave but it offered an early indication of the sensitivities surrounding British symbols in the Irish Free State. When James Connolly observed that independence without a social revolution would amount to little more than painting Ireland's red pillar-boxes green, he could not have known just how many would settle for such an outcome. In *Recollections of a Rebel*, J. J. Walsh, the Free State's first post-master general and one of Cumann na nGaedheal's most nationalist ministers, cited his greening of the post-boxes as among the most notable of his revolutionary achievements.[2] His generation's obsession with symbolic aspects of sovereignty has been widely noted, and equally widely criticised. For example, the concern expressed by republicans in the Treaty debates about the oath of fidelity to the British Crown and other trappings of imperialism is often contrasted with their relative lack of interest in more substantive issues such as partition. Yet, as Joe Lee has observed, such concerns were not unique to Irish republicans – the British government was no less obsessed with symbols in this period. [3]

Why were symbols considered of such importance? Partly because of the different mentality of the era, far removed from the present one when a British cabinet minister can publicly swear an oath to the Crown with his fingers crossed behind his back. However, symbols were also important because they

provided an obvious measurement of sovereignty. The attainment of sovereignty – or failure to achieve it – is most visibly demonstrated by flags, coins,
anthems and other superficial trappings of statehood.[4] In the Irish Free State,
where an incomplete and unsatisfactory measure of sovereignty had been
attained, it was inevitable that such symbols would become contested (just as
they continue to be in present-day Northern Ireland where issues of sovereignty
remain in dispute). Their importance was also exaggerated by the nature of
the distinctive ideology that emerged from the traditions of constitutional
nationalism, Fenianism, republicanism and the Irish-Ireland movement. At
its core was not a commitment to a specific social or economic programme, or
even a particular form of state, but a belief in the importance of asserting the
cultural and political sovereignty of Ireland. Under Cumann na nGaedheal,
symbols of the continued connection with Britain were systematically removed
from public life.[5] This process was accelerated in the 1930s by de Valera whose
popularity was largely rooted in his success in replacing British symbols with
Irish ones, an achievement which enabled him to win the loyalty of all but an
irreconcilable minority of republicans to the twenty-six county state. As a
recent survey concluded, the 'most dramatic changes' that occurred under de
Valera, 'were at the symbolic level'.[6] A less explored aspect of this period concerns the parallel attempts by republicans to suppress symbols and other
expressions of British identity within southern Irish society. This article
considers the motivations of republicans for doing so and the official responses
to such activism.

I

The inter-war campaign against 'British imperialism' must be viewed in the
context of the sectarian violence of the War of Independence, the demor-
alising experience of civil war and the marginalisation of republicans in the Free
State. The fifteen thousand republican internees released by 1924 were faced
with unemployment, competition from demobilised soldiers and discrimination by the Treatyite government. Much of the republican leadership had
been killed in the civil war. The tiny proportion of republicans who remained
IRA activists continued to support de Valera's Sinn Féin (and Fianna Fáil
after its formation in 1926) but important differences remained between
armed and political republicanism. The IRA saw its role as a military one and
lacked much interest, or faith, in political means. The disastrous series of
events after July 1921 reinforced hostility towards democratic politics within
the movement. The IRA's militarism was strengthened by its reorganisation
in 1925 when it withdrew allegiance from the 2nd Dáil (the surviving anti-
Treaty political leadership) and vested governmental authority in its own

army council. This process hastened the divergence between the IRA and those republicans, led by de Valera, who believed in the necessity of winning popular support to return to power. The IRA became a secret army, committed to the use of physical force to achieve its objectives. Its main enemy was not Britain or Northern Ireland but the Free State and its supporters, who were regarded as Britain's garrison in Ireland and most responsible for the humiliation of the Treaty.

Given the scale of the military defeat in 1923, IRA activism was of necessity restricted to recruitment, drilling, propaganda and agitation. Sporadic acts of violence occurred, such as the assassination of Kevin O'Higgins in 1927, but it was not until the end of the decade that the IRA had revived sufficiently to launch a concerted campaign against the police and courts of the Free State. In the meantime, IRA agitation was aimed at those individuals, institutions and symbols most visibly associated with the former regime. The IRA's newspaper, *An Phoblacht*, identified the 'two most blatant and unnecessarily offensive outward symbols of West Britonism in Ireland' as 'Union Jacks and Baden Powell Scouts'.[7] The latter, castigated as 'pets of the CID' and 'dupes of Empire', were ridiculed and occasionally attacked. In September 1928, for example, the Gilmore brothers led a raid on 'British scouts' at Powerscourt, burning their tents and carrying off a quantity of 'military equipment'. Huts belonging to the sea scouts were destroyed, while others were fired on.[8] (Even the Catholic Boy Scouts – a rival of the IRA's youth wing Na Fianna – did not escape criticism due to its 'West-British atmosphere' and fraternisation with 'Imperialist Scouts'.) Other targets of republican invective included the Royal Dublin Horse Show, Freemasons and, more surprisingly, the Knights of Columbanus ('the swanky crust of the toiling masses – a rotten gang of sycophants').[9]

Cinemas which showed war movies, news of Britain's royal family or patronising films of Irish life, provided another soft target. In 1930 the Savoy's inaugural film – which republican students from University College Dublin succeeded in disrupting – was condemned as a 'typically Oirish' travesty. *An Phoblacht* observed: 'As a rule we Irish are too tolerant. Our tolerance has again been abused by Englishmen who come to vilify us and make us pay for seeing ourselves vilified.'[10] (This concept of tolerance as weakness was a recurrent motif in *An Phoblacht* and the mentality of inter-war republicanism.) The Bohemian Picture Theatre in Dublin was bombed after showing a newsreel featuring the Prince of Wales at the 1935 FA Cup Final.[11] The previous year some four hundred men had rushed the Savoy to protest the showing of a Movietone News feature on the wedding of the Duke of Kent and Princess Marina. They stampeded past the uniformed gardaí and armed Special Branch men assigned to guard the cinema, hurling stink bombs, rotten eggs and ink at the screen. A group of protesters took to the stage, shouting

'Remember Casement' and 'Down with Imperialism', before shredding the screen. Some of the audience joined in, several hysterical women fainted, while others ostentatiously clapped the pictures of the royal wedding. Completing the scene of chaos, the Savoy's organist, Philip Dore, attempted to restore calm with his rendition of 'My Dark Rosaleen' as police reinforcements chased after fleeing protesters. Following further protests and raids by Cumann na mBan, the IRA and Republican Congress, the newsreel was pulled from cinemas in Dublin, Kilkenny, Cork and Waterford but shown under heavy police protection in Limerick.[12]

An interesting aspect of such protests was the divergent responses they provoked. After learning of the riot, Tom Casement complained that his brother 'gave his life for the rights of minorities – in the Congo, in Putamayo, and in Ireland. He would have been the first to condemn last night's exhibition of tyranny.'[13] Another correspondent regarded this as 'rather presumptuous': 'What is tyranny to one may surely be freedom to another. At the moment one cannot be truly British and truly Irish . . . The only way that the public have of voicing their feelings regarding cinema films, music hall dramas etc. is by verbal or physical action inside the offending theatre.' He blamed the disturbances on the management for insisting on showing the film regardless of the protest and the laxity of government censorship: 'In any other country in the world enemy propaganda would be stopped at the Customs barrier.'[14] The state was also divided in its attitude to the riot. The investigating officer, Chief Superintendent Clarke, took much the same view as the correspondent to the press: 'I consider that the continual showing of this picture and the attitude of certain sections of the audiences in cheering and clapping it is calculated to lead to disorder.'[15] Urging the banning of the newsreel, he noted: 'Cinema managers in this country who book this film must be prepared to suffer some consequences as they must be aware that such films are distasteful to the majority of their patrons.'[16] Clarke's report was sharply dismissed as 'Bunk!' by the secretary of the Department of Justice who claimed that most of the audience 'did not find the film of the Royal Wedding distasteful. On the contrary they liked it & enjoyed it.'[17]

However, the most popular focus for organised protest against imperialism was the annual Armistice Day ceremony held on 11 November to commemorate the dead of the First World War.[18] By the mid-1920s Armistice (or Poppy) Day parades in Dublin, organised by the British Legion, involved as many as twenty thousand ex-servicemen and ten thousand supporters. Union Jack flags and bunting were displayed outside the city-centre businesses and residences of wealthy Protestants, a visible symbol of the position of economic privilege retained by unionists (or ex-unionists) in the Free State. Armistice Day infuriated republicans who regarded it as a provocative display of British imperialism. Counter-demonstrations were soon organised, with the women's organisation, Cumann na mBan, playing a leading role. *An Phoblacht* described the scenes during the first well-organised protests in 1925:

> Union Jacks were waved, and a part of the crowd sang 'God Save the King' as a prelude to the two-minute silence. With malicious humour smoke bombs were thrown amongst the crowd, and the impressive ceremony fizzled out before the smoke drifted away. Parts of the audience again broke into wavering singing of 'God Save the King,' and the report of further explosions created something of a panic. On the outskirts of the crowd that gathered round the memorial, a big Union Jack was burned by a crowd, many of whom wore the Tricolour of the Irish Republic, to the singing of the 'Soldier's Song'. This crowd, a couple of thousand strong, paraded the city and Union Jackery in Dublin was done. The few Union Jacks that were left out in the belief that Dublin was safe for the Empire were swooped upon and burned, and an aggressive display of the same kind by Trinity boys cost many of them a severe handling. At night time this parade, swelled by thousands, marched through the streets and were greeted everywhere in approval and cries of 'Up Ireland', 'Up the Republic'.[19]

The protests soon won the support not only of the IRA but also of almost all republican and left-wing organisations. Both Sinn Féin and Fianna Fáil supported the demonstrations, linking them to a broader campaign against public expressions of British identity. In 1925, for example, a motion at Sinn Féin's Ard Fheis urged 'action throughout all Ireland against British propaganda being displayed in Cinemas, and also to prevent the display of British emblems, viz: Union Jacks, etc. in public places'. Seán Lemass declared that the 1925 ceremony should be the last 'to popularise the Imperialistic idea amongst the people of their country'.[20] Armistice Day quickly became one of the most important events in the republican calendar, invariably marked by protests, street-fighting and armed attacks on 'British' targets. The republican writer, Rosamund Jacob, recorded the scenes in her diary the following year:

> I found poppy crowds standing in rows observing the silence, & other crowds walking or shouting. A few steps up the Green I perceived an ordered mob of young men marching in the roadway ... and at their head Proinnsias [Frank Ryan] & another, carrying a stick from which trailed a large Union Jack. The grave dignity of P., indulging in this childish sport, was impressive. They turned presently & marched down again, & then got involved with some peelers and between them & the peelers the flag was torn to bits. Then they marched off up Grafton St & Dawson St, growing as they went, & I followed ... The first Union Jack they found was out of the Church Representative Body house in Stephen's Green & it took them a while to deal with it but eventually someone got in & opened the door, and they went up & fetched it down & streeled it in the mud.[21]

In 1928 republicans bombed William III's statue in College Green, Edward VII's fountain in Herbert Park and George II's equestrian monument on St Stephen's Green. (William III's mutilated head was later stolen by armed men from a Corporation repair yard). Republicans fought gardaí and poppy-wearers throughout the day, bringing chaos to the centre of Dublin despite a heavy police presence.[22] Poppy-snatching became a common pursuit. UCD youths sporting Easter lilies descended on Trinity students and other ex-unionists, some of whom concealed razor blades within their poppies. A Protestant boy's home on Grand Canal street was raided by armed men after one of the boys was seen waving a Union Jack from a window.[23] Sinn Féin began a boycott of businesses which flew the 'the blood-soaked banner of England' including the Bank of Ireland, Ulster Bank, Brown Thomas, Weirs & Hayes, Conygham & Robinson.[24] Businesses and residences which flew the Union Jack were attacked. These were rarely lethal but nonetheless frightening, as a police report of a raid by seven republicans on a second-hand bookshop on Ormond Quay indicates:

> One of them asked Mr Morisy if he had any Greek books for sale and was shown one. He then asked for some Irish plays and while Mr Morisy was looking for them another of the men said 'Hand up those Flags' meaning some Union Jack flags which were for sale in the shop. Mr Morisy refused to do so. The man then produced a .45 revolver and pressed it to Mr Morisy's side at the same time hitting him on the face and body with his fist. Mrs Morisy who was also in the shop screamed for help and another man put his hands on her throat and his knee against her stomach. Her two nieces, Christina Hickey and Moira Hickey, then came into the shop and all screamed for help. The raiders then left taking two Union Jacks.[25]

The most serious incident of the campaign occurred when Albert Armstrong, a Protestant who testified against IRA men who removed a Union Jack from his insurance company, was murdered in his home.[26]

The year 1928 marked the high point of the republican campaign against Armistice Day which, as *An Phoblacht* noted, soon became a victim of its own success:

> During the past twelve months, Imperialists in Ireland have learnt a salutary lesson. Gone is the day when they could march boldly and bravely, to honour their king, to flaunt his flag, and to revile 'the mere Irish'. To-day they keep their Union Jacks in the garrets, and have no great inclination to shake the moth-balls out of them.[27]

Although only four Union Jacks (each guarded by armed Special Branch men) were spotted where hundreds once flew, *An Phoblacht* urged vigilance against the more insidious policy of 'peaceful penetration'. It drew attention to efforts by imperialists and clerics to introduce the two-minute silence in Catholic schools.[28] It revealed also that Union Jacks had been waved and 'God Save the King' sung at the service of remembrance in Phoenix Park: 'Dubliners are tolerant of what happens outside the city streets, but next time, they may be provoked into visiting Phoenix Park.' Frank Ryan, the leader of the League Against Imperialism (the republican organisation which organised the counter-demonstration on the eve of Armistice Day), urged militant vigilance all year round: 'Imperialist blockheads are not by nature susceptible to argument, they are susceptible to fear, and must be made feel fear.'[29] Despite its effective suppression, Armistice Day remained an important event for the IRA in the early 1930s. According to *An Phoblacht*, some ten thousand republicans attended the counter protest in 1930, three times the number that attended the ceremony itself which was described as 'fairly quiet' and 'tame' despite some attacks on Protestant businesses.[30] Why was Armistice Day so important to republicans?

II

First, one must consider those motives which republicans denied were connected to their protests. Republicans always emphasised that they were not opposed to commemoration of Ireland's war dead. Rather, they claimed that Armistice Day was not a genuine day of commemoration. In 1925, for example, Seán MacEntee noted 'that English propaganda was cute and cunning. Last year they were asked to allow a section of the community to commemorate their dead. There was no Irishman who would raise an objection to that, but the opportunity was taken of that commemoration to make it a propagandist day of Imperialism . . . next year there would be no display anywhere.'[31] *An Phoblacht* similarly argued that Armistice Day was about jingoistic imperialism rather than commemoration.[32]

> No Republican wishes to mar the solemnity of their commemoration. We, too, know what it is to lose well-loved comrades who fought by our side. We, too, have our widows, our orphans, our mourning parents . . . But there is another side to the story. There is in Ireland a small, but noisy section of the British garrison, which seeks each year to turn Armistice Day into an occasion of imperialist propaganda. These people think that, under police protection, they can safely outrage our national sentiment by flaunting the flag of our oppressor and singing the anthem of the country which holds us in subjection. We warn them once again – we are not out for trouble, but if they invite trouble they will get it.[33]

Republican protests were depicted as a defensive response to aggressive British imperialism. But was Armistice Day, as the League Against Imperialism claimed, a 'flagrant display of British Imperialism disguised as Armistice Celebrations' or were republicans, as was often alleged, actually opposed to commemoration of the war? Some truth lies behind both assertions. As well as uniting mourners of all persuasions, Armistice Day was also the only public occasion when unionists could take to the streets of Dublin to celebrate their British identity in a defiant flurry of Union Jack waving and singing of the British national anthem. *An Phoblacht*, for example, argued that the Trinity students who were prominent participants knew nothing of the war, and that the Irish ex-servicemen who took part were misled by the jingoistic British Legion (just as they had been by Redmond and the British government in 1914):

> Well-fed, young Trinity students in their plus-fours and Oxford bags – untroubled boyish faces. What do they know of war? Children they were when a hundred thousand Irishmen agonised and died in the mud of Flanders. Ex-soldiers, too; veterans of the 'Great War' with their medals on their breasts . . . For four years you [veterans] suffered for them – and for ten years since they have wanted you one day in 365. On Armistice Day, fed and feted. For the other 364 days – slums and starvation.[34]

For a minority of participants (Trinity's rowdy contingent included), the opportunity to publicly demonstrate loyalty to Britain was clearly a central attraction of Armistice Day. The Garda Síochána, despite despising the republicans who organised the counter-protests, nonetheless agreed with their criticism of Armistice Day. Chief Superintendent Edward Duffy (having being berated by an excitable Protestant minister who shouted 'To hell with the Free State') complained to the head of Special Branch, Dave Neligan, that the occasion 'was a definite Imperialistic parade, and not a Commemoration to the war dead, as it ought to have been'. Neligan had previously complained to the Garda Commissioner, Eoin O'Duffy, that it was 'becoming the excuse for a regular military field-day for these persons'. O'Duffy, in turn, suggested the government ban Armistice Day as it was 'more a military display than a bona fide commemoration service'.[35] The president of the Executive Council, W. T. Cosgrave, also acknowledged that nationalists resented 'the exploitation of Poppy Day in Dublin by the most hostile elements of the old Unionist class'.[36] It is important to note, however, that sources both sympathetic and hostile to Armistice Day accepted that this provocative behaviour was confined to a minority of the participants (invariably identified as females), and opposed by the British Legion.[37] For example, General Sir William Hickie, president of the British Legion in southern Ireland, criticised those Protestants who attempted to turn the occasion into another twelfth of July.[38]

Conversely, however, republican claims that they did not object to com-memoration of the war itself do not stand up to scrutiny. The very emphasis republicans placed on this in their anti-Armistice Day rhetoric indicated their sensitivity to the allegation. A close reading of anti-imperialist rhetoric does demonstrate an underlying hostility to commemoration of the war. One *An Phoblacht* article revealingly complained:

> In the Limerick of John Daly and Bishop O'Dwyer there is a circular going the rounds these days. It is an appeal for funds to erect a 'Memorial to the memory of the men of Limerick who gave their lives in the service of the county in the Great War' [to be] unveiled on Armistice Day. If that day were fittingly celebrated in Ireland it would symbolise deception and hypocrisy. It would commemorate in pity those who were sacrificed in a commercial war between John Bull and his German cousins and hypocritically told that they were fighting for small nations.

In this case, commemoration was illegitimate not because of the way it was conducted, or the motives of those who organised it, but because of the nature of the war itself. As one historian noted: 'the rhetorical legacy of Sinn Féin made it impracticable to separate the issues of personal suffering and political conviction, all servicemen living and dead being damned by the flag under which they served . . . For the revolutionary generation war service signified betrayal of the Irish nation'.[39] During the War of Independence ex-servicemen had been a common target of IRA violence and they remained under suspicion in the Free State. Underlying this hostility was an uneasiness about Irish commitment to the war effort. Some two hundred thousand Irish men had enlisted, a figure which far outweighed the numbers involved in 1916 and the War of Independence. Few of those who fought for Britain (or later comme-morated them) did so for explicitly political reasons but the figures were a reminder that tens of thousands of Irishmen had, like Redmond, seen no contradiction between Irish patriotism and support for the British war effort. It was also an unwelcome reminder that until recently the great majority of nationalists supported Home Rule. This unease was not confined to radical republicans, the two-minute silence on 11 November was dwarfed by the state's silence on the subject. In contrast, the British Legion's sale of some half million poppies in the Dublin area in 1924 illustrated the gulf between private and official remembrance of the war.[40] The latter attitude was reflected in O'Duffy's observation that while he did not object to commemo-ration of the war 'there appears no necessity to perpetuate this form of ceremony in the Saorstat'.[41]

Republicans were also careful to emphasise that their protests were not motivated by sectarianism. This claim can be broadly accepted. Frank Ryan, the driving force behind the League Against Imperialism, was an outspoken critic of sectarianism within republicanism, as were other leading figures involved in the protests such as George Gilmore (a northern Presbyterian) and the socialist Peadar O'Donnell. However, the businesses, residences and churches which were attacked on 11 November belonged to Protestants, and the rhetoric of even relatively progressive republicans such as Ryan during Armistice Day was problematic. The discordance between Ryan's anti-sectarianism and comments such as 'Ireland for the Irish; the Empire for Imperialists. Let those who want to honour their king get out to their proper country' seem evident.[42] Figures such as Ryan regarded the republican tradition as progressive because it would welcome Protestants as equals in a united Ireland, but the implication of such rhetoric was clear: Protestants must renounce their political and cultural (if not religious) allegiances to qualify for this equality. The specious argument which *An Phoblacht* editorials often gave – 'Think you it would be possible for the French to hold in Berlin, or the Germans to hold in Paris, an elaborate procession honouring their own dead at the capital of the others country?' – unwittingly highlighted the fact that those who died in the British Army were Irish (whether nationalist or unionist), as were those who commemorated their deaths.[43] The limitations of such thinking must be seen in context; the idea of tolerating conflicting political identities had little support on either side of the border in this period when the War of Independence and civil war remained a vivid memory. Ryan, drawing a rigid if unrealistic distinction between religious and political affiliations, viewed the stripping of Union Jacks from Protestant churches as an anti-imperialist rather than sectarian action, and his Anti-Imperialist League formed part of a broader international grouping of anti-imperialist organisations. Whether rank-and-file republicans (or their targets) appreciated the distinction between Protestant and ex-Unionist targets is more questionable.

Downplaying questions of commemoration and sectarianism, republicans focused on the imperialist threat to justify their protests. *An Phoblacht* argued:

> The Imperialists in our midst have become as aggressive and insulting to the National Ideals as they were before the Wars of Independence . . . They are actively, if in some districts quietly, organising all the anti-National and pro-British elements in the country. They have such organisations as the Legion of British Ex-Servicemen, Freemason Lodges, Baden Powell Scouts, Boys' Brigades, Girl Guides, British Fascisti . . . The Imperialist menace is very real, and it is the duty of Republicans to watch closely its development and ramifications.[44]

The spectre of a far-reaching imperialist conspiracy, backed by Britain, was frequently invoked to justify the suppression of pro-British bodies. It was claimed that the Boy Scouts sought 'to train Irish boys to act as British soldiers in the next Great War, to act as British scouts in the next Anglo-Irish

War, to act as strike-breakers in the next Class War'.[45] Armistice Day was denounced as an attempt 'to strengthen recruiting for the British army'.[46] As ex-unionists clearly represented a politically disempowered (albeit wealthy) minority within the Free State, it might be questioned whether republicans genuinely believed they represented a potential fifth column. A close reading of republican propaganda suggests such doubts did exist. In 1929, by which time most ex-unionists had reconsidered the wisdom of displaying Union Jacks, an editorial in an *An Phoblacht* issue otherwise dominated by the dangers of Armistice Day, pondered: 'Perhaps the warning is unnecessary; perhaps, indeed, we are giving an exaggerated importance to these nonentities. In recent years they have had one or two sharp lessons.'[47] Elsewhere in the same edition, however, the dearth of Union Jacks was attributed to the insidious policy of 'peaceful penetration', thus justifying increased vigilance.

It would be wrong, however, to dismiss any relationship between violent opposition to displays of British identity and a fear of British imperialism re-emerging in the Free State merely because the latter was an unlikely scenario. Charles Townshend noted that it was not until the return of the Treaty ports in 1938, 'a pivotal moment in British history', that Britain formally abandoned the option of reconquest, a notion 'which certainly haunted Irish minds'.[48] Fear, moreover, is related to insecurity, an emotion clearly evident within the political culture of extreme nationalism in this period. The Armistice Day protests originated from a Cumann na mBan-sponsored organisation, the Anti-Imperialist Vigilance Association, which monitored not only politics but the theatre, art, literature, cinema and press for imperialist propaganda.[49] This sensitivity was related to the fact that Ireland had not achieved full independence. The protests were about cultural as much as political sovereignty (and shared much in common with the many Irish-Ireland and Catholic vigilance societies which defended Irish society from other foreign threats in this period). As *An Phoblacht* declared: 'If Ireland were really free, think you, that such a celebration as that of Poppy Day would be permitted or even thought of? . . . What are we going to do to establish Irish-Ireland opinion as master in its own house?'[50] Another example of such thinking is provided by Clann na nGaedheal (also known as the Pre-Truce IRA), one of several veterans' organisations which emerged in this period devoted to a happy combination of self-interest and patriotism.[51] Among other activities, these guardians of the ideals of 1916 lobbied for the proscription of disloyal organisations, censorship of anti-national literature and films, the expropriation of the property and citizenship of individuals who expressed loyalty 'to Kings or Governments outside the state', the playing of the national anthem at theatres and cinemas and the introduction of 'a daily ceremonial in schools combining the National Anthem and the Salute to the National Flag' in a form suitable to 'National Characteristics'.[52] It also lobbied the government to ban Armistice

Day on the grounds that it was a humiliating and dangerous display of imperialism.[53] In contrast to most nationalist bodies, Clann detailed the reasons for its fear of an imperialist conspiracy.

> From the network of Imperial propaganda woven through Press, Cinema, Stage and magazines, it is clearly apparent that a very big organisation exists within the present Free State area, which, operating through the British Legion and kindred allied associations adheres rigidly to alarming and dangerous tactics unchecked which must ultimately endanger the complete national consciousness which is essential to ensure victory.[54]

It believed that 'the recognition of open treason to the Irish people' which toleration of Armistice Day entailed, would 'induce a harmful complex of hopelessness and cause many to despair of victory'. Tolerance for treason would also cause the Irish youth to 'unconsciously absorb part of the Empire recognition complex'.[55] Its vigilance was further justified by the decline of patriotism: 'As a new and much confused generation has grown since 1916, the effects of the great sacrifice are in danger of being lost, and the real National question allowed to fall into the degrading obscurity which made the sacrifice imperative to ensure the awakening of proper National consciousness at that time.'[56] Similar rhetoric appears in the protests of another old IRA body (the National Association of the Old IRA) which complained that Armistice Day was organised 'to insult the memory of the dead who died in the National struggle and to insult the vast majority of their countrymen by insolent ruthless contempt of their traditions, rights, faith and National independence'. It added that there was no nation where extreme penalties were not imposed on citizens guilty of treason. Again, at the heart of the sensitivity to Armistice Day was the fact that only partial sovereignty had been gained despite the 'overwhelming mandate' for complete separation since 1916: 'There can be no doubt as to the will of the people on the matter. Still less can it be assumed that Imperial expressions in Ireland are within the realm of legitimate politics . . . In Ireland, above all places, there can be no room for dual allegiances, and much harm has already been caused by this abuse of liberty.'[57]

As the rhetoric of such groups suggested, many of those involved were cranks. However, as J. H. Whyte noted in a different context, 'One can learn something of the tendencies in a society by observing on which particular fringe of it the lunatics break out.'[58] In the 1920s, the campaign against Armistice Day united every republican and left-wing party in the state, from Sinn Féin to the communist movement. Only Labour and the governing Cumann na nGaedheal party did not participate in anti-imperialist protests, and the latter's distaste for Armistice Day was clear.[59] The objections of the

National Army and Department of External Affairs to 'the disgusting scenes of pro-Britishness' at the Dublin Horse Show suggests such attitudes were fairly widespread.[60] An acrimonious dispute over the playing of the British national anthem at Trinity College in 1929 also provoked surprisingly extreme rhetoric among mainstream nationalists. The *Irish Independent* complained 'our kindness is being mistaken for servitude', while the *Limerick Leader* demanded that if ex-unionists could not demonstrate loyalty 'steps should be taken sooner or later to compel them to give full allegiance to the country that is supporting them'. The *Irish News*, a little richly given its northern Catholic readership, observed: 'if they do not regard themselves as citizens of the Irish Free State, let them get out'.[61] Moreover, there was no opposing tendency calling for toleration of displays of British identity in the Free State (hardly remarkable when considered in the wider context of the treatment of minorities with suspect allegiances in other inter-war European states). The nearest such views came to expression was by Frank MacDermot, a senior Fine Gael politician with a tendency to offer rational assessments of the national question (which, no doubt, accounted for the brevity of his Dáil career). Writing in 1935, three years after the election of Fianna Fáil, MacDermot observed

> that at present King George V, as King not of England but of Ireland, is an integral part of the Irish Free State Constitution; that Mr. De Valera and his colleagues are his ministers; and that all the members of the Dáil but three have sworn allegiance to him. I have repeatedly expressed my preference for complete separation, as compared with continuance of a dishonourable pretence. But, by one road or another, to real acceptance of the Crown we must come if we are ever to get rid of Partition.[62]

The other reasons offered by republicans for the suppression of British symbols can be more briefly noted. Ex-unionists were disliked by republicans and provided convenient targets for rhetorical – and physical – abuse. Consider, for example, the description of the sponsors of a war memorial (or a 'Monument to National Perfidy' as *An Phoblacht* dubbed it) in Merrion Square: 'As our readers are aware, the whole Poppy Day, War Memorial, Boy Scout stuff is an attempt to hold Ireland in the British Empire and to gain for the promoters the kudos that their Imperial masters are wont to extend to their mongrel slaves.'[63] Many nationalists considered the Union Jack, which incorporated the cross of St Patrick symbolising the union of Ireland and England, an inherently offensive symbol. Frank Ryan objected to the flying of the Union Jack in the south on the grounds that in the north 'if a man flies the Tricolour, the police at once order him to remove it . . . We are too damned tolerant.'[64] That unionist repression of nationalist symbols in Northern Ireland infuriated republicans is understandable, that emulation of its intolerance was the best response which one of the more intelligent republicans of this period could suggest is less so. But the protests were less about partition than the humiliation and resentment that southern republicans felt about the Treaty. It should also be recalled that republicans like Frank Ryan viewed their actions in the context of the international anti-imperialist movement. The League Against Imperialism (the Irish section of which organised the annual protests) was formed in 1927 at a Comintern-sponsored Congress of Oppressed Nationalities in Brussels attended by Ryan, along with anti-colonial organisations such as the Indian and African National Congress parties.[65] However, as Stephen Howe has observed, despite such affiliations most Irish republicans tended not to identify themselves as part of a broader anti-colonial movement as they did not view Ireland's case as analogous to colonial-settler states such as Australia or non-white colonies such as India. 'So far as "imperialism" was invoked at all by Irish nationalists as a general explanatory category beyond Ireland's own shores, it was not as a set of expansionist practices, forms of exploitation or institutions of colonial rule but as an attitude of mind, a popular enthusiasm to be lambasted among the Irish just as among the British public.'[66]

The most powerful reason for the popularity of anti-imperialist protests among republican leaders – their usefulness in mobilising popular support against the Free State – was rarely admitted. Republican propaganda instead blamed the Free State authorities for permitting imperialist demonstrations. *An Phoblacht*, for example, challenged '"Free Staters" who are opposed to Union Jackery to lift one finger against it. We tell them that were it not for their police, there would not be one Union Jack flown in the twenty-six counties.' The following year it noted: 'If they had withdrawn from Dublin, even for one half hour, that Two Minutes' Imperial Silence would certainly have been a perpetual one.'[67] In reality, as was noted, the Garda had little sympathy for such events but the decision of the government to permit them was too good a propaganda opportunity for republicans to miss. The most potent aspect of Armistice Day was its symbolism. By forcing the government and police to defend poppy-wearers, republicans could depict the Free State authorities as the defenders of British interests in Ireland – precisely the role that republicans attributed to them. The independent republican journal *Honesty*, Fianna Fáil's newspaper *The Nation* and the nationalist periodical *The Leader* also blamed the government's 'slavish cringing before the old enemy' for imperialist displays.[68] The protests also permitted an impressive show of unity among otherwise deeply divided republican and socialist organisations. Armistice Day was the only occasion when the leaders of Sinn Féin, Fianna Fáil, the IRA and the communist movement shared a public platform.[69] (In contrast, ownership of republican commemoration ceremonies such as Bodenstown was usually contested by rival organisations, frequently leading to unseemly brawls). Armistice Day gave radical republicans, an increasingly marginal force, a genuinely popular occasion to mobilise mass support for its objectives. The opportunity provided by anti-imperialist demonstrations to unite republicans against the Free State accounts for the radically different nature of Armistice Day protests following the election of Fianna Fáil in 1932. De Valera, who had previously embraced this perennial opportunity to demonstrate Fianna Fáil's radical roots, now inherited the onerous duty of protecting imperialist demonstrators from his former comrades.

III

The events of Armistice Day, 1932, demonstrated that the underlying target of anti-imperialist protests was the Free State rather than ex-unionists. Although de Valera, eager to win radical republican support for his attempts to reform the Free State, had ended the proscription of the IRA, lifted the ban on *An Phoblacht* and released republican prisoners from jail, the IRA escalated its campaign against imperialism. In March the IRA's chief of staff, Moss Twomey, defined the IRA's attitude towards the new government. Resolving not to stand aside to allow his more constitutionally minded comrades breathing space to implement its programme, Twomey announced 'a mighty drive against British rule and Imperialism and all that these connote, politically and socially in Irish life'. The ostensible, and somewhat lame, target of this drive was 'avowedly British and bitterly anti-Irish organisations such as the British "Boy" Scouts which is a powerful military organisation'. The underlying purpose, however, was clear: 'It is important that the position of the Irish Republican Army in the leadership of the national struggle should be seen under a clear light. Even when Parliamentary efforts are achieving concessions, the leadership of the Freedom Movement remains with the revolutionary movement.'[70] Following his release from Arbour Hill, Frank Ryan expressed similar sentiments in characteristically intemperate style to some thirty thousand supporters at College Green:

> A good many people were mourning that [election] day – the little Britishers – who were very quiet now and had to roll away their Union Jacks in moth balls. These people thought they were going to put an end to Republicans once and for all, but instead they had put an end to themselves. They had now gone forever, but there was just one thing more that they should do and that was to follow the example of Judas and take a rope.[71]

Ryan made two important points. First, he broadened his definition of imperialists to include the former Cumann na nGaedheal government: 'These people had said that they would hang some of them, persecute more and jail them, but they were changed and sorry men now and had been put out of public life and would never come back.' Secondly, as Special Branch noted, he made it clear that the IRA would challenge de Valera for the leadership of republicanism: 'Frank Ryan in the course of his speech asked the crowd did they want two Armies, and when the crowd shouted "No" he said, "Very well, we will have one army – the I.R.A."'[72]

The IRA army council's Easter statement continued on the same lines: 'The power of the Imperialists remains very active in our midst. We feel it our duty to issue a warning that endeavours will be made to drive the new Ministry of Southern Ireland, step by step, into conflict with any movement which aims at the complete undoing of the Treaty . . . It is, therefore, the clear duty of all National organisations to combat and destroy these subversive influences which promote internal strife and help to maintain foreign domination.'[73] Decoded, this characteristic example of solipsistic republican logic asserted that the IRA was aware that the escalation of its campaign against imperialist targets would bring it into conflict with de Valera's government. Several weeks later, the exasperated Minister for Justice, James Geoghegan, stated that he regarded commemorative processions, whether its participants were 'adorned with red poppies or with Easter lilies' as a public nuisance.[74] The IRA widened and escalated its anti-imperialist campaign during the summer, calling for attacks on banks, chambers of commerce, large industrial concerns and newspapers. Fianna Fáil's position remained ambiguous – several of its TDs attended an anti-imperialist rally at which copies of the *Cork Examiner* were burned.[75]

As always, anti-imperialist rhetoric climaxed on Armistice Day, but it was noticeable that were now few references to the ex-unionists who had previously formed the focus of the protest (and few of whom took to the streets any longer). More attention was paid to the fact that de Valera (no longer represented at the anti-imperialist rally) had assured Cumann na nGaedheal that its right to hold public meetings would be protected. Frank Ryan disagreed, infamously declaring: 'No matter what anyone said to the contrary, recent events showed that while they had fists, hands and boots to use, and guns if necessary, they would not allow free speech to traitors.' Peadar O'Donnell told the audience that every time Cosgrave 'or any imperialist' tried to hold a meeting, they should be pulled from the platforms. Again, the underlying target of the campaign was not the defeated treatyites but Fianna Fáil, which was winning the competition for grassroots republican support. *An Phoblacht* accused de Valera of substituting 'a false idea of democracy for National Sovereignty' by allowing imperialist meetings, an example of the IRA's ambiguous attitude towards democracy.[76] Republicans tolerated a certain degree of political opposition but only within the parameters of acceptance of rather narrowly defined political principles. This intolerance was shared by even relatively progressive republicans such as George Gilmore who told one activist he 'was not for free speech all round, but only for it for deserving people like working class organisations'.[76]

Just as the IRA had forced Cumann na nGaedheal to protect ex-unionists, de Valera was now compelled to choose between defending Treatyites or confronting republicans. A memorandum to de Valera outlined the government's unpalatable options. If they allowed Ryan and O'Donnell to indulge in such threats, the government would be blamed if people were murdered. However, such rhetoric could not be prevented without resort to the panoply of draconian measures which Cumann na nGaedheal had used with so little success. Moreover, it would infuriate extreme republicans and expose Fianna Fáil to the mockery of the opposition: 'There is no easy or pleasant course for the Government in this dilemma. My advice is to give the Ryans and O'Donnells a last warning that the Government will not allow intimidatory acts or intimidatory language and will not only prosecute . . . but will, if necessary, strengthen the law for the purpose of effectually blotting out this menace to the peace of our country.'[78] De Valera, until recently the star attraction of this annual menace to the state, remained reluctant to use coercion. His minority government had depended on radical republican votes in the last election, many grassroots Fianna Fáil supporters sympathised with the IRA's campaign and de Valera hoped a combination of conciliation and reform could yet win radical republican loyalty to the state. The popularity of the 'No Free Speech for traitors' campaign was a central factor in the emergence of the Blueshirts in late 1932, which reorganised itself into a popular volunteer force to defend Treatyite meetings. *An Phoblacht* now openly linked the campaign against imperialism to a broader attack on Fianna Fáil, accusing the party of lacking the courage to fight imperialism in Ireland. Frank Ryan was more explicit at the 1933 anti-imperialist meeting: 'When they tore down the symbols of Imperialism on Armistice Day, they should remember that these were but the symbols and that the structure of Imperialism still remained to be uprooted. Whoever would lead the country out of the Empire, the present Fianna Fáil would not do it.'[79]

Although the IRA, with its eye on the bigger picture, had revised its definition of imperialists to include Treatyites and, increasingly, Blueshirts, extreme nationalist organisations continued to agitate against Armistice Day. De Valera's decision to permit the commemoration provoked the ire of Clann na nGaedheal. In early November 1932 its general secretary, Gerald Loughrey, wrote to de Valera to request an end to 'these humiliating displays', in particular the suppression of the British Fascisti who had become annual participants in the parade.[80] The Minister for Justice, James Geoghegan, sought advice from his police commissioner, Eoin O'Duffy, who complained about the 'grave disturbances' and 'severe strain on police resources' which Armistice Day entailed. He particularly resented the 'almost exclusively young girls' who provocatively waved Union Jacks 'in the faces of citizens passing by in the course of their business'. O'Duffy recommended a range of restrictions, including a ban on the display of the Union Jack (not only the flag but its image on uniforms, badges and collection boxes), permits for each parade, poppy sales to be limited to two days and the proscription of words of command and other trappings of militarism.[81] The cabinet accepted all but the last of these, presumably on the grounds that such restrictions might also be applied to IRA parades.

This did little to satisfy Clann na nGaedheal which continued to demand the banning of the British Fascisti on the grounds of 'Maintenance of Order' and 'Morale of the Nation'.[82] From 1933 De Valera did ban the Fascisti from the parade but notwithstanding this small success, and the decline of ex-unionists as a visible presence, Clann na nGaedheal's demands grew more radical (and detached from political reality). Quoting Patrick Pearse ('Every man or woman within the nation has normally equal rights, but a man or a woman may forfeit his or her rights by turning recreant to the nation') and Fintan Lalor ('If he refuses [allegiance to Ireland] than I say – away with him – himself and all his robber rights and all the things himself and his rights have brought into our island'), Clann na nGaedheal requested de Valera to consider its legislation to impose patriotism on the British Legion:

> the proposed legislation will be framed to deal, in the first instance, with this menace, and will be of such a nature to empower the representatives of the people to deal with the group leaders as my Executive strongly recommends – that they forfeit all rights of citizenship and are dispossessed of whatever property they may hold.[83]

De Valera declined the suggestion, offending Clann na nGaedheal with his opinion that their views were 'submitted from a narrow outlook'. Clann responded that its proposals were offered as friendly advice 'based on a legitimate interpretation of the National leaders' teaching'.[84] Notwithstanding its extremism, Clann na nGaedheal expanded in the years following de Valera's coming to power, winning acceptance of its policies by the Irish-American Fenian off-shoot, The Shamrock Club. A well-attended national conference was held in 1934 to agree an agenda and establish branches of the 'Pre-Truce IRA' in every county in the Free State. (It was strongest in Ulster, Leinster and Connacht, and claimed over twenty branches in the ex-serviceman stronghold of Waterford alone). It decided to prioritise four objectives:

1   Against Imperial organisation, penetration and propaganda;

2   On behalf of old comrades who have been the victims of economic distress;

3   Against the folly of unseemly commemoration ceremonies which only mark division, and mock the teachings of the National leaders; and

4   Against new movements which are based on sectional foundations.[85]

The focus of the first objective remained Armistice Day. De Valera's unco-operative attitude in allowing imperialists to hurl 'insult in the face of the Irish people' was viewed with much gravity. The second objective concerned not only charitable works for distressed former comrades but securing preferential employment for pre-truce volunteers to counteract the advantages enjoyed by 'the pampered anti-national type of applicant for employment'. It supported expediting the granting of pensions to pre-truce IRA men ('the people of the country who were for the country would be getting only a little of their dues') but all resolutions relating to financial issues were withheld from the press to avoid 'the charge of being simply out on a material issue'. Their first duty, its president commented, 'was to preserve for the Nation the one organisation which was above criticism or reproach and which, for the sake of the Nation, must be kept so'.[86] The conference's preoccupation with attaining national unity through the regulation of commemoration was striking. The suppression of 'anti-national' commemoration was seen as a way of uniting republicans, as was its call for acceptance of the 1916 Proclamation and non-partisan commemoration of national occasions. The dynamic behind the organisation's obsession with anti-imperialism was similar to that of the IRA – the suppression of ex-unionists was seen as a means to reunite the Irish separatist movement. The irony that the one issue believed potent enough to reunite republicans was the one which most clearly demonstrated the implausibility of genuine national unity was presumably overlooked.

Clann na nGaedheal achieved little success. Despite its message of non-partisan unity, it fell all too easily into the category of the 'little, self-obsessed groups' which it set out to replace.[87] The stream of correspondence to de Valera's government became increasingly one-sided. It came to a virtual halt when de Valera discovered that its secretary was a civil servant. (De Valera ordered him to quit the organisation and transferred him to another department).[88] Clann na nGaedheal's attempts to enlist support from the Catholic hierarchy also provoked a sharp response. Cardinal MacRory, the Primate of All-Ireland, rejected the idea of binding Ireland to 'the views of those long dead and gone' and the organisation's extremist separatism: 'while you want freedom from English interference, you seem ready to deny freedom to Irishmen to determine their country's status. I will never stand for that though I consider myself as good an Irishman as any of you.'[89] A number of other groups claiming roots in the old IRA continued to attack de Valera for permitting Armistice Day parades but their efforts increasingly focused on self-interested material issues rather than efforts to reunite Irish separatism.

IV

By the mid-1930s, anti-imperialist protests ceased to attract much interest. The violent protests of the 1920s had succeeded in ridding Union Jacks from public view, and the smaller, more discreet, ceremonies which followed presented less of a target. The underlying reasons for anti-imperialist protests had also dissipated. Their pre-1932 popularity was rooted in their ability to unite opponents of the Free State in an impressive, if ephemeral, display of solidarity. This no longer proved possible after de Valera's election which hastened the decline of anti-Free State republicanism, a process mirrored by the decline of the anti-imperialist movement. De Valera's success in removing the humiliating legacy of the Anglo-Irish Treaty (the oath, annuities, governor-general, Crown and Free State constitution) reconciled most republicans to the southern state. Astute republicans had long been aware of this possibility. The IRA was forced to support de Valera's reforms, while realising that his success would undermine its own support. Within weeks of de Valera's election, for example, *An Phoblacht* worried about the imminent demise of the oath:

> While every Irish citizen must welcome the ending of the humiliation it is well too to consider possible consequences. Would its elimination make for increased morale and give encouragement to the people to press forward for full freedom – the complete undoing of the 'Treaty'? Or would it be used by some elements to make the other humiliating terms and restrictions of that 'Treaty' more acceptable by the people?[90]

The IRA failed to depict Fianna Fáil as mere Free Staters, though not from want of trying. Its demise was hastened by schism and decline. The inter-war IRA (a Dublin-led body) exploited issues such as annuities, unemployment and partition but its popular support had stemmed from resentment of the humiliations imposed by the Treaty and the legacy of the civil war. Despite advancing the objectives of the Irish revolution – unification and Gaelicisation – with as little success as Cosgrave, de Valera succeeded in reconciling all but a tiny rump of southern republicans to the twenty-six county state. Future support for the IRA would depend on partition and northern grievances rather than rejection of the southern state.

Studies of commemoration invariably raise similar themes, most notably what was forgotten as much as what was remembered. Armistice Day fell hostage to extremists on both sides – polarised between republicans intent on disrupting the event and nostalgic supporters of Empire. The memory of the tens of thousands of nationalist Irishmen who fought, and died, in the First World War was largely overlooked in the public sphere. The IRA's campaign against Armistice Day was not its finest hour. Republican attitudes to commemoration of the First World War highlighted the inconsistencies, evasions and ambiguities inherent within inter-war republican ideology. Underlying republican allegations that commemoration of the war constituted support for British rule was a sense of insecurity in the face of the annual reminder of the widespread support which had once existed for Home Rule. Such uncertainty about the commitment of the Irish population to an uncompromising vision of republicanism was understandable, particularly after Fianna Fail's decision to work within constitutional politics. The specious analogy between Armistice Day in Dublin and German commemoration of war-dead in Paris indicated a more deep-rooted cultural insecurity, one that helps to explain the otherwise nonsensical targeting of groups such as the girl guides as enemies of the republic. Implicit, and occasionally explicit, in these comparisons was not only a rejection of the historical reality that nationalist Ireland had supported Redmond in 1914 but a refusal to accept that a minority of Irish people adhered to a British identity as well as – or instead of – an Irish one: 'Such exclusivist thinking about national identity, on both sides of the nationalist-unionist divide, continues to bedevil politics in Ireland'.[91] The evasions and intolerance necessitated by such a solipsistic outlook contrast with a more honest acceptance of the complexity of identities by present day republicans who view commemoration of Ireland's war dead with lack of interest rather than hostility.[92] The relationship between republicanism and the Crown continues to evolve. Northern republicans oppose the use of symbols such as the Crown and Union Jack in the institutions of the renegotiated northern state but the absence of protest during the recent visit of Queen Elizabeth II demonstrated a softening of attitudes in other respects.[93] More radically, echoes of Frank MacDermot's comment that 'to real acceptance of the Crown we must come if we are ever to get rid of Partition' were discernible in the comments of Bertie Ahern, the Taoiseach and leader of Ireland's largest republican party, Fianna Fáil, welcoming a debate on the possibility of Commonwealth membership permitting the coexistence of Crown and republic in a united Ireland.[94]

Notes

1   *Official Report: Debate on the Treaty between Great Britain and Ireland* (Dublin, n.d.), 5 Jan. 1922, p. 261.

2   J. J. Walsh, *Recollections of a Rebel* (Tralee, 1944), pp. 63–4.

3   J. J. Lee, *Ireland 1912–1985: Politics and Society* (Cambridge, 1993 edn), p. 51.

4   For the clash between British and Irish national anthems see Ewan Morris, '"God save the king" versus "The soldier's song": the 1929 Trinity College national anthem dispute and the politics of the Irish Free State', *Irish Historical Studies* 31, 121 (May, 1998), pp. 72–90.

5   *Round Table*, Sept. 1929, quoted in Morris, 'God save the king', p. 85.

6   Charles Townshend, *Ireland: The Twentieth Century* (London, 1998), p. 136. See Seán O'Faolain, *De Valera* (London, 1939), *passim*, for discussion of the importance of the symbolic to de Valera.

7   *An Phoblacht*, 1 Sept. 1928.

8   National Archives (NAI), Department of Justice (DJ) H280/36; *An Phoblacht*, 15 Sept. 1928. U. MacEoin, *The IRA in the Twilight Years 1923–1948* (Dublin, 1997), p. 153.

9   *An Phoblacht*, 15 Feb. 1930. See *An Phoblacht*, 21 July 1927, 22 Sept. 1928 and 14 Sept. 1929 for criticism of the Catholic Boy Scouts. For the Knights, see *An Phoblacht*, 9 June 1928.

10 *An Phoblacht*, 15 Feb. 1930.

11 *Irish Press*, 14 May 1935; NAI, DJ 8/198.

12 NAI, DJ 8/72, 8/101.

13 *Irish Press*, 5 Dec. 1934.

14 *Irish Press*, 6 Dec. 1943.

15 Clarke to Commissioner, Crime Special, 4 Dec. 1934 (NAI, DJ 8/72).

16 Ibid.

17 Margin notes, ibid.

18 J. Leonard, 'The twinge of memory: Armistice Day and Remembrance Sunday in Dublin since 1919', in R. English and G. Walker (ed.), *Unionism in Modern Ireland* (Dublin, 1996); B. Hanley, 'Poppy Day in Dublin in the '20s and '30s', *History Ireland* 7, 1 (Spring, 1999).

19 *An Phoblacht*, 13 Nov. 1925.

20 *An Phoblacht*, 20 Nov. 1925.

21 Diary of Rosamund Jacob, 11 Nov. 1926 (NLI, MS 32582/58).

22 Miscellaneous police reports (DJ 8/684); MacEoin, *The IRA*, pp 154–5. Venues guarded by the police included poppy depots, cinemas showing war films, royal statues and war memorials.

23 NAI, DJ 8/73.

24 *An Phoblacht*, 29 Sept. 1928.

25 Garda report, 11 Nov. 1930 (NAI, DJ 8/684). Morisy may have been targeted due to his membership of the British Fascisti (his name appears on a membership list compiled by Chief Supt. G. Brennan, 12 Apr. 1933) (NAI, Department of Taoiseach (DT) S11168).

26 MacEoin, *The IRA*, p. 159.

27 *An Phoblacht*, 9 Nov. 1929.

28 *An Phoblacht*, 16 Nov., 9 Nov. 1929.

29 *An Phoblacht*, 16 Nov. 1929. For Ryan's role see F. McGarry, *Frank Ryan* (Dundalk, 2002).

30 *An Phoblacht*, 15 Nov. 1930; NAI, DJ 8/684.

31 *An Phoblacht*, 20 Nov. 1925.

32 *An Phoblacht*, 3 Nov. 1928.

33 *An Phoblacht*, 9 Nov. 1929.

34 *An Phoblacht*, 10 Nov. 1928

35 Duffy to Neligan, 12 Nov. 1928, Neligan to O'Duffy, 7 Nov. 1928, O'Duffy to secretary, Department of Justice, 21 Nov. 1928 (NAI, DJ 8/684).

36 Quoted in K. Jeffery, 'The Great War in modern Irish memory', in T. G. Fraser and K. Jeffery (eds) *Men, Women and War: Historical Studies*, XVII (Dublin, 1993) p. 145.

37 O'Duffy to secretary, Department of Justice, 21 Sept. 1932 (DJ 8/684); *Ulster Herald*, 16 Nov. 1929, quoted in *An Phoblacht*, 23 Nov. 1929 and *The Irish Times*, cited in *An Phoblacht*, 16 Nov. 1929.

38 Jeffery, 'The Great War', p. 149

39 D. Fitzpatrick, 'Commemoration in the Irish Free State: a chronicle of embarrassment', in I. McBride (ed.) *History and Memory in Modern Ireland* (Cambridge, 2001), p. 191.

40 Fitzpatrick, 'Commemoration'; Leonard, 'Twinge of memory', pp. 102, 105–6.

41 O'Duffy to secretary, Department of Justice, 8 Nov. 1928 (NAI, DJ 8/684).

42 *An Phoblacht*, 15 Nov. 1930.

43 *An Phoblacht*, 23 Oct. 1925.

44 *An Phoblacht*, 31 March 1928.

45 *An Phoblacht*, 3 Aug. 1929.

46 *An Phoblacht*, 3 Nov. 1928.

47 *An Phoblacht*, 9 Nov. 1929.

48 Townshend, *Ireland*, pp. 150–1.

49 A. Matthews, 'Cumann na mBan and the birth of the Easter lily as a Republican symbol', paper read at Republicanism in Modern Ireland conference, NUI Maynooth, 11 May 2002.

50 *An Phoblacht*, 23 Oct. 1925. The answer to this question would surely have been in the affirmative. It was not until the twenty-six county state became more secure in its identity that it could afford a more honest remembrance of the First World War. Moreover, it is difficult to see how a united Ireland in which Irish-Ireland was master, and the public expression of the British identity of its minority suppressed, could have existed.

51 Several Clann na nGaedheal leaders, including Liam Tobin and Frank Thornton, had been members of the Irish Republican Army Organisation responsible for the army mutiny in 1924, a body which similarly combined patriotism and self-interest.

52 Miscellaneous letters (NAI, DT S11168).

53 Gerald Loughrey to de Valera, 5 Nov. 1932 (NAI, DT S11168).

54 Loughrey to de Valera, 15 Mar. 1934 (NAI, DT S11168).

55 Loughrey to de Valera, 5 Nov. 1932, 12 Oct. 1933, 15 March 1934 (NAI, DT S11168).

56 Loughrey to de Valera, 9 Nov. 1934 (NAI, DT S11168).

57 S. MacRaghnáill, honorary secretary, Old IRA to de Valera, 6 Nov. 1936 (NAI, DJ 8/684).

58 J. H. Whyte, *Church and State in Modern Ireland 1923–1979* (Dublin, 1984 edn), p. 165.

59 See, for example, criticism of imperialism and Armistice Day in the Cumann na nGaedheal newspaper, *The Star* (15 June 1929). The Irish Free State was the only Commonwealth state to refuse to contribute to the Imperial War Graves Commission, which tended, among others, the graves of Irish servicemen who died in the war. Neither the government nor the governor-general participated in the Armistice Day ceremony in Ireland in this period (See Fitzpatrick, 'Commemoration in the Irish Free State', *passim*).

60 Morris, 'God save the king', p. 77.

61 *Irish Independent*, 13 June 1929; *Limerick Leader*, 15 June 1929; *Irish News*, 10 June 1929, quoted in Morris, 'God save the king', p. 84.

62 Press cutting, *c.*July-Aug. 1935 (NAI, DT S11168).

63 *An Phoblacht*, 25 Nov. 1925. Similar attitudes about ex-Unionists were voiced in Fianna Fáil newspaper, *The Nation* (22 June 1929): 'They live and thrive in our midst, and yet they hate and detest us; their highest wish, if their mean hearts had the courage to express it, is to see this country again enslaved and pauperised.'

64 *An Phoblacht*, 1 Sept. 1928.

65 D. Ó Drisceoil, *Peadar O'Donnell* (Cork, 2001), p. 51.

66 S. Howe, *Ireland and Empire: Colonial Legacies in Irish History and Culture* (Oxford, 2000) pp. 60, 43–9.

67 *An Phoblacht*, 1 Sept. 1928, 16 Nov. 1929.

68 Morris, 'God save the king', p. 84.

69 *An Phoblacht*, 15 Nov. 1930.

70 *An Phoblacht*, 12 Mar. 1932.

71 *An Phoblacht*, 19 Mar. 1932.

72 Police report of Republican meeting, 13 Mar. 1932 (NAI, DJ 8/698).

73 *An Phoblacht*, 2 Apr. 1932.

74 *An Phoblacht*, 20 Apr. 1932.

75 *An Phoblacht*, 4 June, 9, 23 July 1932.

76 *An Phoblacht*, 19 Nov. 1932.

77 Diary of Rosamund Jacob, 28 Apr. 1936 (NLI, 32,582/78).

78 Unsigned memo, *c.*Nov. 1932 (NAI, DJ 8/684).

79 *An Phoblacht*, 18 Nov. 1933.

80 The British Fascisti was an imperialist organisation with twenty-five active members in Dublin dismissed by Special Branch as social-climbing card-players.

81 O'Duffy to Minister for Justice, 21 Sept. 1932 (NAI, DT S3370).

82 Loughrey to de Valera, 21 Mar., 3 May, 6 May, 12 Oct., 3 Nov., 1933 (NAI, DT S11168).

83 Loughrey to de Valera, 15 Mar. 1934 (NAI, DT S11168).

84 Loughrey to de Valera, 10 May 1934, ibid.

85 Clann na nGaedheal (Pre-Truce IRA), 'Report of National Convention, 1934' (Armagh Diocesan Archives, Clann na nGaedheal folder, box 9, XII Political, MacRory papers).

86 Clann na nGaedheal (Pre-Truce IRA), 'Report of National Convention, 1934', pp 4–5, 10–11.

87 Clann na nGaedheal (Pre-Truce IRA), 'Report of National Convention, 1934', p. 3.

88 Miscellaneous correspondence, 1934–8 (NAI, DT S11168).

89 Cardinal MacRory to Gerard Loughrey, 21 July 1934, MacRory papers.

90 *An Phoblacht*, 23 April 1932.

91 Morris, 'God save the king', p. 90.

92 This is not to suggest that commemoration of Irish servicemen who died in the British army is no longer contentious. For example, during the summer of 2002 Waterford council was divided on a proposal to commemorate local men who died in the First World War. However, like so much else in the wake of the Good Friday Agreement, northern republican attitudes are undergoing considerable revision and the case for reclaiming the legacy of nationalists who served

in the British army is increasingly heard. See, in particular, the thoughtful statement by Sinn Féin's Lord Mayor of Belfast, Alex Maskey, following his decision to lay a wreath at the cenotaph in Belfast on 1 July 2002 in honour of those who died in the Somme ('The Memory of the Dead: Seeking Common Ground", 27 June 2002, RM Distribution: Irish Republican News and Information (http://irlnet.com/rmlist)). This shift in policy has been accepted with surprising alacrity from members of an organisation which had considered war memorials, British Legion headquarters and Remembrance Day ceremonies suitable targets for bombs. See, for example, Martin Meehan's recent criticism of Belfast City Council's neglect of British army war graves in Belfast City Cemetery as an insulting fiasco (*North Belfast News*, 26 Oct. 2002).

93 For objections to royal visits a century earlier see S. Pašeta, 'Nationalist responses to two royal visits to Ireland, 1900 and 1903', *Irish Historical Studies* 31, 124 (Nov. 1999), pp. 488–504.

94 *The Irish Times*, 27 Nov. 1998. Aptly, the main proponent of this idea was Fianna Fáil minister, Eamon O Cuiv, grandson of the man who did so much to define Ireland's relationship with the Crown. De Valera, always ambiguous on the Commonwealth question, believed that the southern state's departure had hindered the cause of Irish unity. Despite contributions from Mary Robinson and Nelson Mandela, the anticipated political debate was something of a damp squib, confined largely to the usual suspects within the pages of *The Irish Times*. Fintan O'Toole argued in favour of Commonwealth membership while John Waters suggested its southern advocates were mainly 'certified lunatics or descendents of Blueshirts who have wet dreams about shaking hands with the queen of England' (*The Irish Times*, 4, 1, Dec. 1998). My thanks to Éanna Ó Caollaí for these references.

CHAPTER 6

IRA Veterans and Land Division in Independent Ireland 1923–48

* * *

Terence Dooley

INTRODUCTION

The importance of the role of the land question in the Irish revolution, 1917–23, has often been lost on historians of the period. In their introduction to *Ireland: The Politics of Independence, 1922–49,* for example, Mike Cronin and John M. Regan argue that

> There is little evidence of a social component within the Irish revolution and less again in its settlement. Such potential as there was for social upheaval had to a great extent been defused by the transfer of land back to native ownership under a series of reforming land acts at the end of the nineteenth and the beginning of the new century. The conservativeness of the Irish revolution was underpinned by a rural peasant proprietorship, nationalist in outlook but classically liberal in its economic interest.[1]

This is much too simplistic an analysis of a very complex issue. There is, in fact, overwhelming evidence of a social component in the revolution and just as much evidence to suggest that the settlement of the land question from 1923 onwards was seen to be central to the restoration of law and order in Irish society. The potential for social upheaval had not been defused by the British land purchase acts from 1870 to 1909. The widely held misconception that the 1903 Wyndham Land Act effectively solved the land question in Ireland has blinded historians to the fact that the creation of a mass of peasant proprietors actually led to immeasurable long-term problems. By 1922, an average of around 65 per cent of all agricultural holdings in each county in Ireland came under the definition of 'uneconomic' as set out by the Land

Commission, that is below £10 valuation or roughly twenty acres of 'reasonable' land. When one goes back to 1917 and adds to these uneconomic holders the 114,000 tenant farmers who between them occupied approximately 3 million acres and who had not yet benefited from the land purchase acts, one can see that there was a great deal of potential for social upheaval in rural Ireland.[2]

Towards the end of 1917, the fledgling Sinn Féin Party moved to exploit this potential. Its leaders saw the possibility of consolidating the support it was gathering as a result of its anti-conscription stance by appealing to the more traditionally emotive subject of the land question. In its bid to capture the imagination of the Irish electorate in preparation for the forthcoming general election, Sinn Féin promoted the idea that the 'true remedy for the land problem' was the 'exclusive control of our own resources which sovereign independence alone can win'.[3] By exploiting the land question in order to promote political change, Sinn Féin leaders ensured that the merging of the land and the national questions would once more become inevitable. A new phase of land agitation was subsequently born when prominent party members such as Eamon de Valera, William T. Cosgrave, Darrell Figgis and Laurence Ginnell (a veteran of the land war era) travelled throughout the country promoting agitation for the break up and redistribution of estates and large grazier farms.[4] They concentrated their efforts in western counties such as Mayo, Sligo and Clare as well as upon the grazing areas of East Galway, Roscommon and further east in Kildare, Offaly, Westmeath and Meath. In these areas, disgruntled uneconomic holders and labourers (most of whom themselves were the sons of farmers) lived side by side with large graziers. The former classes were amenable enough to Sinn Féin land policy rhetoric (even if it was not properly defined) to join the party and the Irish Volunteers (later the IRA) in significant numbers, many in the belief that when the revolution had ended they would benefit by being rewarded with land. In February 1918, for example, the county inspector for Galway East Riding reported: 'Sinn Fein is now being worked in this Riding as an agrarian movement for the forcible possession of lands. . . . This new phase of Sinn Fein will bring many young men into the movement which had no attraction for them heretofore'.[5] Developments in this direction were given further impetus that month when Eamon de Valera told his audience at a meeting in Elphin, County Roscommon, that every Sinn Féin club should form a company of the Volunteers not only to prevent conscription but also 'to help to divide the land evenly'. Later that month in the same county, notices were posted by local Sinn Féin clubs that they would be responsible for the equitable letting of estates on conacre: 'in the name of the Irish Republic'.[6] Again, this was significant because, for the first time, independence (if it was to be gained in the form of a republic) became synonymous with the equitable redistribution of land.

Increasingly, from the beginning of 1918, locals in many areas used the authority of elements of the republican movement in order to enhance their claims to land and to bolster their authority. In February 1918, lands taken over in Roscommon by groups of agitators had notices declaring 'By order of the Irish Republic' posted on them.[7] In March 1918, a notice was posted on Patrick Deviney's land at Gort in Galway that it had been taken over by the Irish Republic; it was actually taken over by Deviney's brother who had recently been evicted from this farm.[8] In July 1920, Thomas Armstrong in Monaghan received a letter ordering him to give up his farm and '£300 excess profits' in the name of the Irish Republic. The police suspected a former holder of the farm who had been evicted some time previously for the non-payment of rent.[9] From the beginning of 1918 to the end of the War of Independence, anonymous letters, often signed 'IRA', sometimes 'Sinn Fein', demanded recipients throughout the country to surrender all or part of their lands, while posters opposing lettings on the eleven month system were placed upon piers signed 'By order of the Dail' or 'By order of the IRA'.[10]

Many of the major players in the War of Independence and other contemporary commentators later emphasised that it was the lower strata of the farming class who offered most support.[11] In Clare Michael Brennan tells us that he 'hadn't the slightest interest in the land agitation, but I had every interest in using it as a means to an end . . . to get these fellows into the Volunteers'.[12] Rural IRA leaders were very much attuned to the needs of the people they purported to represent. In Cork, Liam Deasy was educated at national school to rid him 'of the attitude of servility and subservience towards the landed gentry'.[13] He was quick to acknowledge 'the small farmers and cottiers of West Cork and elsewhere who, throughout the entire campaign, sheltered and fed our fighting men, often at the price of great hardship and loss to themselves'.[14] He felt that without them victory would not have been achieved – the underlying notion being that they deserved some form of reward as a result. Tom Barry resented the fact that the rich fertile areas around Bandon, Clonakilty and Skibbereen were 'in the hands of a small minority, and the large majority of the people had a hard struggle for existence'. He despised the type of lifestyle that characterised big houses, as well as 'the sycophants and lickspittles, happy in their master's benevolence [who] never thought to question how he had acquired his thousand acres, his cattle and his wealth, or thought of themselves as the descendants of the rightful owners of those robbed lands'.[15] 'Many a time', wrote Dan Breen of Tipperary, 'I walked for three or four hours without meeting even one human being'. He concluded that 'Landlordism, the willing instrument of British rule had wrought this desolation. I renewed my resolve to do my share in bringing about the change that must come sooner or later.'[16]

Recent studies of the socio-economic backgrounds of IRA members in rural areas have found that it was the small farmers, the landless and the labourers who offered most support to the IRA and that the large farmers held aloof. Peter Hart, for example, notes that hostility towards the IRA 'was strongest in North and East Cork – "cow country" – where agricultural prosperity was most pronounced'.[17] Joost Augusteijn has shown that 'the IRA in Mayo was entirely dominated by farmers', that this dominance was true to a lesser extent for Wexford, while in Tipperary farmers and labourers were almost equally represented.[18] Augusteijn contends that 'the results for Mayo demonstrate that "below average" farmers, whose land was valued at around £4, were more likely to join the IRA than the poorest'.[19] The point he misses here, however, is that those who lived on farms with a £4 valuation or below could hardly be any poorer. When the Land Commission began to increase the size of uneconomic holdings, it was its objective to bring them up to a valuation of at least £10. If the latter figure is a more realistic threshold, 355 of the Volunteers out of a total of 408 identified by Augusteijn were uneconomic holders. While not intending to doubt the patriotic motives of these to join the IRA, there is the strong possibility that many were also motivated by considerations of improving their socio-economic position.

II

In December 1918, Sinn Féin won a resounding victory at the general election, capturing seventy-three seats. The deputies refused to take their seats at Westminster and instead established their own parliament, Dáil Éireann. At a sitting on 4 April 1919, Alistair MacCabe, seconded by Countess Markievicz, moved the following resolution:

> That this assembly pledges itself to a fair and full redistribution of the vacant lands and ranches of Ireland among the uneconomic holders and landless men. That no purchase by private individuals of non-residential land in the Congested Districts, or other land essential for the carrying out of any such schemes of land settlement as the Dáil may decide upon, which has taken place since Easter Monday, 1916, be sanctioned now or subsequently by the Irish Republican Government. That this resolution be taken as conveying a warning to those who have recently availed themselves of the crisis in national affairs to annex large tracts of land against the will and interests of the people.[20]

After discussion (the records of which are not available), this motion was withdrawn as the question of land policy had yet to be discussed by the Department of Agriculture. But the motion itself is significant. First of all, a democratically elected government, representing an Irish republic, considered that land redistribution was one of its first priorities. Vacant lands undoubtedly referred to untenanted and demesne lands, still in the possession of traditional landlords. It was to be expected that these would be targeted, given that they were owned by a class that was representative of what the republic aimed to overthrow. Targeting the ranches suggested perhaps a more socialist approach, but more significantly the fact that the Dáil suggested that these lands should be redistributed amongst landless men as well as uneconomic holders was effectively dangling a carrot in front of younger sons of farmers as well as labourers, thereby inviting them to partake in the prospective rewards of a political revolution. Finally, there was also a warning to those who were grabbing land. Agitation had taken on such a life of its own that there was clearly a fear that it would undermine Sinn Féin's primary aim of securing political independence.

The problem with agrarian agitation as it developed from 1917 was that it no longer focused on landlords, as had been the case in the late nineteenth century. Instead it threatened to divide the rural classes pitting smallholders against strong farmers and labourers and the landless against both. This could have serious repercussions for the military wing of Sinn Féin that was attempting to attract recruits to the Volunteers. As the IRA stepped up its military campaign in 1920, localised agrarianism began to detract from its efforts.[21] In June 1920, the Dáil decreed that:

> The present time when the Irish people are locked in a life and death struggle with their traditional enemy, is ill-chosen for the stirring up of strife amongst our fellow-countrymen; and that all our energies must be directed towards the clearing out – not the occupier of this or that piece of land – but the foreign invader of our country.[22]

Individual Sinn Féin TDs went to their constituencies to plead for restraint and to warn of the consequences of failure to do so. Brian O'Higgins, for example, told the people of West Clare:

> After the victory has been won the Dáil will do everything to do justice to all, so that no Irishman will have to go to seek a livelihood far from his native land. . . . But this must be clearly understood, any individual who, after today, continues an endeavour to enforce his claims, to give rise to disputes, to write threatening letters in the name of the Republic to a fellow-countryman, must be aware that in so acting he is defying the wishes of the representatives elected by the people and is injuring the national cause.[23]

Since May, a system of Sinn Féin arbitration courts had been set up ostensibly to deal with land disputes. At the same time, the Dáil ordered that 'the forces of the Republic be used to protect the citizens against the adoption of high-handed methods by any such person or persons' engaged in agrarianism.[24] For a time, the Sinn Féin courts and IRA worked together on quelling rural unrest.[25] In the short term, they were relatively successful but when the civil war broke out in 1922, agrarianism once again reared its ugly head, this time like a hydra.[26] The anti-Treaty section of Sinn Féin refused to accept the legitimacy of the new state. In the west, the IRA went predominantly anti-Treaty and drew the bulk of its support from small farmers.[27] To what extent this was a political decision is difficult to gauge. The IRA had not been particularly active in the west during the War of Independence, but agrarian agitation had been extreme. As the Treaty did not promise any economic gains to the landless and the uneconomic holders, the anti-Treaty faction of the IRA was perhaps perceived as being more likely to provide this.[28] From County Mayo, Col. Maurice Moore wrote a revealing letter to the Minister for Defence in May 1922 stating that:

> The anti-Treaty politicians and IRA, finding themselves in a hopeless minority, have adopted a policy very dangerous to the country and to the present ministry, though it has not been openly avowed. They are now making a bid for support through an agrarian movement.[29]

In December 1922, Patrick Hogan, Minister for Agriculture, pointed out:

> To produce chaos the Irregulars smashed up the transport of the country even though that was unpopular. A result which would be the same in kind though perhaps less in degree, would be produced by the wholesale seizure of land and it would have the advantage of being much more popular, in fact quite in the best tradition. The 'land for the people' is almost as respectable an objective as the 'Republic' and would make a much wider appeal.[30]

But obviously, land grabbing was much too widespread for all of the blame to be laid at the door of anti-Treatyites. In March 1922 William Rochfort, a local landowner in the Clogheen area of Tipperary where agitation was out of control, informed the Minister for Home Affairs that 'the men in question have no connection with the anti-Treaty party'.[31] Indeed, many people who played no role whatsoever in the political revolution were involved in land agitation. The early 1920s witnessed a dramatic growth in land committees, landless associations and evicted tenants' associations throughout the country. The activities of these associations and committees ranged from canvassing politicians to threatening violence on landowners on behalf of individuals or families or, indeed, whole communities who wanted lands divided.[32]

By December 1922, Patrick Hogan, Minister for Agriculture, was convinced that dealing with land seizures was no longer a concern of the Department of

Home Affairs: it was now a matter for the army. The time had come for the government to take 'immediate and drastic action against people who [had] seized other people's land' and to consider whether seizures of land should be regarded as a bar to the acquisition of land in the future under legitimate means. Hogan proposed that in early January 1923 the army should simultaneously clear three or four grabbed farms in each county and transport the seized cattle for sale in Dublin (but that the owners should not be arrested at that stage). As this would obviously create enormous resentment towards the soldiers involved, particularly if they were from the area, Hogan suggested that the raids be carried out by 'flying columns' made up of men selected from outside the county.[33] By April, Hogan was praising the work of these so-called Special Infantry Columns, particularly in Galway, and advocating the intensification of operations throughout the country: 'If this is not done the present dishonouring class war will continue and the house of every large farmer and land owner will be burned and agrarian outrage of all forms will be rampant for the next few years.'[34]

The flying columns did much to quell the agrarian unrest. But not everybody welcomed their tactics. Peadar O'Donnell later claimed that it was the 'city-minded' Sinn Féiners – suspicious of the 'wild men on the land' – who were responsible for quelling the growing agrarian agitation of the early 1920s. However, when they used the IRA to do so, there was a consequence: 'Many an IRA man in jail in '22 and '23 cursed his use as a defender of pure ideals to patrol estate walls, enforce decrees for rent, arrest and even order out of the country leaders of local land agitations.'[35]

III

The first significant debate on providing land for the IRA took place in the Dáil on 1 March 1922, shortly before the civil war began. David Kent (Cork, Sinn Féin, later Coalition Republic) urged

> That it be decreed [by Dáil Eireann] that all lands which were in the occupation of enemy forces in Ireland and which have now been evacuated, except those that may be retained as necessary training grounds for the IRA, be divided up into economic holdings and distributed among landless men; and that preference be given to those men, or dependents of those men, who have been active members of the IRA prior to the Truce, July 1921.[36]

Kent argued that the first duty of the Dáil to the people of Ireland (specifically the landless and the unemployed) was to fulfil the promises on land redistribution it had made in the past. The division of military lands, he claimed, was a step in the right direction; the break up of large estates would follow. He went on:

> I want to make myself perfectly clear that in giving the land to landless men, preference should be given to active members of the IRA who, during the trying times of the last two or three years, have given their services to the country. . . . These men and their dependents are entitled to anything we can do for them. These men came out not for any pecuniary gain, but for love of country. And the first duty of a nation should be to the soldiers who fought for them.[37]

He accepted an amendment from Constance Markievicz (Dublin, Sinn Féin, later republican) that as well as being members of the IRA, allottees should also have a working knowledge of farming.[38]

If such a policy was to be pursued on a much wider level, would all IRA members be entitled to land? Richard Mulcahy, the Minister for Defence, supported Kent's qualification clause that prospective IRA allottees should be those who saw active service prior to the truce of 11 July 1921. So-called 'trucileers', those who had joined the IRA in great numbers immediately after the Anglo-Irish truce, were not to be included. At this stage there was no argument.[39] Then again, by March 1922, there were still hopes of avoiding a civil war. When the civil war had ended the question of which IRA members were deserving of land had become a far more complex one.

IV

David Kent's proposal was never implemented, largely because of the outbreak of the civil war the following month. However, in 1923, when the Cumann na nGaedheal government began restoring law and order, the resolution of the land problem through the compulsory acquisition and redistribution of lands was prioritised as one of its main objectives. When Patrick Hogan, Minister for Agriculture, formulated the terms of the 1923 Land Act and set out the hierarchy of allottees to whom land was to be given, there was no mention of the IRA. The civil war arguably did much to change the notion that IRA veterans were entitled to land. A pragmatist such as Hogan undoubtedly realised the potential dangers of legislating that land should be given to those who had fought in the IRA, particularly if due regard was not to be paid to their previous farming experience. Hogan believed that the maximum number of uneconomic holders, particularly in the designated congested areas of the west, should be catered for at the expense of the minimum number of landless men. In 1926, he had to travel to his own county, Galway, because of agitation on the Pollock estate by landless locals who objected to the bringing in of migrants. These migrants had given up their holdings elsewhere in the county in order to help relieve congestion. As such they were entitled to alternative holdings elsewhere but the landless men in the vicinity of the Pollock estate felt that they should have first preference. Hogan described the difficulties he and the Land Commission, faced:

> It would be easier for the Land Commission to go into a district, divide an estate, make friends with the people there, including, if you like, a few super-landless men and dispose of the land in that way . . . We shall have to try and stand up to any odium that we may incur by reason of taking in congests instead of landless men to estates which are being divided.[40]

The 'few super-landless men' that Hogan referred to were probably republicans who had risen to prominence in the local IRA, whose sympathies had been with the anti-Treatyites, and were now fuelling the land agitation. Hogan despised such tactics, which undoubtedly made him more determined to resist calls for land for IRA veterans, or indeed for any class that he considered undeserving of allotments. He was, in fact, extremely suspicious of the IRA's use of the land question. Peadar O'Donnell had 'a contact' in Hogan's office who supplied him with scraps of information. From these O'Donnell deduced that 'Hogan seemed to consider the IRA was lurking in the shadows'.[41] However, as we shall see, this did not mean that Free State IRA veterans were ignored in land division schemes.

From the government's point of view, the lack of political coherency amongst agrarian agitators was fortunate.[42] They formed no political party and remained largely politically impotent while the stronger farmers and the middle classes formed the political elite of the new state. This new elite showed little interest in specifically rewarding those small farmers, labourers and landless men who had joined the IRA, some in the hope of being rewarded with land.

Initially, the party to which IRA veterans obviously looked to provide them with a political framework was Sinn Féin. But after the general election of 1923, Sinn Féin failed to make any significant advances.[43] By 1925, it was in disarray and eventually split with many of its members later drifting to Fianna Fáil under Eamon de Valera. As such the old IRA was voiceless within the Dáil. There was, for example, no recorded mention of land for IRA veterans in the Dáil until December 1925 when John Nolan (Limerick, Cumann na nGaedheal) made the point that:

> there is one class who seems to be nobody's children and they are the ex-army men of the old Volunteers. I think if any class of people are entitled to consideration as regards land, they have first claim, because the Act of 1923 would not have been in

existence at all, and we would not be here, were it not for them. They seem to have been forgotten in every department, and I hope when the minister sends his inspectors out that he will give them directions to have these men given special consideration.[44]

Rather significantly, only D. J. Gorey (Carlow-Kilkenny, Cumann na nGaedheal) and David Hall (Meath, Labour) responded to Nolan's remark. Gorey rather flippantly referred to 'the new class [of allottee] who has been brought into the discussion – the national heroes'.[45] Hall, who was supportive of Nolan's suggestion, took exception and responded that 'had it not been for some of those heroes whom Deputy Gorey was hitting at he would not be here today'.[46]

Gorey's flippant remark epitomised the Cumann na nGaedheal government's attitude towards the old IRA that had been causing so much disgruntlement amongst those who had fought in the independence struggle. In January 1923 the government's reluctance to reward IRA veterans for their efforts prompted General Liam Tobin among others to establish the organisation that became known as the old IRA.[47] It was not a political move; it was more an attempt to bring to the government's attention the widespread grievances of a body of men who felt that they had not been compensated for the sacrifices they had made during the War of Independence. While Tobin and his allies were embittered by the fact that they had been gradually excluded from key positions within the army, there were hundreds, if not thousands, of rank and file veterans, who felt just as aggrieved about the lack of employment opportunities available to them (especially in the public sector) as well as the slow progress in the area of land division. Outside the Dáil, such grievances gave rise to a dramatic growth in old IRA associations at local level, composed mainly, it would appear, of old republicans.[48] In 1928 an old IRA association was formed in Westmeath because there were 'a good many of the men who did their bit in the Anglo-Irish war unemployed in this area. . . . [and] there are several other grievances that need redressing'.[49] By the mid-1920s there were too many like Paddy Hennessy, formerly of the third Kerry Brigade, who died destitute in Liverpool of TB and was, according to the IRA's newspaper, *An Phoblacht*, 'as much a victim of the slave state as any soldier who died in action'.[50] In the mid-1920s, this newspaper continuously criticised the land division policy of the Cumann na nGaedheal government ('that preferred bullocks to people'[51]) and referred back to the teachings of Fintan Lalor.[52] A preliminary survey suggests that old IRA organisations were strongest in counties such as Tipperary, Laois, Limerick, Offaly and Galway where a high proportion of large estates were yet to be divided and pre-truce IRA men could still hope to receive parcels of land.[53]

At the Fianna Fáil Ard Fheis in 1934, a speaker from County Offaly made the bold claim that under the Cumann na nGaedheal administration 'most of the people who fought against the republic in the civil war were placed in mansions and on broad acres, while other men were left out in the cold'. Unfortunately there are no statistics available to confirm how much land IRA veterans received from the Land Commission between 1923 and 1932. However, there is a good deal of evidence to suggest that those veterans who benefited most during the Cumann na nGaedheal administration were predominantly Free Staters. In 1925 a Land Commission official in charge of dividing an estate in Sligo gave the lands to

> ex-officers of the Free State army, some of who were living miles away, and in receipt of pensions from the government. Two ex-captains of the Free State army, each in receipt of a pension of £70 per year, received allotments on the Knockbrack farm. Several other members of the Free State army were brought in from other estates and were given portions of this farm, with the result that the unfortunate congests on the mountain-side were deprived of the land . . .[54]

A document drawn up by the Old IRA Association of Meath in the 1930s listed 'Free State army pensioners and gratuitants (who took up arms against the Republican troops) and who are resident in County Meath and environs'. At least ten of these had reputedly received land in Meath, although the size of allotments was generally not specified. Amongst these was Seán Boylan who reputedly received fifty acres from 'a "grateful" Land Commission.' (According to an earlier Dáil debate Boylan had allegedly received 140 acres of the Cloncurry estate in Kildare much to the chagrin of the local Fianna Fáil TD, Donal Ó Buachalla, who wanted to know why the land had not been divided amongst the small holders in the area.[55]) A former captain in the Free State army, named Haughey, who was referred to as 'a Mayo migrant', received another farm and Sylvester Duffy from Monaghan, an ex-captain in the same army, received 60 acres.[56] To this day there remains a part of the Cloncurry estate between Athgoe and Newcastle known as the 'Free State' because those who received land divisions there in the mid-1920s were allegedly former Free State army officers.

v

It was the growth in the land annuities conflict in the 1920s that seems to have convinced de Valera that a more radical approach to land division would consolidate support for his party.[57] At Fianna Fáil's first ard fheis on 24 November 1926 in the Rotunda, de Valera declared that the party's first economic priority would be 'to break up the large grazing ranches and distribute them amongst young farmers and agricultural labourers' and 'establish as many families as practicable on the land'.[58] During a political rally in Mayo in the lead up to the general election of 1932, de Valera launched a stinging attack on the land division policy of Cumann na nGaedheal, ironically (or perhaps deliberately) in the county where the Land League had first taken root in the 1880s:

> What about the rich lands? Have they been divided? In Meath, the richest land in Ireland, 5 per cent of farmers own 41 per cent of the land. These are the farmers who own 200 acres each; 631 persons own 234,575 acres: 631 own practically a quarter of a million acres of the best land in Ireland . . . In Tipperary 485 persons own 200,000 acres and in Kildare 6 per cent of farmers own over 172,000.[59]

De Valera, like all of his political colleagues – and opponents – fighting for survival in rural constituencies knew only too well the necessity of wooing the electorate with promises of land division. With the growing proliferation of old IRA societies in many areas from the mid-1920s (the membership of which was drawn from the same social classes – small farmers, labourers and clerks – as the rank and file of Fianna Fáil), it became fashionable for politicians to make promises that members of the old IRA would be rewarded for their past sacrifices. In 1935, for example, Dr Conn Ward, Fianna Fáil parliamentary secretary to the Minister for Local Government, told a rally in Monaghan:

> The [Fianna Fáil] government appreciated their [the old IRA's] work in the struggle for freedom and hoped to reward them under the Pensions Act. He would see that those who fought for their country had first claim in the division of land in the county, and they would also have first preference in the division of large ranches in Meath and Roscommon.[60]

At least partly as a result of such promises, Fianna Fáil was promised the support of old IRA organisations throughout the country after its victory in the general election of 1932. In 1933, for example, the Meath Old IRA Association declared:

> Every one of the members feel bound by the oath of allegiance to the Irish republic taken by him on entering the Old Irish Republican Army and in pursuance of that continuing allegiance the members are encouraged to support and aid the Fianna Fáil movement as the present dominant and active national movement striving towards the goal of Republican freedom for Ireland.[61]

In January 1933, the Roscommon Old IRA declared that by voting for Fianna Fáil the electorate was 'taking a step in the right direction and for the making of a peaceful and prosperous Ireland'.[62] The same month, the East Waterford Old IRA Men's Association expressed their support for Fianna Fáil.[63] But this support was largely conditional upon the reversal of the perceived discrimination against old republicans during the Cumann na nGaedheal administration. In April 1933, the Tipperary Old IRA, for example, demanded that their members should get first preference in any appointments in the county as 'the Cosgrave gang were being catered for long enough in the way of land, pensions and positions'.[64]

Since 1923 there had been considerable resentment and disillusionment amongst old IRA members (who, it should be emphasised, were predominantly republican in their sympathies) regarding the division of lands. This is exemplified by the following resolution passed by the Tipperary Old IRA in 1933:

> Governments in the past have proved themselves notoriously ungrateful and convinently [sic] forgetful of the men who made them and as our only hope of compensation is through the medium of land, we mean to see it, as far as in our power lies that a reoccurence [sic] of this treatment is not meted out to those who gave the best years of their lives to make this country a land without footing or shelter for slaves.[65]

One former IRA captain of the 7th Battalion of the Tipperary No. 1 Brigade had applied for a farm to the Land Commission in 1924. He was the eldest son of a farmer but as he had been effectively on the run from 1917 to 1923 while his younger brother ran the farm, he thought it only right that he should relinquish his stake in it. The Land Commission initially allotted him a farm in Tipperary but subsequently reneged on the deal. Some time later he learned that the farm had been allotted to the brother-in-law of Patrick Hogan, the Minister for Agriculture. In 1934, he wrote to the Leix–Offaly Fianna Fáil TD, Paddy Boland:

> I could get no money to get out of the country & all the wise people round were sneering at me for making as they said, a fool of myself losing the best years of my life for nothing . . . while those who took no part had got into the best of positions. Can you understand what that feels like?[66]

The Meath Old IRA Association also complained that, under the Cosgrave administration, old IRA men (meaning old republicans) had been victimised in the allocation of farms while lands were given to Free Staters. Now they demanded 'the preferential treatment, all else being equal, of Old IRA members in the division and allotment of lands' in recognition of their IRA service and compensation for losses during such services.[67] On 2 October 1932, a conference of the South Tipperary Old IRA in Thurles passed a series of resolutions proposing *inter alia* that the 1923 Land Act should be abolished; that the ranches of Tipperary should be distributed immediately amongst local uneconomic holders and landless men with 'first preference [to] be given to Republican soldiers'; that the farm at Castlefogarty offered for sale by the Land Commission should be handed over to a republican soldier; and, finally, that the two migrant families brought on to the Bailey and Carew estates should be removed and replaced by local landless men and uneconomic holders.[68]

If IRA veterans' claims were to be catered for, the right men, so to speak, had to be placed in strategic or influential positions. In his Land Commission memoirs, P. J. Sammon claimed that a new CEO, Paddy Brennan, joined the Acquisition and Resales Department in the spring of 1933. He had passed the CEO grade examination that was 'open to applicants with certain pre-truce IRA service'.[69] The same year, the number of land commissioners was raised from four to six. One of the new appointees was Eamonn Mansfield who 'displayed an unflagging zeal in performing his new duties. In particular, he showed a special interest in all those applicants for land who claimed to have pre-Truce service.'[70] Sammon recalled being summoned to Mansfield's office in the late 1930s to find him 'in his shirtsleeves . . . beavering away at some applicants who had claims for pre-Truce IRA service. His trouble was that some of these did not figure amongst those selected for parcels.'[71] Mansfield's official views on land division policy clearly illustrate that his sympathies lay with IRA veterans of the War of Independence.[72]

In 1933, the new government drafted a memorandum on land policy for the Irish Land Commission which stipulated that the hierarchy of allottees was to be changed: discharged estate employees were to get first priority followed by evicted tenants, uneconomic holders in the immediate vicinity of an estate, 'landless men of a deserving class in immediate proximity' and finally, migrants. National service in the old IRA was to be taken into consideration in the landless class.[73] In another memorandum written around the same time, the Land Commission was told by Frank Aiken, the Minister for Lands, to place more emphasis on the landless men than the congests; his reasoning being to relieve unemployment.[74] But Aiken may have had in mind the provision of more land for landless IRA veterans and certainly some of these were hopeful that Aiken would exert some influence in land division schemes in his own constituency of Louth. In March 1933, when the Knockabbey estate was being divided, a constituent wrote to him from the Mills of Louth (a townland not far from Louth village): 'As you know I have taken part in the Tan War and Civil War and still is [*sic*] chairman of Tallanstown Cumann F[ianna] F[ail]'.[75]

In May 1935, Commissioner S. J. Waddell issued 'strictly private and confidential' instructions to the Land Commission inspectorate that widened the scope to provide land for veterans. National service in the pre-truce IRA was now to be taken into consideration in each class of allottee. This meant that congests with pre-truce IRA service were to be given preference over those who had none and the same applied across the board with other classes of allottees. While Waddell's instructions made it clear that it was to be difficult for anybody with a pension (or other source of income) to receive land, he specified that 'Pre-Truce IRA men who have been awarded small pensions for national service under *Saorstat* Pensions Acts are not affected if eligible for land and capable of working it'.[76]

There was still a difficulty in determining whether claims by IRA veterans were legitimate or not. When the policy of land for veterans became public, it was inevitable that there would be considerably more men (and in some cases women) claiming to have seen active service in the pre-truce period than had been the case. Indeed, it was difficult for the government to determine what constituted active service. Did one have to have taken part in an ambush in which members of the crown forces had been killed or was it enough to have carried dispatches? Was the cutting of roads or the purchasing of arms as important as the shooting of a member of the RIC?[77] As the government faced similar difficulties with regard to the issuing of military service pensions to IRA veterans, the Minister for Lands recognised that one could work in conjunction with the other. In 1936 he decided that preferential treatment for IRA members should be 'definitely confined to men with pensions and to men in respect of whom the army pensions authorities are prepared to issue certificates of first-class meritorious service'.[78] In November, the Executive Council agreed that an applicant should have 'outstanding IRA service' before he could be considered.[79]

VI

One does not have to be a cynic to realise that it is one thing for politicians to promise land for everybody when they are out of office and quite another to deliver upon these promises when they take office. And so it was with Fianna Fáil, as with Cumann na nGaedheal before them. For the first three years or so of its administration, Fianna Fáil attempted, in some areas at least, to stand by its land division pledges. These years seem to represent the heyday of land allotment to IRA veterans. But how accurate was the Fianna Fáil claim, as issued through the Office of the President in 1937, that 'in addition to provision for pensions, the gov[ernmen]t has, as no doubt the Old IRA organisations are aware, given special consideration to Old IRA men in the important matter of land division'?[80] Again, no statistics are available but it is probably safe to conclude that Fianna Fáil was much more favourably disposed to IRA veterans, particularly anti-Treatyites, than their predecessors in government. In 1935, the editor of the *Meath Chronicle* wrote:

We are able to give the names of some of the allottees on the Deerpark and at Dunmoe and for those of us who lived in and had a fair share of our being in the resurgent years from 1916 to 1922 and 1923, it is pleasant to see amongst them brave men and brave families that took their full share of the perils of that glorious if dangerous epoch . . . families that sheltered the soldiers of the Republic when the hounds of England were at their heels . . . Too long were many of these men forgotten and the land minister can rest assured that there are few indeed who begrudge the restoration of the land to the men, and to the breed of men, who fought and wrought and bled for Ireland.[81]

Two years later at a meeting of Dunboyne Fianna Fáil cumann, David Hall, an old IRA member and president of the cumann, announced that during the previous two years 'not a single Old IRA man who had made application for land was turned down'.[82] To appease local opposition to a migration scheme at Emly in Tipperary in 1942, the Land Commission set aside the O'Connor estate for locals including five old IRA men.[83]

How much of a political smokescreen were such divisions? Certainly, by the late 1930s, there were a number of high-ranking officials and civil servants who were pragmatic enough to realise that allotting land based on military service did not make sound economic sense. In 1936, a Land Division Committee (composed of members of the Land Commission and civil servants from other governmental departments working in an advisory capacity to the Minister for Lands), which had been established by the government to push forward the scheme of acquisition and redistribution, decided that IRA men should be at the bottom of the hierarchy.[84] In May 1937, Gerald Boland, the Minister for Lands, was asked if he was aware of a resolution passed by members of the Tipperary Old IRA

alleging that a hostile element within the Land Commission was deliberately endeavouring to obstruct the government's declared policy of settling suitable Old IRA men on the land; whether he has instituted an inquiry into the allegation, and with what result; and, if not, if he will state what action he intends to take in the matter.[85]

Boland replied that he was aware of the resolution but unimpressed by its questioning of the impartiality and loyalty of the staff of the Land Commission and that he had no intention of taking any further action.[86] There is the possibility that even at this early stage, the Fianna Fáil government was aware that many of those old IRA men who had received parcels of land were not capable farmers. Referring to the landless category (which originally was the only category to cater for old IRA allottees), the minister said: 'These should be men of a good type who have experience of the working of land and who have sufficient capital or stock to enable them to work the land allotted to them.'[87] For years afterwards the Fianna Fáil government was criticised for 'slipping up', and for allotting land to people 'who should never have got it' or 'who did not intend to work it properly'.[88]

Ultimately, Fianna Fáil proved as disappointing to land-hungry IRA veterans as Cumann na nGaedheal. While its commitment to land redistribution was clear in the early years of its administration, it became increasingly aware of the need to avoid antagonising the middling to large farmers who had been so adversely affected by the Economic War. Faced with conflicting demands, Fianna Fáil did not deliver to the small farmer and labourer classes all that it had promised.[89] While a number of small divisions continued, the Emergency effectively put a stop to large-scale land division from 1939 to 1947. When Sean Moylan became Minister for Lands in August 1943, his policy regarding land division was based on sound and practical economic and agricultural sense. Shortly after taking up his position as minister, Moylan wrote to de Valera outlining his proposals regarding allottees. He strongly urged that only farmers were deserving of lands. Uneconomic holders should be given primacy, the allotment of three to ten acre plots to cottiers and labourers should be stopped and there was to be serious reconsideration of the allotment of lands to the landless.[90] Notwithstanding his own high profile in the IRA during both the War of Independence and the civil war there was absolutely no mention of special consideration for old IRA men. In 1944, he pointed out that

> Land is not given to applicants merely because of IRA service; they must first have the necessary qualifications ordinarily looked for, and then, within the various classes of ex-employees, congests, migrants and so on, national service entitles a man to special consideration.[91]

During the 1940s, Fianna Fáil government representatives met with organisations representing the old IRA from different localities, including representatives of the United Conference of Old IRA Organisations,[92] but nothing concrete came from these discussions. Old IRA members increasingly looked for patronage in the form of jobs rather than land.[93] Fianna Fáil's tough anti-IRA stance undoubtedly contributed to a change in policy. Fighting the IRA at one level did not stand easily with rewarding IRA veterans on another level. By the end of the war, the Minister for Lands argued that giving land to the landless was a waste of resources.[94] Subsequently, a new Land Act was passed giving the Land Commission power to deal with unsatisfactory allottees and a new department was set up within the commission to process transactions. Moylan proposed to restrict the granting of holdings to landless men to the absolute minimum. From the late 1950s, the old IRA stopped lobbying for land and concentrated more upon their pension entitlements.[95] It had become obvious that they had received all the favouritism in respect of land division that they could hope for. Writing in 1957, an embittered Seosamh Ó Cearnaigh, a member of the Leinster Council of the Old IRA, complained to de Valera:

> Over a year ago we decided that we would not in future seek any concessions from any of the political parties which constituted an Dáil at that time, and we wish to let you know that we still adhere to that decision. We are convinced more and more of the hostility of successive governments to the pre-Truce IRA. This was very evident in the allocating of land and positions in which we did not even get equal treatment with the rest of our countrymen.[96]

Notes

1   J. M. Regan and M. Cronin, 'Introduction: Ireland and the politics of independence 1922–49, new perspectives and re-considerations', in J. M. Regan and M. Cronin (eds), *Ireland: The Politics of Independence, 1922–49* (Hampshire, 2000), pp. 1–2. See also J. Augusteijn, 'Motivation: Why did they fight for Ireland? The motivation of volunteers in the revolution', in Augusteijn (ed.), *The Irish Revolution, 1913–1923* (Basingstoke, 2002), p. 104.

2   *Dáil Debates*, vol. III, col. 1925–75, 14 June 1923.

3   L. MacFhionnghail [L. Ginnell], *The Land Question* (Dublin, n.d. [1917]), pp. 18–19.

4   Inspector General's confidential monthly report (IGCMR), Dec. 1917 (Public Record Office (PRO) CO904, monthly police reports). Writing in 1917, Ginnell claimed that 'the vast majority of the young landless men in the ranching districts desire the distribution of these lands as reparation for the past, for the general good of the country, for historical and other reasons transcending the cash value of the land' (MacFhionnghail, *Land Question*, p. 15).

5   County inspector's confidential monthly report (CICMR), Co. Galway ER, Feb. 1918 (PRO, CO904, monthly police reports).

6   IGCMR, Feb. 1918.

7   CICMR, Co. Roscommon, Feb. 1918.

8   CICMR, Co. Galway WR, Mar. 1918.

9   Précis of agrarian outrages, 23 July 1920 (PRO, CO 904, police reports).

10   Numerous county inspectors refer to these types of notices in their monthly reports from the beginning of 1918 onwards; see also the memoirs of Arthur Shiel, a judge of the Sinn Féin arbitration courts (*The Irish Times*, 11 Nov. 1966).

11   E. O'Malley, *On Another Man's Wound* (Dublin, 1979 [1st edn 1936]), pp. 123, 144; P. O'Donnell, *Not Yet Emmett* (Dublin, n.d.), p. 1; E. Childers, *The Constructive Work of Dáil Éireann: no. 1* (Dublin, 1921), p. 12; *An Phoblacht*, 11 June 1926.

12   Quoted in M. Hopkinson, *Green against Green: The Irish Civil War* (Dublin, 1988), p. 45.

13 L. Deasy, *Towards Ireland Free: The West Cork Brigade in the War of Independence 1917–21* (Cork, 1973), p. 1.

14 Ibid., p. 162.

15 T. Barry, *Guerilla Days in Ireland* (Dublin, 1991 [1st edn Cork, 1949]), pp. 6–7.

16 D. Breen, *My Fight for Irish Freedom* (Dublin, 1981 [1st edn 1924]), p. 100.

17 P. Hart, *The IRA and its Enemies: Violence and Community in Cork, 1916–23* (Oxford, 1998), p. 143.

18 J. Augusteijn, *From Public Defiance to Guerilla Warfare: The Experience of Ordinary Volunteers in the Irish War of Independence, 1916–21* (Dublin, 1996), p. 359.

19 Ibid., p. 361.

20 *Minutes of the proceedings of the first parliament of the Republic of Ireland, 1919–21*, 4 Apr. 1919.

21 [Erskine Childers], *The Constructive Work of Dail Eireann: no. 1* (Dublin, 1921), p. 10.

22 Quoted in ibid., p. 18.

23 Quoted in S. Briollay, *Ireland in Rebellion* (Dublin, 1922), p. 60.

24 Childers, *The Constructive work of Dail Éireann, no. 1*, p. 18.

25 CICMR, Co. Meath, June 1920.

26 For more details, see T. Dooley, *The Decline of the Big House in Ireland* (Dublin, 2001), pp. 127–31.

27 D. Seth Jones, 'Land reform legislation and security of tenure in Ireland after independence', *Eire-Ireland* XXXII–XXXIII, (1997–8), p. 117.

28 Henry Patterson has convincingly argued that while agrarian radicalism was being put down in the east and midlands, the smallholders of the west still believed that the resolution of their agrarian grievances depended upon the victory of the republicans. Tom Garvin observes that some IRA leaders believed that the fear among Volunteers of losing land promised to them was the main reason why the IRA would not settle for anything less than the Irish republic. H. Patterson, *The Politics of Illusion: A Political History of the IRA* (London, 1997 [1st edn 1984]), p. 24; T. Garvin, *1922: The Birth of Irish Democracy* (Dublin, 1996), pp. 44–5.

29 Col. Maurice Moore to Minister for Defence, Richard Mulcahy, 9 May 1922 (Military Archives (MA), A/3126).

30 Patrick Hogan, memo on land seizures, 22 Dec. 1922 (MA, A/7869).

31 William Rochfort to secretary, Minister for Home Affairs, 7 Apr. 1923 (National Archives (NA), Dept. of Justice files (DJ) H5/56).

32 See, for example, public notice issued by Kyleavallagh and Kyleoughan (Land Committee, April 1922, NA, DJ H5/123). This subject will be dealt with in more detail in a forthcoming publication by this author on the work of the Irish Land Commission from 1923.

33 Memo on seizures of land [by Patrick Hogan], 22 Dec. 1922 (NA, Dept. of Taoiseach files (DT) S1943). These Special Infantry Columns will be dealt with in more detail in a forthcoming publication by this author.

34 Patrick Hogan to W. T. Cosgrave, 7 April 1923 (NA, DT S3192).

35 P. O'Donnell, *There Will Be Another Day* (Dublin, 1963), pp. 19–20.

36 *Minutes of proceedings of Dáil Éireann*, 1 Mar. 1922, p. 144.

37 *Minutes of proceedings of Dáil Éireann*, 11 Mar. 1922, p. 144.

38 Both Kent and Markievicz were supported by Art O'Connor, former director of agriculture, on the point that if there was going to be land for the landless it should only be for those who had given 'good service to this country during the past two years' (ibid., p. 160).

39 Ibid., pp. 160–1.

40 *Dáil Debates*, vol. 16, 1358, 17 June 1926.

41 O'Donnell, *Another Day*, p. 48.

42 Art O'Connor, 'A brief summary of the work done by the agricultural department from April 1919 to August 1921', n.d. (University College Dublin Archives (UCDA), Richard Mulcahy papers, P7A/63).

43 T. Garvin, 'Nationalist revolution: Ireland 1858–1928', in *Comparative Studies in Society and History* XXVIII (1986), p. 492.

44 *Dáil Debates*, vol. 13, 1109, 2 Dec. 1925.

45 Ibid.

46 Ibid., 1151.

47 E. O'Halpin, *Defending Ireland* (Oxford, 1999), p. 46.

48 At various stages these included the Reunited IRA Association or Reunited Irish Republican Pre-truce Forces Association, as well as a host of other organisations at local and national level. In the late 1930s, the National Association of Old IRA was formed to reunite the factions and 'to restore to the nation that unity of purpose and solidarity of organisation which, twenty years ago, brought forth the highest qualities of self-sacrificing patriotism in our people'. By the early 1940s the United Conference of Old IRA Organisations had taken under its wing The Old Cumann na mBan, The Association of Old Fianna Eireann, Association of Irish Citizen Army, National Association of the Old IRA, the 1916 Veterans' association; Association of the Old Dublin Brigade and so on; National Association of Old IRA, *Dublin Brigade Review* (Dublin, n.d.), p. 74; R. Muldoon, 'Report of IRA Old Comrades Association, all-Ireland convention, 16 July 1933' (NA, DJ 8/718).

49 T. J. Keenan to Piaras Beaslai, 10 Mar. 1928 (National Library of Ireland (NLI), Piaras Beaslai papers, MS 33,947(8)).

50 *An Phoblacht*, 27 Nov. 1925.

51 *An Phoblacht*, 29 Jan. 1926.

52. *An Phoblacht*, 14, May, 28 May 1926; 22 Apr. 1927.

53 This will be dealt with in a forthcoming publication by this author.

54 *Dáil Debates*, vol. 29, 666,18 Apr. 1929.

55 *Dáil Debates*, vol. 28, 1019, 7 Mar. 1929.

56 List of members in battalion areas deserving of land allotment with suggestions as to estates for acquisition in those areas, n.d. [*c.* 1934?] (UCDA, Frank Aiken papers, P104/2886).

57 See Patterson, *The Politics of Illusion* pp. 37–50.

58 *Fianna Fáil: 1926–51: The Story of Twenty-five Years of National Endeavour and Historic Achievement* (n.d. [1951]), p. 6. This principle was to be enshrined in article 45.2 (v) of the 1937 constitution which stated as a directive of social policy: 'That there may be established on the land in economic security as many families as in the circumstances shall be practicable.'

59 *Mayo News*, 6 Feb. 1932; quoted in ibid., pp. 50–1.

60 *Meath Chronicle*, 19 Jan. 1935.

61 T. E. Duffy, 'Old Irish Republican Army Organisation: County of Meath and environs: report and schemes with appendices presented to President De Valera and his government for consideration', May 1933 (Aiken papers, P104/2887). The president of the Fianna Fáil cumann in Navan, Henry O'Hagan, was a member of the old IRA (*Irish Press*, 17 Jan. 1933).

62 *Irish Press*, 18 Jan. 1933.

63 *Irish Press*, 16 Jan. 1933.

64 P. J. Davern to Frank Aiken enclosing resolutions passed by United Republican Association of County Tipperary, 2 Apr. 1933 (Aiken papers, P104/2875).

65 Enclosed in P. J. Davern to Frank Aiken enclosing resolutions passed by United Republican Association of County Tipperary, 2 Apr. 1933 (Aiken papers, P104/2875).

66 E. Q. to Paddy Boland, n.d. [*c*.1934] (Aiken papers, P104/2875).

67 List of members in battalion areas deserving of land allotment with suggestions as to estates for acquisition in those areas (Aiken papers, P104/2886).

68 Report of Thurles conference of IRA, 2 Oct. 1932 (UCDA, Moss Twomey papers, P69/54 (37)).

69 P. J. Sammon, *In the Land Commission: A Memoir 1933–78* (Dublin, 1997), p. 2.

70 Ibid., p. 11.

71 Ibid.

72 Eamon Mansfield, 'Observations on memo by Department of Lands', 21 June 1943 (NA, DT S14399).

73 Govt. memo on land policy, prepared for secretary of Irish Land Commission, n.d. [1933] (NA, DT S6490(A)).

74 Frank Aiken memo on Land Bill 1933, n.d. (Aiken papers, P104/3298).

75 J. S. to Frank Aiken, 25 Mar. 1933 (Aiken papers, P104/2247).

76 Inspectorate notice no. 11/35, signed by S. J. Waddell, chief inspector, 4 May 1935 (NA, DT S6490(A)).

77 Representations by County Clare Old IRA Association: administration of Military Service Pensions Act, 1934 (NA, DT 97/9/331).

78 Memo by Minister for Lands for Executive Council on land division policy, 21 Aug. 1936 (NA, DT S6490(A)).

79 Department of lands: land division policy, 17 Nov. 1936 (NA, DT S6490).

80 Draft letter from Maurice Moynihan to chairman of Old IRA Convention, *c.* 21 Jan. 1937 (NA, DT S9240(A)).

81 *Meath Chronicle*, 16 Mar. 1935.

82 *Meath Chronicle*, 16 Oct. 1937.

83 *Dáil Debates*, vol. 86, 28–33, 24 Mar. 1942.

84 Report of Land Division Committee, 21 May 1936 (Aiken papers, P104/3388).

85 *Dáil Debates*, vol. 66, 2043, 4 May 1937.

86 *Dáil Debates*, vol. 66, 2043–4, 4 May 1937.

87 Memo prepared by Minister for Lands for Executive Council on land division policy, 21 Aug, 1936 (NA, DT S6490(A)).

88 See speech of Senator Sweetman, *Seanad Debates*, vol. 31, 1175–82, 3 Apr. 1946.

89 P. Bew, E. Hazelkorn and H. Patterson, *The Dynamics of Irish Politics* (London, 1989), p. 77.

90 Sean Moylan to Eamon de Valera, 1 Sept. 1943 (NA, DT S12890A).

91 *Dáil Debates*, vol. 93, 1905, 2 May 1944.

92 For units affiliated to this organisation, see note 48 above.

93 Government memo on old IRA preferential treatment, 12 Nov. 1942 (NA, DT S9240(A)); Seosamh Ó Traithigh, secretary of United Conference of Old IRA, to Éamon de Valera, 8 August 1942 (NA, DT S9240(B)).

94 Dept of Lands memo on land division policy, Apr. 1947 (NA, DT S6490(B/1)).

95 See, for example, John A. Costello to Sean Dowling, 14 Mar. 1957 (NA, DT, S9240(B)).

96 Seosamh Ó Cearnaigh [Joseph Kearney] to Eamon de Valera, 7 June 1957 (NA, DT S9240(B)).

CHAPTER 7

British Intelligence, the Republican Movement and the IRA's German Links 1935–45

* * *

Eunan O'Halpin

INTRODUCTION

This chapter attempts to explore how much British intelligence agencies knew or surmised about the republican movement's links with Germany before and during the Second World War, and the impact of such knowledge upon British policy towards Ireland. The timing as well as the fact of British knowledge and supposition is crucial, particularly in terms of assessing the influence of raw intelligence and of intelligence analysis on key policy makers including Winston Churchill.

The chapter is based largely on material in the Public Record Office (PRO) in London, including recently released code-breaking and other documents. The releases are in three main categories: (a) records of the British security service MI5, including the in-house Irish section history compiled in 1945–6, which are in the PRO class KV which was first opened in 1998; (b) records of the code-breaking organisation GC&CS in the PRO class HW, a series which was first opened in the early 1990s; and (c) Dominions Office files previously withheld but eventually opened in 2001 and 2002 in the DO130 and DO121 classes. I have also used the papers of Churchill's intelligence adviser Major Desmond Morton (PREM7).

I have written elsewhere on much of the material in the first two categories noted above, but those contributions were completed before the latest tranche of Dominions Office files became available.[1] Crucially, these include both GC&CS documents and a good deal of analytical material on Ireland produced by the Secret Intelligence Service SIS or MI6, together with correspondence between the Dominions Office and SIS on various Irish security issues. The GC&CS material in these files includes a large body of intercepts of German diplomatic traffic to and from Dublin, the first such set of British diplomatic decrypts that I know of (the process of declassification of GC&CS diplomatic material generally has not yet reached the late 1930s). The SIS material is particularly useful for two reasons: firstly because it remains British policy generally never to release SIS records, and secondly because the documents in the Dominions Office files form two nearly continuous time series of intelligence assessments on Ireland covering much of the war period and based on the best information available to SIS headquarters at the time, including decodes, reports from SIS's Irish networks, and scraps of material from SIS agents and other sources in Europe. These documents give a fairly detailed picture of the output of an SIS headquarters country section – in this case '16-land', the shorthand for Ireland – and consequently they are of interest to historians of SIS generally as well as of the more particular matters of Irish republicanism and of Anglo-Irish relations.

The new SIS material is complemented by the recent release of a large number of MI5's pre-war and wartime 'PF' files, that is the personal case files of individual suspects and enemy intelligence personnel. Included in the 2001 releases were the very important files on the pre-war Dublin based German agent Mrs Gertrude Brandy, and, unexpectedly, on a hapless young Breton traitor Guy Vissault de Coetlogon, who was involved in German efforts to get Breton nationalists and Irish republicans working together and who displayed a surprising if sometimes jumbled knowledge of the personalities and politics of the curious Irish republican-Celtic studies milieu.[2]

I have also made some use of material long available in Irish intelligence records in the Military Archives in Dublin.

BRITISH INTELLIGENCE ORGANISATION AND IRELAND BEFORE THE WAR

The evidence suggests that before the outbreak of war Britain had no organisation in Ireland capable of actively gathering intelligence on the Irish state, on the republican movement, or on foreign espionage. The British Isles formed a common travel area with a shared system for issuing visas to aliens wishing to visit either state, but this matter was dealt with adequately if inefficiently by sharing watch lists of suspects and undesirables and by periodic correspondence between Dublin and London. Apart from occasional contacts on matters such as suspected communist activities, once the civil war was over there was no dialogue on security questions. Furthermore, Britain had no diplomatic representation in Dublin before September 1939. When de

Valera first came to power in 1932 the British were so alarmed that they started decoding Irish diplomatic cable traffic and, after MI5 had declined the opportunity, SIS established 'not an Intelligence Service, but a very restricted information service. The reports furnished by this service did not do more than give a limited cross section of private opinion on current events of political and public interest in Eire'.[3] It seems likely that this series was designated 'QRS', as the Dominions Office files include QRS reports from 1942 to 1944 numbered sequentially from 195 to 212.[4] Judging by this material, SIS up to 1939 was in effect simply carrying out what would normally be a diplomat's task of sending home confidential reports. At some point SIS also established an Irish section at headquarters, but up to 1939 this was almost certainly only part of the workload of a single officer. For most of the war it seems to have been the responsibility of Mrs K. M. Archer, who up to 1940 was an MI5 officer specialising in communist activities and Soviet espionage.[5] Its main function was to collate material having any bearing on Ireland which was picked up anywhere in the world, and from 1931 to 1938 it also received information about 'events and suspect individuals in Northern and Southern Ireland' from the RUC, although that force 'was not well equipped to study foreign organisations and activities in Eire'.[6] From 1938 the RUC dealt directly with MI5, but that organisation did not have a presence in Dublin and until 1939 did not even have an Irish desk where problems of Irish security might be systematically studied. In summary, before the outbreak of war, Britain had no one on the ground in Ireland to liaise with the Irish on security questions, to conduct covert inquiries about foreign activities in Ireland, or to spy on the republican movement or on the Irish state.

In May and June 1938 an MI5 officer did visit Dublin in the guise of a 'Fascist minded young journalist attached to a press agency specializing in Service articles'. This was after an Irishman had disclosed to the War Office that he had been recruited in Dublin to secure Irish informants in the British armed services by a visiting German, Kurt Wheeler Hill. The MI5 officer was successfully introduced by his informant 'to the German Club where he attended a supper at the Red Bank Restaurant at which Dr Mahr', the director of the National Museum and the head of the Nazi party's Ausland organisation in Ireland, 'made a speech'. Unfortunately Wheeler Hill soon disappeared back to Germany and the contact never flowered. MI5 informed the Irish of this episode when they established what they termed 'the Dublin link', that is liaison with the Irish authorities, in the autumn of 1938.[7] Before war broke out the shared assumption of both MI5 and SIS was apparently that if war with Germany did break out the Irish would be willing to act in tandem with Britain on espionage and security matters and that British agencies would not operate independently in Ireland for fear of the political repercussions if their activities came to light. These assumptions are visible in the first major case of German espionage involving Ireland which came to light in 1938, that of Mrs Gertrude Brandy.

A POTENTIAL FIFTH COLUMN?
THE IRA AS A GERMAN PROXY, 1935-9

It might be thought that the IRA's insurrectionary potential would have loomed reasonably large in the minds of British military and security officials studying problems of home defence which might arise in the case of a war with Germany. Until the spring of 1938, such a war would have been assumed to include operations based on the Irish ports and unspecified other facilities guaranteed to Britain under the Anglo-Irish Treaty of 1921. In those circumstances, even the least imaginative staff officer would surely have factored in the likelihood of IRA action against British targets. Even after the April 1938 Anglo-Irish agreement ended British defence rights in independent Ireland, there was an obvious danger that the republican movement would take the opportunity to make trouble in Northern Ireland and in Britain, whether through sabotage or espionage. Yet it appears that, until very late in the decade, Britain had no inkling of the IRA's sporadic contacts with Nazi Germany which were initiated in 1935. It may be that the idea of a serious renewal of the First World War Irish separatist–German link which had produced the 1916 Rising was discounted in the changed circumstances of an independent Ireland, despite how difficult and unpredictable a dominion Mr de Valera's was proving to be.

The evidence on pre-war British appreciations of the IRA's intentions, capabilities and alliances is very confused. As early as 1927, SIS reported indications that the organisation had, through international communist circles, established contact in 1922 with 'the German espionage service'.[8] This seems unlikely: the IRA had in fact reached agreement with the Soviets in 1925 to gather military intelligence in the United Kingdom, an episode of which the British seem never to have become aware. In 1927 republicans also formally resolved to take the Russian side in any future Anglo-Soviet war.[9] In 1933 a Russian émigré reported that the IRA had concluded a pact with the Comintern (the Soviet controlled Communist International) under which large quantities of arms were to be delivered to Ireland, a report which SIS was inclined to discount because of its general suspicion of 'White Russian information' as 'the sources were so uncontrolled, so liable to produce tendentious matter and to be vitiated at their source' by Soviet penetration.[10] These scraps suggest that after 1933 SIS and MI5 may have regarded the Soviet Union, rather than Nazi Germany, as the IRA's most likely future ally. Yet in December 1935 a decoded Italian diplomatic telegram from Dublin to Rome indicated that the

Italian minister had persuaded IRA leaders to organise propaganda in the United States in support of his country's attack on Abyssinia. It is not known how British agencies interpreted this second hand evidence of Irish republicanism's ideological elasticity. Even when the first traces of German intelligence interest in Ireland were noted in Whitehall, they do not appear to have been construed in terms of a possible IRA–German alliance: a Joint Intelligence Committee (JIC) document of June 1937 on 'German activities in the Irish Free State' analysed evidence in terms of the possibility of Germany seeking a military understanding with the Irish government, not with the IRA which then appeared a predominantly left-wing movement.[11]

There is no evidence to indicate that up to 1939 any British (or Irish) defence or security agency actively contemplated the possibility that Germany was forging links with the republican movement for development during a future war against Britain. It seems that it was not until the IRA launched the 'S-plan' that the possibility of German manipulation was seriously considered. An early War Office advocate of irregular warfare dismissed the 'completely futile and puerile attempts at sabotage being carried out by the IRA in England', and did not argue the possibility that the activity was German inspired or assisted.[12] Despite its apprehensions about German designs, and its unfolding knowledge of German intelligence activities concerning Ireland, MI5 concluded that there was

> no evidence that German agents had been responsible for the IRA bombing campaign, though there were grounds for thinking that the Germans in Dublin . . . had made approaches to the IRA leaders as to the possibility of co-operation in the event of war between Germany and England. They were inclined to regard the danger of Germany organizing sabotage with the assistance of IRA terrorists as a very serious one.[13]

GERMAN ESPIONAGE AND IRELAND UP TO 1939

On 29 April 1938 an SIS officer wrote to MI5 about recent arrests in Prague and New York which had disclosed the existence of a German espionage network which was in communication with Mrs Jessie Jordan in Dundee and Mrs Gertrude Brandy of Dublin.[14] While this case was under investigation, the Irish gave their first intimation of concern about German covert activities, though the possibility of a German-IRA linkup was not strenuously canvassed. The British were concerned that Germany might be planning to use Ireland as a base for intelligence gathering on the United Kingdom, and the Irish were alarmed at the implications for Anglo-Irish relations. On 31 August 1938 Guy Liddell of MI5 met the Irish High Commissioner in London, J. W. Dulanty, and the secretary of the Department of External Affairs, Joseph Walshe. The latter

> expressed the concern of the Eire Government about German activities in Eire and their desire to set up a Department similar to the Security Service. The Security Service representative expressed his readiness to assist them in every possible way and promised to supply a memorandum on the subject. Walshe said that the new Eire counter-espionage Department would be under the Eire Department of Defence and it was agreed that exchange of information would be made between the Security Service and the Eire counter-espionage Department on the activities of Germans in Eire.[15]

These overtures provided MI5 with the opportunity to apprise the Irish of the Brandy case. Further investigation of Mrs Brandy revealed that she was in receipt of letters from a French naval officer, sous-lieutenant Marc Aubert of Toulon, who was supplying intelligence on the French Mediterranean fleet in return for cash to fund his expensive mistress. Mrs Brandy had apparently been drawn into this clandestine work after the death early in 1937 of her husband R. L. Brandy, a German import agent in Dublin who, post-war American analysis of captured German records revealed, had been recruited 'as an espionage agent and had submitted a number of reports' to the naval intelligence arm of the Abwehr.[16] As investigations proceeded, a British photostat of an intercepted letter addressed to Mrs Brandy 'created a tremendous impression in the Deuxieme Bureau' and in French naval circles.[17] A senior MI5 officer prepared to brief the French on the ramifications of the case, and a British security officer based in Paris was advised that

> for internal political reasons, it is very difficult to pursue enquiries [in Ireland] and the observance of the utmost secrecy is most earnestly requested . . . The US authorities have given an assurance that they will do their best to exclude Mrs Brandy's name and address in the current proceedings in New York.[18]

MI5 had two reasons for enjoining particular secrecy: they hoped that further investigation of Mrs Brandy would yield more information about German espionage in Europe, and they desperately wanted to avoid embarrassing the Irish authorities with whom tentative contact had just been established. This had already resulted in some enquiries in Dublin about the Brandy family, the findings of which were sent to MI5 in mid-October. After a meeting with the Irish army director of intelligence on 5 November, Colonel Hinchley Cooke of MI5 noted:

> Spent most of the morning with Colonel Archer. Explained to him the situation

that had arisen in connection with Mrs BRANDY and discussed with him the possibilities. It is quite clear to me that at the present moment Colonel Archer (a) is certainly not prepared to act against Mrs BRANDY under the Official Secrets Act; (b) is quite unable satisfactorily to intercept her correspondence and therefore quite rightly is not proposing to do so; (c) is very dubious as to how far he can safely employ the police in attempting to shadow.

I am quite satisfied that he is anxious to help in any way he can, but I think we were right in getting him over as the information from Paris will undoubtedly strengthen his hand with the authorities in Ireland in order to get them to come round to his point of view as to what he requires in the way of personnel and powers.

I promised to let him know if and when we got any detailed information from Paris.[19]

The Brandy case showed both London and Dublin that Ireland could be used by Germany, not in this instance because of a republican link, or even contiguity with the United Kingdom, but simply as an innocuous location through which to route communications from agents in target countries. Since such activity involved neither espionage nor any other act directed against the Irish state, it was probably not even illegal.

A second line of British enquiries into pre-war German preparations for espionage and subversion was that of the possible manipulation of Celtic minorities in Britain, France, Belgium and Ireland. So far as can be judged, London did not raise this possibility with the Irish until well after the war had started. Yet it was an element in the first major pre-war break into German preparations for espionage in Britain. This was the case of Arthur Owens – 'SNOW' as he became known in the parlance of the Double Cross system which he did a great deal to create. 'SNOW' was a Welsh engineer with business contacts in Germany. From 1936 he worked both for SIS and for German intelligence, and in 1938 disclosed to the British that he had been recruited by the Germans to collect intelligence and to establish networks of informers. Amongst tasks given him by his German controllers shortly after the outbreak of war was the forging of a link with Welsh nationalists with a view to an eventual insurrection, an arrangement which MI5 put in place using a retired police inspector in lieu of a genuine activist. This ruse enabled MI5 to control German efforts to harness Welsh separatists for intelligence gathering and sabotage purposes throughout the entire war.[20] It must have been clear to MI5, if the Germans were minded to use so insignificant and unproven an entity as the Welsh nationalist movement, that they had parallel ideas for the rather more experienced IRA.

British investigation of German attempts to manipulate national minorities continued during the war. This involved some curious intersections of personalities and causes, including the Irish: the secret history of the MI5 section dealing with the security of merchant navy personnel states that:

> One of our intended double agents, GWLADYS, was in touch with the Pan-Celtic Union in Dublin [excised] the German-controlled Breton autonomist organisation in Rennes. This [excised] provided GWLADYS with a very good motive for getting in touch with the Germans, which he later succeeded in doing. We had given GWLADYS considerable training in the United Kingdom, and we arranged with him to join the Welsh nationalists and spend a certain amount of time with them in order to acquire the right background . . . He was introduced by them to the Scottish nationalists, and was able to talk intelligently about their work to the Pan-Celtic Union in Dublin. Our reason for preparing GWLADYS with this background was that we knew from Special Sources [German intelligence decodes] that the enemy were interested in the breton autonomist organisation, which was connected with the Pan-Celtic Union.[21]

More details about Germany's efforts in this direction involving Ireland emerged in the interrogation in 1944 of the ill-fated young Breton, Guy Vissault de Coetlogon, whose alarming claims to have seen German agent reports emanating from Ireland in the summer of 1943, at a time when the British and Irish authorities believed that they had complete control over German espionage in Ireland, were carefully analysed but eventually dismissed as confused by MI5.[22]

THE BRITISH DISCOVERY OF GERMAN–IRA LINKS IN 1939

By the time of the Munich crisis in the autumn of 1938, the Brandy and other cases confirmed that Germany was aware of 'the possibilities of Eire as a base for operations'. Early in 1939, after the initiation of the IRA's 'S-plan' bombing campaign in Britain, reports began to come in of IRA-German contacts.[23] In July 1939 SIS reported that

> on the 20th and 25th June a conference had taken place in Berlin between Admiral Canaris, head of the Abwehr, a representative of the German War Office, and a responsible member of the IRA who was said to have reported on the bombing campaign in Britain. Canaris was reported to have undertaken to supply him with arms and funds.
>
> A report dated 20th July was received through the Foreign Office which came from the Czech Consul in Dublin that, on that date, the German Minister with three members of the Nazi Party in Dublin had left Dublin for a personal meeting with the leaders of the IRA at Inver, County Donegal. The preliminary arrangements for this meeting were said to have been made by Theodor Kordt, the Counsellor at

the German Embassy in London, who had visited Ireland for that purpose, and further that General O'Duffy, former leader of the Blue Shirts, a para-fascist organization in Ireland, had also been responsible for the arrangements . . . It was also learnt that Dr Hempel . . . visited London on the 23rd July, saw Kordt, and left for Germany on the 25th, returning on the 29th July to Dublin. This information was passed to the Dublin link . . . It was thought unlikely that the IRA would attend such a large meeting in an out of the way place where it would certainly attract attention, and though O'Duffy was known to be pro-German and pro-Fascist, it was considered unlikely that the IRA would co-operate with him.

In August a report was received from the same source that Dr Hempel was in touch with Henry Francis Stuart and his brother-in-law Sean MacBride, on the question of organizing an Irish legion to fight for Germany against Britain. This information was passed to the Dublin link, and they were informed that the source was a Czech servant in the German Legation. This information reached the Secretary of External Affairs, Joe Walsh, who informed the Dominions Office that the source was utterly unreliable. Later, a report was received from the Dublin link saying he thought the information was poor and that Walshe spoke of the informant as a "villainous type". He added that the Eire police had received their information about the Inver meeting . . . from a newspaper editor in Dublin who was known to be a friend of the Czech Consul.

This report and the enquiries which followed showed how difficult it was, even with the assistance of the Dublin link, to obtain any definite information about the activities of the Germans in Ireland. There is little doubt that Joe Walshe feared that the Czech informant in the German Legation might prove embarrassing to the Eire Government, and though in this case it is doubtful whether the information of the meeting with the IRA at Inver was correct, he did his best to discredit the informant in the eyes of the British and, it is believed, later informed the German Minister, who sacked him.[24]

A difficulty with these initial exchanges with the Irish was that the allegations concerned were so circumstantial as to be quite easily discredited in detail. This may well have contributed to a degree of complacency on the part of the Department of External Affairs, in control of Anglo-Irish security liaison at all times, which was only shattered with the arrival of Herman Goertz just as the Low Countries were invaded and France attacked in May 1940.

THE IRA AS IRELAND'S FIFTH COLUMN, 1940–1

In his first letter as prime minister to President Roosevelt, Winston Churchill on 15 May 1940 warned that 'we have many reports of possible German parachute or airborne descents in Ireland', a reflection of the alarm felt in

London at Ireland's vulnerability to a sudden attack, and sought the immediate dispatch of 'a United States squadron to Irish ports'.[25] That this was not
scaremongering on Churchill's part is reflected in a further warning which
reached him on 29 May. Major Desmond Morton of SIS, who had been
installed in 10 Downing Street as his personal assistant for intelligence matters,
reported on the first meetings of Lord Swinton's 'Executive Committee on
Security Defence' – that is, the umbrella security policy body which soon
became known as the Security Executive. He told Churchill:

> The most urgent matter which has arisen so far concerns the situation in Eire . . .
> The War Office states categorically that the IRA is well armed and well organized,
> whereas the Eire Defence Forces are little short of derisory. There is information
> that a number of Germans have landed surreptitiously in Eire since the outbreak
> of the war and that there has been a regular communication service by wireless and
> other means between Eire and Germany. A rising in Eire is now thought likely at
> any time. It is known that the Germans have plans to land troops by parachute and
> aircraft, who might reach Eire flying very high over this country and so escape
> interception, but even if there was no immediate German assistance forthcoming
> it is probable that the IRA could overcome the Eire forces by themselves, together
> with such German aid as has already arrived.
>
> The Secret Services have a great deal more detailed information, much of
> which has fitted into place as a result of the arrest in Eire a few days ago of an
> individual named HELD, who had in his possession a wireless transmitting set,
> and a number of papers showing that he was a German intelligence, sabotage and
> revolutionary agent. Finally, Dutch Police Officials and Army Officers who have
> got to this country as refugees have disclosed other particulars of a German plan
> to invade Ireland which came to their knowledge during the period that Holland
> was neutral.[26]

This was a rather poor summary of a mélange of fact, surmise and erroneous
reportage – Held was an Irishman and IRA sympathiser who had visited
Germany earlier in the year, and the American currency, equipment and
radio found in his house belonged not to him but to the newly arrived German
agent Herman Goertz, whom the police swoop had failed to catch – but the
conclusions drawn that Germany was mounting espionage operations in
Ireland, that she had established a link with the IRA, and that that organisation was willing (if not very capable) of co-operating in the event of a
German attack, were not far wide of the mark.

In the following month SIS finally established a clandestine presence in
Ireland through the appointment of Captain C. S. Collinson as Passport
Control Officer (PCO) in charge of the newly established British Permit
Office in Dublin. Collinson was a career intelligence officer who had served as

a PCO in Paris before the war. In conjunction with Lieutenant Commander Clarke of the British Trade Commissioner's Office he established a network of informants in Dublin and other key centres. Furthermore, through an employee of the credit control agency Stubbs Gazette he mounted a large number of individual inquiries focusing on suspicious aliens and on allegedly pro-Axis elements, both republican and ex-Blueshirt. These inquiries continued until March 1945 – one of the last of the one thousand eight hundred and eighty two commissioned was into the background of 'T. L. MULLINS who, according to the "Irish Press" of 19.2.45, has replaced Seamus DAVIN as General Secretary of the Fianna Fáil party'.[27] Significantly, Collinson reported to SIS's counter-intelligence section V, headed by the vice chief of SIS Colonel Valentine Vivian. This reflected SIS's main Irish priorities, which were to do with countering the Axis espionage threat rather than with penetrating the Irish state machine or with manipulating Irish affairs. Collinson's presence meant that London now had a means of checking on suspicious activities in Ireland, and on balance that was probably of benefit both to Britain and to Ireland. It was partly for that reason, and also because the Irish calculated that to stamp out his organisation would only prompt the British to create another one, that G2 was content simply to penetrate and monitor Collinson's networks. This was achieved without anyone in SIS or MI5 realising the fact.[28]

In mid-September 1940 the JIC concluded that a German attack on Ireland, either as an adjunct to an assault on Britain or as a means of 'extension of the blockade . . . as a substitute for the invasion of Great Britain', would be supported by the IRA, 'the nucleus of which is believed to consist of some 2,000 to 3,000 men, all well armed'.[29] Later estimates of IRA strength and effectiveness painted a radically different picture: in August 1941 the Admiralty director of intelligence reported that, due to vigorous police action in both parts of Ireland, the IRA had all but dissolved and no longer posed any insurrectionary threat.[30] But the republican movement could, with its cross-border and cross-channel ties amongst Irish communities and war workers in the United Kingdom, potentially still do serious damage to British interests through sabotage and, more significantly, through espionage. Furthermore, the Dublin diplomatic missions of the Axis powers and of sympathetic states such as Vichy France and Spain provided credible means by which intelligence gathered by republicans could be channelled back to Germany. The problem was most acute in respect of the German Legation once it became known at the beginning of 1941 that it housed a clandestine radio transmitter.

THE LIMITS OF ANGLO-IRISH SECURITY
CO-OPERATION ON IRA–GERMAN LINKS

A good deal has been published about the development of close Anglo-Irish security co-operation in the course of the Second World War. What needs to be stressed, however, is that this took place subject to a very clear interdict on any discussion of republican activities as such. G2 was under instructions not to disclose details of IRA plans and activities to MI5 other than where there was a clear link to Germany; instead the British were to be assured that the Irish security authorities had matters well in hand and would ensure that republicans could do no damage to British interests. This was an obvious impediment to full and frank exchanges, because the reality was that militant republican activities frequently intersected with pro-Axis ones, not least in attempts to gather intelligence for the German war effort. The Irish government was anxious to downplay the IRA's capacity and intentions as a kind of green fifth column for the Third Reich. They did not want to lend support to British fears on these lines even if they privately shared them, because to do so would weaken the state's case that independent Ireland was no threat to British security even with an Axis diplomatic presence in Dublin. The difficulty in operating this policy was that it impeded joint investigation of republican collusion with Germany even though that was plainly a major worry for both governments. The policy also had the defect that the British might, through their own sources of intelligence in Ireland and in the United Kingdom, acquire real or apparent evidence of IRA collusion with Germany and confront the Irish with it. After the Garda raid on the house of Stephen Held, Dan Bryan of G2 persuaded Fred Boland of External Affairs to inform the British quickly because they would assuredly otherwise get a garbled and alarmist version of the seizure themselves.[31] The fact that G2 had to be highly circumspect in discussing republican engagement with Germany was a recurrent problem in Anglo-Irish security dialogue.

This lacuna was, however, partly compensated by another channel of information exchange, that between the two police forces on the island. The political sensitivities which debarred Anglo-Irish discussion of the republican movement did not apply in respect of north–south relations. According to the MI5 Irish Section history, Garda action against the IRA after 1939 was conducted 'in close touch with the Royal Ulster Constabulary', a claim borne out by the observations of the RUC and of the Admiralty director of intelligence in 1941.[32]

Even as trust built up and as the tide of war changed decisively, there was also reticence on the British side. In preparing papers for a meeting to discuss the recently captured German agents John Kenny and Joseph O'Reilly in January 1944, Cecil Liddell sought clearance to show Dan Bryan various documents including 'a note on the SD prepared by Trevor Roper . . . none of the information on this is based on most secret material', as well as material on O'Reilly's known contacts in Germany other than 'one or two items . . . which may have to be excluded owing to their being based on SIS sources'.[33]

THE IMPACT OF CODE-BREAKING ON BRITISH
INTELLIGENCE ASSESSMENTS OF IRISH AFFAIRS

It is now clear that arguably the most important diplomatic decode carried out by GC&CS relating to Irish affairs involved not any German traffic – decipherable from December 1942 onwards – but a cable from the Italian Embassy in Washington to the Italian Legation in Dublin in December 1940, conveying a message from the Ministry of Foreign Affairs in Rome. This spoke of 'facilities for a connection by wireless telegraph with DUBLIN via BERLIN. These facilities are at present for the use of the Ministry of Foreign Affairs only'. Colonel Vivian of SIS was in no doubt about the importance of this communication:

> I have had this thoroughly considered and we have come to the conclusion that it undoubtedly affords complete proof that the German Minister in Dublin is operating a wireless set . . .
>
> As regards the possibility of taking any steps to prevent or protest, I have obtained an authoritative finding that in no circumstances can we risk for one second the Most Secret Message, which forms the subject of your letter . . . I am, however, considering what other grounds we can find, which can be put forward in order to support a representation to the Eire Government, and will let you know if I find anything promising.[34]

Thus began the lengthy saga of British efforts to deal with the enormous problem of the German Legation transmitter in Dublin. Discussion of that lies outside the scope of this paper, except in so far as it became possible for SIS and MI5 to conduct a retrospective analysis of much though not all of Hempel's cable and wireless communications since 1939. This diplomatic material, termed 'PANDORA' in British documents, came on stream in January 1943 shortly after GC&CS broke the German diplomatic code. Berlin-Dublin communications were distributed thereafter as a fortnightly 'Summary of most secret information from Dublin'. While the cable com-munications of the Italian, Vichy French and Japanese representations in Dublin were also read, it is clear that it was PANDORA which transformed British views of the problem of German activities in Ireland, and the associated question of German-IRA links, and it played a crucial role in policy making until the autumn of 1944.

In considering Britain's mastery of Hempel's communications after December 1942, it is important to realise that British code-breakers did not have a complete backlist of his encoded communications since 1939: only a proportion of the illicit radio traffic had been intercepted and recorded by either the British or the Irish signals interception services, and as is often the case with transmissions there were often gaps and garbles in such material as was caught. Furthermore, there may have been gaps in the British records of his cable traffic although it passed through London. In addition, Britain was very severely constrained in her management of the information gleaned from 'most secret sources' by the imperative of not disclosing to the Irish or anyone else the precise nature of that knowledge, for fear of jeopardising the secret of her code-breakers' success.

In August 1943 MI5 forwarded an analysis of what PANDORA indicated about Irish government knowledge of Herman Goertz's activities and his dealings with the IRA in 1940–1. While based on an incomplete set of decodes, the analysis submitted for the information of the Dominions Secretary and Deputy Prime Minister Clement Attlee

> sets out fully in chronological order the story of this affair so far as it has at present been possible to disentangle it. Generally speaking, the conclusion is that there is no adequate evidence of any Irish Government implication with German activities. On the contrary, the Irish authorities appear with reasonable success to have been able to check German intrigues with the extremist IRA element.[35]

The decodes did, however, confirm that Goertz had been in touch with the IRA, and that through them he had obtained a replacement wireless set which was operated for him by Tony Deery. Through this

> GOERTZ was able to communicate in cipher with his employers in Germany. The date on which GOERTZ first started his W/T communications is not known; but it was probably in July 1941. PANDORA shows that he was in touch with the German SS [secret service] in August 1941, presumably by W/T (See IR 0363) . . .
>
> On the 27th November 1941 GOERTZ was arrested . . . a watch was kept on the house and Pearce [*sic*] Paul KELLY, a Northern IRA man, who came to visit GOERTZ, was also arrested. This shows that GOERTZ was still in touch with the active members of the IRA and was probably collecting information about Northern Ireland through them and transmitting it by means of DEERY's set to Germany. Some confirmation of this view has been obtained from a copy of four cipher messages which came into the hands of the Dublin police early in 1942. These messages are in GOERTZ's cipher. The decypher shows a reference to the arrest of Charles McGLADE, a Northern IRA leader, who was captured in October 1941, and probably dates the sending of these messages. The other messages refer to the

arrival of the Americans at Derry and the construction of an aerodrome by the Eire authorities at Limerick. There are, too, references to GOERTZ's set being in danger, and a request for £2,000. He asks whether his employers in Berlin intend to support the efforts of the IRA. If not, the Germans would lose hundreds of thousands willing to help them. If yes, why do they refuse GOERTZ the bare means of existence.

More worryingly, however, reading of Hempel's ongoing traffic in the spring of 1943 indicated that he

is now convinced that Eire's neutrality is secure and possibly as a result he is now ready to show a greater activity in espionage activity. See in this connection the documents tagged A and B; the latter shows that he has been in touch with IRA extremists in Northern Ireland . . .

On the German Minister's activities generally, they [MI5 and SIS] are doing their best to try to obtain some independent evidence, in a shape that can be used, to prove that the Minister is engaged in intrigues with the IRA. If this can be done, it seems reasonable to suppose that the Eire Government will be willing to get rid of him at once.[36]

The fortnightly SIS analyses of 'most secret information' in the Dominions Office files are distinguished by their balanced approach to the matters under scrutiny. Where apparent evidence of Irish government perfidy or of IRA-German co-operation appears it is duly mentioned, but generally this is balanced with comments or references to other material. The material pointed to a number of firm conclusions:

(a) Hempel was very wary of the IRA, which he regarded as incompetent and insecure, and was most reluctant to have anything to do with the republican movement despite overtures from the northern IRA, arguing that to do so would risk expulsion by the Irish government

(b) Hempel was in receipt of occasional titbits of war information picked up casually in Dublin. He relayed this to Berlin for what it was worth, but declined to solicit intelligence either from the IRA or from anyone else

(c) Hempel had refused Berlin's request to use his radio to send messages, but had undertaken to do so if he obtained vital operational intelligence about Allied invasion plans. For this purpose he arranged at the end of 1942 for a German wireless technician interned in the Curragh to come to work in the Legation

(d) The IRA was not, so far as was known, communicating intelligence to Germany independently of the Legation

(e) Hempel was under severe pressure from the Irish government about his transmitter, and he anticipated that he would eventually be forced to hand it over on pain of the closure of the legation.

MI5's analysis of Hempel's traffic led Attlee to write to Churchill setting out the case against forcing the issue of the German Legation transmitter with the Irish authorities. He pointed out that since 1941 the radio had been used on 'only one occasion . . . a weather report sent on the 11th February 1942'. If

> the Germans were deprived of the known transmitter, they or the IRA might succeed in setting up another transmitter elsewhere in Ireland which might be available at an actual time of emergency and might not by that time have been discovered . . .
>
> The actual information which the German Minister has so far been able to collect and telegraph does not suggest that hitherto he has been able to secure any information seriously likely to hamper or injure our operations. The close watch which the Irish Security authorities keep on his movements and contacts, in co-operation with our Security authorities, can go some way to prevent his having much greater success in future.
>
> There was also the danger that too much pressure might run 'the risk of compromising our knowledge of the German cipher and the value of the information which we are now obtaining and shall in the future obtain therefrom'. The aim of British policy should be to wait until other evidence of German intrigue, and of links with the IRA, could be found which would provide 'grounds that can be publicly used' to demand the closure of all the Axis legations.[37]

This advice clearly irritated Churchill, who responded by first reproving Attlee for insecurity: 'your minute . . . referring as it does to the most secret sources, ought not to have come to me other than in a locked box'. He grudgingly acknowledged the strength of Attlee's argument:

> I think we must endure this abominable state of things for the present. The entry of the United States into the war has changed the picture, and it may be possible to take a stronger line against Southern Ireland and to force them to dismiss the enemy representatives they harbour. Their conduct in this war will never be forgiven by the British nation unless it is amended before the end. This in itself would be a great disaster. It is our duty to try to save these people from themselves.[38]

The saga of the eventual Irish demand in December 1943 for the surrender of the German Legation radio has been dealt with elsewhere.[39] Here we need only note that the intelligence agencies analysed Hempel's messages in a balanced and professional fashion, and also provided policy makers in the

Dominions Office with the raw material on which those assessments were based. This contrasts with the manner in which German diplomatic decodes concerning Ireland during the First World War were manipulated by the director of naval intelligence 'Blinker' Hall to bounce the government into action which he thought appropriate.[40]

OTHER SOURCES OF SIS INTELLIGENCE ON IRELAND, 1940–5

Initially, SIS suffered from the fact that in 1939 it had no organisation in Ireland for intelligence gathering. Consequently undue weight was sometimes attached to alarmist reports from what documents refer to as 'loyalists', that is pro-British people. It is, it must be stressed, completely wrong to leap from indications that some Irish residents passed on rumours and political comment to Britain to the accusation that in so doing they were spying. Nor does it make sense to label people such as Elizabeth Bowen, who wrote very able reports on elite opinion in Ireland for the Ministry of Information between 1940 and 1942, as being engaged in 'espionage'.[41] Once Captain Collinson began his operations in the latter half of 1940, and as MI5–G2 co-operation deepened, so a more realistic picture of the extent and limits of Axis activities and of IRA–German collaboration began to emerge in Whitehall.

We now have a good run of SIS documents on Ireland. These are the QRS reports 195 to 212, covering the period from May 1942 to December 1944. These bimonthly political analyses of affairs in Ireland, drawing on all sources available to SIS headquarters, are generally balanced in tone. In September 1942 it was reported that

> the Eire authorities . . . have lately increased the numbers of releases on parole of members of the IRA. So far it is understood this policy has proved itself justified. There is a complete split between the IRA personnel still interned in the Curragh. The left-wingers are wholeheartedly in favour of an Axis defeat by Soviet Russia. The opposing faction, numbering about 220, are in favour of collaboration with the Axis and are hoping steadfastly for the defeat of the United Nations. The remaining minority are diehard republicans who are neutral as regards the split of the larger groups.[42]

Succeeding reports emphasised the IRA's complete eclipse, and correctly treated the espionage issues which arose in 1943 – the Andrews-Eastwood case and the arrival of the German agents John Kenny and Joseph O'Reilly – as unconnected with extremist republicanism. SIS did, however, note an apparent confluence of fascist and republican ideology in the nativist party Coras na Poblachta and in Gearoid O'Cuinnegain's quasi-fascist Ailtirí na hAiséirghe, reporting contacts between the latter group and the German Legation as well as referring to potential Quislings such as Ernest Blythe, J. J. Walsh, and Dan Breen. In September 1943 a QRS report stated that Breen

> is a frequent visitor to the private residences of both Hempel and Thomsen [the secretary of the German Legation]. We now have a circumstantial report that he is a regular informant of Hempel on matters connected with the extremist IRA and he has been described as a paid intelligence officer of the German Legation . . . Another potential Quisling, General O'Duffy, is ill in a Cork nursing home, suffering, it is said, with acute alcoholic poisoning.[43]

A few months later SIS reported that

> the extremist IRA is still quiescent . . . 'Ailtiri na hAiseirghe' is still fighting to increase its influence and hold the ground already gained. The organization, or at any rate its 'Fuhrer', Gerald Cunningham, seems to have fallen foul of his erstwhile champion Ernest Blythe. Blythe in 'The Leader' has suddenly rough handled Cunningham and recommended that he retire from the leadership on account of his poor qualities as a public speaker.[44]

In December 1944, SIS noted a shift in Blythe's approach, citing his endorsement of continued Irish membership of the Commonwealth. Although the IRA appeared a dead duck, Ailtirí na hAiséirghe was still providing some cause for concern. The party

> is making a big drive amongst young people all over Ireland. It is possible too that 'Ailtiri na hAiseirghe' is being used as a breeding ground for the IRA, and that membership of the one may in a number of cases lead to membership of the other organization. It is known that the Government is becoming anxious about the activities . . . and the man in the street wonders why, since it is avowedly Fascist, the organization has not been prohibited as an illegal body. Actually the very strong Nazi flavour which permeated 'Ailtiri na hEiseirghe' in its early stages, has lately given way to a policy based rather on the administration of SALAZAR.[45]

Material from the other main seam of SIS intelligence on Ireland, the reports of its Irish networks under the control of Captain Collinson, is harder to come by although it was plainly absorbed into composite summaries prepared by Mrs Archer and circulated to MI5 and the Dominions Office. One notable exception is a rather hostile analysis of de Valera prepared by SIS's Irish 'representative', presumably Collinson. This depicted de Valera as a menace to Allied interests, spoke of his 'political crookedness', and remarked that his attitude to the IRA was ambivalent: 'Here they are an offence to his vanity and his government. In Northern Ireland they are brave if slightly misguided patriots'. Given that, 'is it fair to lay it down that de Valera is our safest friend as long as the war lasts?'. While the 'Fine Gael Party has many faults which it would be absurd to pass over', it would surely be more amenable to British reason. If the Irish ports 'are to be obtained without bloodshed, would it not be better to see an Eire Government with whom negotiations could be carried out rather than one dominated by a man incapable of any form of compromise?'[46] Collinson's argument does not appear to have carried much weight in Whitehall, where the Dominions Office continued to take its line very largely from Sir John Maffey in Dublin.

In retirement, Collinson reflected on his Irish experiences in commenting on a series of newspaper articles on German espionage in Ireland (most likely a serialisation of Enno Stephan's *Spies in Ireland*), sent to him by his former subordinate in Dublin. He

> read with interest the batch of newspapers and was able to follow the articles . . . They do not give much information that we did not possess at the time, apart from the main workings of the services in the enemy country. There were, you will recall, a number of similar activities which are not recorded, but they possibly originated from a different service than that of which the author of the articles examined the records. On the whole, the most consoling impression from a reading of these 'revelations' is that however many trips, blunders and stupid failures we ourselves were responsible for, the other side produced far greater and far graver ones and, in fact, lost a host of golden opportunities by crass ignorance and sheer incompetence.[47]

Collinson's modesty in acknowledging the possibility of British 'trips, blunders and stupid failures' was well judged, since by far the most detailed information available on the work of his organisation between 1940 and 1945 lies not in the British PRO but in the Irish Military Archives.[48]

Despite their mastery of German communications from January 1943 onwards, and their close liaison with the Irish, it is unlikely that British agencies ever learned the full extent of republican intelligence gathering directed against British interests, however amateurish these efforts might have appeared to professional intelligence officers. A striking example of a disciplined IRA attempt to provide useful material is the fourteen page single spaced memorandum and map setting out targeting information on Belfast for the Luftwaffe, a document seized by the Garda when they arrested an IRA courier in Dublin in October 1941. The Northern IRA's covering note explained that

> On the map enclosed are marked the remaining and most outstanding objects of military significance, as yet unblitzed by the Luftwaffe.

If left, as now, without a final Blitz, the city still constitutes a strong link in Britain's defence; while on the other hand, if the objectives marked are bombed . . . as thoroughly as the other areas in recent raids, Belfast will be rendered a negative quantity in Britain's war effort.

SPECIAL NOTE: Re the symbol coloured light blue, it may be noted that the road thus marked, is the Fall's Road, the chief site of Nationalism; while the square is the Prison, where some 300 to 400 Irish Republican Soldiers are imprisoned.[49]

There is no trace of this chilling communication in the British records, and it is reasonable to infer that the Irish sat on it because of its explosive nature. For their part, the British also kept plenty of secrets from the Irish authorities both during and after the war. They were anxious lest any evidence of SIS's clandestine Irish operations inadvertently come to light, and they did not want to disclose techniques of intelligence gathering which were still very useful. In August 1945 Sir John Maffey raised the possibility of disclosing to de Valera in strict confidence some of the contents of Hempel's communications in order to bring home the point that the German legation had indeed been a mortal threat to British security. He argued that this might influence Irish policy in a future war, where Ireland might again be neutral and the IRA might still pose a threat to British interests. The idea was eventually turned down on the advice of SIS, who advanced two interesting arguments. The first was, predictably enough, that the game was not worth the candle because it would jeopardise the security of a vital and ongoing British capability. The second point was that although Hempel's traffic showed his willingness in an extreme situation to collect and forward operational intelligence, it was not all that damning. De Valera could as easily draw comfort from the fact that Hempel generally honoured his undertakings to the Irish government, particularly regarding the use of his radio, as be shocked at his willingness to break his word should circumstances demand it. Furthermore, the intercepts showed Hempel to be particularly doubtful about the IRA, continually warning Berlin not to place any faith in them either as intelligence gatherers or as guerrilla fighters. Sir John Stephenson of the Dominions Office noted SIS's objections: 'As Colonel Vivian says, the argument cuts both ways since the German Legation did not in fact get hold of, and pass on, anything of really first class importance to the Germans'.[50]

CONCLUSION

In the decade before the war, British intelligence on the IRA's external links was fragmentary, and was analysed primarily in terms of what it disclosed about the organisation's relationship with international communism and with the Soviet Union. Like the Irish authorities, the British were slow to realise that the IRA, in common with other European minority nationalist movements, would be attractive and willing partners for Nazi Germany. When the fact of IRA–German collusion was demonstrated in May 1940, British estimates of the strategic implications were understandably alarmist. But the evidence also shows that, as intelligence on German–IRA links improved in the course of the war, so did the analysis of the nature and extent of the threat which these posed to Allied interests. As the department responsible for Irish relations, the Dominions Office was supplied not only with political intelligence summaries and analyses but with raw intelligence such as decodes – most importantly Italian and, from January 1943, German traffic. This material played a crucial part in framing British policy on Ireland, and its effect was generally to counter rather than to support the more alarmist construction which Churchill in particular was apt to place on reports of Axis intrigue and German-IRA links.

In terms of the wider history of British intelligence in the Second World War, the records discussed here suggest that, in respect of Ireland if not elsewhere, the main agencies and departments involved – the security service, the intelligence service, the code-breakers, and the policy makers in the Dominions Office – worked together in a reasonably harmonious manner, took account of each other's positions, were of one mind on the nature and implications of the Germany-IRA relationship, and did not embark on any solo runs or attempt to use material to discredit a rival. The only inter-service dogfights involving Irish operations of which there is evidence concern the irregular warfare agency SOE, and they are outside the ambit of this paper.[51]

This leaves us with two questions. To what extent did republican enthusiasm for Germany reflect ideology rather than opportunism? And just how dangerous were the IRA's attempts to help Hitler win the war through sabotage, propaganda and intelligence gathering? The ideological issue merits separate discussion, although my own conclusion is that Nazism was even more alien to Irish republican doctrine than the revolutionary socialist ideology which it periodically affects to embrace. That the IRA-German link proved a grave threat to Irish neutrality is manifest. The evidence of the depth of British (and American) unease about the republican movement's potential to damage Allied interests is clear, as is the role which good intelligence, in combination with vigorous Irish repression of the IRA, eventually played in keeping those fears in proportion and in supporting the case for a policy of critical engagement with the Irish government rather than openly coercive measures. There is some irony in the fact that, despite its wartime Nazi links, Irish republicanism largely escaped post-war odium in the United States and elsewhere, in part because much of the excellent evidence which was available to the British on the IRA's inept efforts to help Germany came through intelligence sources and techniques, particularly code-breaking, which were considered too valuable to disclose.

Notes

1   E. O'Halpin, '"Weird prophecies": British intelligence and Anglo-Irish Relations, 1932–3', in M. Kennedy and J. M. Skelly (eds), *Irish Foreign Policy 1916–1966: From Independence to Internationalism* (Dublin, 2000), pp. 61–73.

2   TS of Vissault's statement, n.d., Oct., and MI5 to G2, 12 Nov. 1944 (Public Record Office (PRO), KV2/303).

3   'MI5 Irish section history', p. 3 (PRO, KV4/9).

4   These are in PRO, DO121/85. There is one gap: 199 (Sept.-Oct. 1942) is missing.

5   Mrs Archer (née Jane Sissmore) debriefed the key Russian defector Walter Krivitsky in December 1939. Archer to Vivian (SIS), 10 Nov. 1939 and 9 Feb. 1940 (PRO, KV2/802).

6   'MI5 Irish section history', p. 9.

7   'MI5 Irish section history', pp. 35–7. On Mahr and other Germans resident in Ireland before the war, see D. O'Donoghue, *Hitler's Irish Voices: The Story of German Radio's Wartime Irish Service* (Belfast, 1998).

8   Undated memorandum, with [illegible], SIS, to MI5, 20 Apr. 1927 (PRO, KV3/11).

9   E. O'Halpin, *Defending Ireland: The Irish State and its Enemies since 1922* (Oxford, 1999), pp. 72–5.

10 Vivian (SIS) to Miss Sissmore (MI5), 7 July 1934 (PRO, KV2/819).

11 Decode of Loda Fé (Dublin) to Foreign Ministry, Rome, 9 Dec. 1935, HW12/198; 'German activities in the Irish Free State', 21 June 1936, JIC 36 (36), CAB 56/3. I am grateful to Ambassador Sir Ivor Roberts for his help in securing access to this material.

12 Text of lecture by Brigadier Marshall, 12 June 1939, PRO, HS8/261. This document is one a small number surviving from the War Office think-tank MI (R) which laid much of the doctrinal groundwork for the irregular warfare activities of the Special Operations Executive (SOE) during the war.

13 'MI5 Irish Section history', pp. 31–2.

14 S. M. (SIS) to Hinchley Cooke (MI5), 30 Apr. 1938 (PRO, KV2/356).

15 'MI5 Irish Section history', p. 6.

16 Cimperman (American Embassy, London) to Ms Paine (MI5), 21 May 1946 (PRO, KV2/356).

17 ? (SIS) to Hinchley Cooke, 19 Oct., copied to PCO Paris, 15 Oct. 1938, ibid.

18 Ibid.

19 'Liam Report', undated but with TS minute dated 14 Oct., and note by Hinchley Cooke, 5 Nov. 1938, ibid.

20 F. H. Hinsley and C. A. G. Simkins, *British Intelligence in the Second World War, vol. 4: Security and Counter-Intelligence* (London, 1990), pp. 41–2; J. C. Masterman, *The Double-Cross System in the War of 1939 to 1945* (New Haven, 1972), pp. 40–1.

21 'MI5 B1L section history', p. 7 (PRO, KV4/26). B1L was responsible for security investigations amongst merchant seamen. According to Guy Liddell, it was not a great success: 'I think the initial project miscarried'. Liddell to Curry, 28 May 1945, ibid.

22 TS of Vissault's statement, n.d., Oct., and MI5 to G2, 12 Nov. 1944 (PRO, KV2/303).

23 Hinsley and Simkins, *British Intelligence*, p. 17.

24 'MI5 Irish Section history', pp. 32–3.

25 Churchill to Roosevelt, 15 May 1940, in F. L. Lowenheim, H. Langley and M. Jonas (eds), *Roosevelt and Churchill: Their Secret Wartime Correspondence* (London, 1975), p. 95.

26 Morton to Churchill, 27 May 1940 (PRO, PREM7/7).

27 Unsigned note, 26 Feb. 1945 (Military Archives (Dublin) G2/X/1091).

28 O'Halpin, *Defending Ireland*, pp. 238–9.

29 JIC (40) 286, 18 Sept. 1940 (PRO, CAB81/98).

30 Note by director of naval intelligence on his visit to Ireland, 16 Aug. 1941, JIC (41) 335, with COS (41) 291 (PRO, CAB79/13).

31 O'Halpin, *Defending Ireland*, p. 244.

32 'MI5 Irish Section history', p. 18; O'Halpin, *Defending Ireland*, p. 207.

33 Liddell to Vivian, 8 Jan. 1944 (KV2/119). I discuss Anglo-Irish signals intelligence cooperation in a comparative context 'Small states and big secrets: understanding sigint cooperation between unequal powers in the Second World War', in *Intelligence and National Security* 17, 3 (2002), pp. 1–16.

34 Decode of Colonna (Washington) to Italian Legation, Dublin, 28 Dec. 1940 (decoded 1 Jan. 1940), and Vivian (SIS) to Stephenson (Dominions Office), 25 Jan. 1941 (PRO, DO121/84).

35 Stephenson to Machtig, initialled by Attlee, 25 Aug. 1943 (PRO, DO121/86).

36 Stephenson to Machtig, 12 Apr. 1943, ibid.

37 Attlee to Churchill, 3 May 1943 (PRO, DO121/84). 11 February 1942 was the date of the dramatic passage of the *Scharnhorst* and the *Gneisenau* up the English Channel, and it was widely believed that a weather report from Dublin indicating that poor visibility was to be expected had contributed to the German decision. However, intelligence analysis indicated that the key information came from German weather aircraft in the Atlantic. O'Halpin, *Defending Ireland*, pp. 189–90.

38 Churchill to Attlee, 5 May 1943 (PRO, DO121/84).

39 E. O'Halpin, 'Irish-Allied security relations and the "American Note" crisis: new evidence from British records', *Irish Studies in International Affairs* 11 (2000), pp. 71–83.

40 E. O'Halpin, 'British intelligence in Ireland, 1914–1921', in C. Andrew and D. Dilks (eds), *The Missing Dimension: Governments and Intelligence Communities in the Twentieth Century* (London, 1984), pp. 55–77.

41 This groundless assertion is contained in J. Lane and B. Clifford (eds), Elizabeth Bowen: *'Notes on Éire': Espionage reports to Winston Churchill; with a review of Irish neutrality in World War 2* (Aubane, 1999). The reports, which are lucid pieces of political reporting of elite opinion as garnered in interviews with prominent Irishmen, were sent to the Ministry of Information, from where a selection were circulated to the Dominions Office. The authors provide no evidence that they were either intended for or ever reached the prime minister, still less that they constitute evidence of 'espionage'.

42 QRS report no. 198, 1 Sept. 1942 (PRO, DO 121/85).

43 QRS reports no. 198, 200, and 202, 1 Sept. 1942, 1 Jan., 1 May and 1 Sept. 1943, ibid.

44 QRS report no. 208, 1 May 1944, ibid.

45 QRS report no. 212, 31 Dec. 1944, ibid. This is the latest report in the file.

46 [Excised, but probably Mrs Archer] (SIS) to MI5, 18 June 1943, and enclosed documents nos I to III written respectively by an unnamed academic, a newspaper editor, and 'our representative' (PRO, KV2/515). I am grateful to Gerry Hughes of the Department of International Politics at Aberystwyth for bringing this to my attention.

47 Collinson to X, 3 Sept. 1962 (letter in possession of X's family, to whom I am very grateful for sharing their recollections of their father's wartime work).

48 Military Archives, G2/X/1091.

49 Undated IRA documents seized by the Garda from Ms Helena Kelly at 42 Frankfort Avenue on 20 Oct. 1941 (Military Archives, G2/1722 (the Goertz file)).

50 Stephenson to Machtig, 17 Aug. 1945 (PRO, DO121/89).

51 O'Halpin, '"Toys" and "whispers"'; see also E. O'Halpin, 'Hitler's Irish hideout: a case study of SOE's black propaganda battles', to appear in M. Seaman (ed.), *SOE in the Second World War* (London, 2005).

CHAPTER 8

An Army of Our Fenian Dead

Republicanism, Monuments and Commemoration

* * *

Anne Dolan

In 1954 a group of men dug a hole in Tyrellspass, County Westmeath. Holes had been dug in Tyrellspass before; there was nothing unusual about that. But this particular hole in the ground was a little different. At dawn on Easter Sunday morning, while the men and women of Tyrellspass slept soundly in their beds, a TD began to dig. No one was to see him, only the select band who came with him would ever know that he was there. After a swift half hour's work this small gathering left behind a four-foot wooden cross.[1] They set it in cement and quickly sped away in what was soon reported to be an 'official car'.[2] The TD in question returned later that day along with about four thousand others. He laid a wreath and commemorated all who died for the freedom of Ireland.[3] No one mentioned at the ceremony that this TD had broken the law.

Colonel Boyd-Rochfort owned this small piece of land, as he did most of the rest of Tyrellspass. He had refused a request from Westmeath County Council to purchase this small area of land for the purpose of erecting the memorial. He objected because he wanted to preserve what he called the 'village green'; he wanted to keep it, in his own words, as 'it had been for centuries'.[4] He was used to quaint local children gambolling about there, and, as an old soldier himself, he was sympathetic to 'the two Protestant families' who had no wish to look from their windows upon an unsightly memorial to what they considered an unpleasant affair.[5] In many ways the colonel could do little else. He was more familiar with the royal enclosure at Ascot than Westmeath County Council offices and, beyond perhaps betting on the Derby and St Leger winners his brother trained, he had nothing in common with the members of the IRA commemorative committee. In rather measured pique, the colonel wrote to the *Irish Press*. He complained that the Fianna Fáil TD in question, Michael Kennedy, had seized private property and took possession furtively at daybreak . . . against the known wishes of a number of the inhabitants of the village and neighbourhood, and contrary to the strong views openly expressed by the clergy. I leave these facts to the judgment and opinion of all people interested in the preservation of Tyrellspass Green and to seeing that justice and not force prevails in this country.[6]

For Kennedy this was merely another round of the great struggle for Irish freedom. He had told Westmeath County Council 'that the memorial would be erected at the Green despite the Colonel's attitude, even had he [to] go there to dig the foundation of it himself'.[7] If nothing else Kennedy was true to his word, true even though most of the memorial committee had accepted Boyd-Rochfort's objections and opted instead for a memorial in the church-yard. With the 'whole village under the landlordship of the Colonel', Kennedy seemed determined to wage his own war of independence, grasping the memory of the republican dead and thrusting it wilfully under the protective wing of Fianna Fáil.[8] Commemoration was a mild and perhaps humorous means to his chosen end. There was not much to fear from a TD running around Tyrellspass with a spade in the middle of the night.

Six years later a committee gathered in Cork to erect a memorial to the men of the county's No. 1 Brigade IRA.[9] A further three years brought the three thousand pounds that Seamus Murphy's twenty-five foot cross cost, another three years brought the president, Eamon de Valera, to the repub-lican plot in St Finbar's cemetery to unveil it.[10] There was mass, a parade, marching bands and eight thousand people standing in the cemetery in the rain.[11] They listened as the president paid tribute to 'each one of them [who] gave his young life and all its love and promise so that our nation might be free'.[12] De Valera spoke of Terence MacSwiney and Thomas MacCurtain, of the dead of 1919–23, even of the dead of 1924. No one seems to have told him, however, that John Joe Kavanagh was also buried in the plot and thus included in the commemoration. He had been shot on 3 August 1940 trying to escape from Cork jail.[13] He had been, as one less than objective observer put it, 'gunned down by de Valera's police'.[14] While the president concluded that 'the people of Cork have reason to be proud of every name inscribed here', matters were a little more complicated than that.[15]

The night before the unveiling ceremony a man's body had been found in St Finbar's cemetery. It had been decapitated, injured past recognition. The man's name was Desmond Swanton. He had come with his colleague, Gerard Madden – who escaped with a partially severed leg – to blow up the memorial to the Cork No. 1 Brigade.[16] Swanton and Madden were both members of the IRA, both active in Northern Ireland, both sworn to the idea of the republic that to all intents and purposes had inspired the memorial committee in the first place.[17]

Swanton was quickly added to the National Graves Association's 'roll of honour'. According to *The Last Post* he was 'killed in an explosion in Cork'.[18] If nothing else it was an accurate description of his death. But for an organisation devoted to the memory of the republican dead and pledged to the erection and maintenance of commemorative monuments, it was a slightly disingenuous one. It was more convenient to say nothing more of the matter, easier to ignore the fact that one wing of the republican family was prepared to die in order to exclude its siblings from the memory of the great republican dead.

Historians make snide comments about republicans squabbling like children at the gates at Bodenstown.[19] Like TDs digging holes in the middle of the night, the strutting figures at Wolfe Tone's grave are easy targets. Granted there is too much of the 'I'm the biggest and best republican of them all' for it to be taken completely seriously. But Desmond Swanton's death, even Michael Kennedy, TD, with spade in hand, should provoke a little more than this snide complacency about the republic and the memory of its dead. Indeed such complacency can lead to rather crude conclusions. After 1926 it all seems rather too simply inscribed. There is Fianna Fáil on the one hand, the 'Republican party', bowing its 'slightly constitutional' head at republican graves,[20] and then there is the rest, the men and women known variously and vaguely as 'Sinn Féiners', the IRA, extremists or republicans. In effect, there was a scramble for the dead, and Fianna Fáil are generally considered the winners, taking Bodenstown, Arbour Hill, and recently, even Kevin Barry, leaving the more obscure republican graves for hardier souls who wish to climb up Benbulben or march to Araglen.[21] The pro-Treatyites are never really considered. It seems easier to forget that men like W. T. Cosgrave had been 'out' in 1916, and that maybe a glimmer of republicanism remained there still. Indeed, *An Phoblacht* rather unfairly berated him for laying a wreath on his own forebear's grave in 1925. Cosgrave was deemed unworthy of the man who had been hanged in 1798.[22] But there are perhaps enough complications without opening such an inconvenient can of worms. Another problem is that the commemorations have come to be viewed with an increasing degree of distaste. They are considered in terms that imply that there is something inherently malevolent in them, that they should not be taken seriously or given credence because they are the work of that shadowy body called the National Graves Association that no one knows or cares to find out very much about. That no one really wants to is also part of the problem. The 'troubles' in Northern Ireland, the studies charting the neglect of the memory of the Great War dead[23] and the sense of disgust provoked by an often largely unsubstantiated caricature of a parochial Ireland crucified by its nationalist and religious pieties have all served to banish years of republican ritual and commemoration to an awkward wilderness. To consider them as nothing more than recruiting grounds for the IRA seems more than a little short-sighted.

It underestimates the complicated relationship between Fianna Fáil and the men and women who are known only by vague terms like 'republican' and 'extremist'. It fails to understand this relationship – particularly at a local level where the lines were not as clearly drawn as many would have liked. Most of all, it fails to look beyond a sense of disgust that has as much if not more to do with contemporary politics as it has with the men and women of the time. Much as we may not like it now, we have to be prepared to concede that there may have been a sense of pride, a need to glorify the 'great dead who died for Ireland', that there was a need to remember that men died fighting for a freedom that we have come in our rather smug complacency to consider misused. It may not have been dreadfully sophisticated, but there were still eight thousand people standing in the rain in St Finbar's cemetery,[24] four thousand in Tyrellspass[25] and many more at gatherings all over the country without the promise or excitement of a president to unveil a statue or the allure of the great martyrs at Bodenstown and Glasnevin cemetery. This has to be at least acknowledged. And somewhere in the middle of all of this there was also an instinct that was as basic as a family needing to remember their son, or father, of a town needing to be proud that it did its bit for Ireland. It seems unfair to condemn this unthinkingly because our sensibilities may have been offended, for example, by Sinn Féin's recent 'Tirghrá' or because others cringed at the old fashioned nationalism that reared its head in October 2001 and buried Kevin Barry and the nine other Volunteers whose names most people just could not remember.[26]

In early May 1961 the Cork memorial committee received a letter from Con Coffey in Mallow. Folded in with the small, dirty piece of paper were 'tree shillinges'. He wrote: 'I woud sende more but I havent it. I am ounley working man . . . I am sending thauses fuw shillings for galaint men huw gave ther lives for Ireland God have mircey on ther souls and all huw gave ther lives for Ireland . . . '.[27] The letter was barely literate; the money was sent even though the man clearly could not afford to give it. And there were more letters like his. £2 2s. came from John J. O'Leary in Fermoy,[28] £28 14s 7d from a church gate collection at Blarney and Waterloo.[29] There was £2 from Dublin,[30] £5 from Derry,[31] $50 from a priest in New York.[32] The intention had been to raise the money from the contributions of old members of the brigade – that 'we should take the major part of the responsibility ourselves' – but despite this sense of duty the committee soon conceded the need for a public appeal.[33] When New York's Cork County Association sent $10, the committee's faith in the kindness of strangers legitimately waned. If 'an Association calling themselves REBEL Cork' could respond in such a miserly fashion, there seemed little hope for the public who had no tangible connection with the county or the brigade.[34] One veteran sent his donation along with his misgivings: 'I doubt . . . that a monument will mean much to the people of today, or that their heirs are worthy of them. I doubt if many now recall Tadhg Barry or Mickey Barrett or Charlie Daly. Nor do I ever hear mention of "Topsie" Coughlan, Dáithi Cottes, Martin Lynch or George Heffernan – to name some of those who survive.'[35] But reservations aside, the money did come, and in comparison to some of the other memorial committees, the money came quite quickly. By September 1961 they had enough. The haste was almost indecent in terms of the committees that took almost thirty years to find the couple of hundred necessary pounds. That three thousand pounds came in less than a year is possibly the best clue as to why an IRA man tried to blow the monument up.[36]

One of the first letters among Florence O'Donoghue's correspondence relating to this memorial is a copy of one he wrote on 18 November 1960 in which he detailed a bequest left by J. J. Walsh of five thousand pounds for the erection of a memorial to the Cork Brigade. The committee wanted to get their hands on the money. They did not, however, want to go along with the scheme planned by Walsh's executor, the county manager J. Wrenne, to honour the dead with a statue of the Virgin Mary: 'As the IRA was not a sectional organisation this was an unsuitable type of memorial'.[37] This was all very broad-minded, as indeed was their willingness to accept money from a former Free State postmaster-general, no matter how much he might have mended his ways and returned to the Fianna Fáil fold. However, it is notable that J. J. Walsh never made it into the republican plot in St Finbar's cemetery. His is the grave closest to it, almost loitering on the outskirts, still tainted by his erroneous Cumann na nGaedheal days. But O'Donoghue's letter closed on a less broad-minded note. If it wanted, the committee could fight for the money: 'A public controversy could of course be started, but it seemed undesirable'.[38] Public bickering over a bequest would not endear them to prospective donors who might be required to contribute a little more. Squabbling openly with other committees was not to be countenanced. So the search turned elsewhere. The GAA was appealed to – with £25 casually mentioned in the letter as an appropriate type of contribution.[39] The Anti-Partition of Ireland League in London was canvassed and willingly obliged.[40] Na Fianna sent £40 but only after the committee had weeded out what it considered the bad element that had crept into the local Fianna group. O'Donoghue explained:

The Fianna has lost most of its decent lads – dropped out or pushed out . . . leaving a bunch now of whom most of us are distrustful. Meaney is a genuine ex-Fianna boy, but not a good type. No one is sure whether Hurley was ever in the Fianna, he is an ex Free State Army and a publicity merchant. These two run their small bunch of followers. In recent years they have gone around to all kinds of commemorations, laying wreaths etc. and always manage to get newspaper publicity for themselves. They made several efforts to start a Brigade memorial, but no one took any notice of them. Their sources of finance are a bit of a mystery. Most of our lads feel that their reputation is not too good and we are better off without them.[41]

Indeed, the committee could afford to do without them. It had turned to Joseph McGrath. At this point McGrath was known for his generous contributions to commemorative projects, at least to ones involving his former Commander-in-Chief, Michael Collins. To be fair to McGrath though, he had always employed former anti-Treaty foes at the Irish sweepstakes. It seems that when there was all that money to be made it suddenly became a lot easier to forget who might have killed Noel Lemass. But the committee was still reticent about approaching him. They discussed if he should be approached and if so then by whom.[42] The expectation even reached the following peak:

> You can be sure too that Joe McGrath will do the needful as he has done, it dawned on me, he may ask 'how much more do you want' and give me a cheque for same . . . Thinking over Joe McGrath's note you can now count away ahead of the figure you expected, but be prepared for what I expect from Joe . . . a cheque for the balance . . . [43]

A cheque for £200 eventually arrived on 24 August 1961. But at this point the committee had more than enough.[44]

The complication did not arise because McGrath was a contributor, or because an attempt had been made to stake a claim on the bequest of J. J. Walsh. The complication arises when some of the letters that accompanied the various donations are put in the context of the appeals to men like McGrath and the committee's unanimous decision to invite Eamon de Valera to perform the unveiling.[45] With his ten pounds Jim Whelan sent the following message: 'The work of the men you honour is only half done, for there are those who hindered in the time of danger and now boast openly that they rule – so perpetuating the hideous Border'.[46] Another came from Jack Barry in New York. He requested that the committee make a public statement in the press as to what policy it was proposing concerning the unveiling of the memorial:

> I don't want any group to use those occasions for political expedencey [*sic*], it is all too clear in our memory, what happened when the bodies of the two exiled Priests, were taken back to Cork. The Ministers of the Free State Government and the Free State Army were invited there by the Committee in charge of the burial. This was the same Free State Government and Free State Army that deported those two noble Priests a few years previous, except for a few changes in the personal [*sic*]. It is truly said; when men compromise on their religion or their nationality they will go to any extreme to justify their actions, hence we see the honour and principles of brave men who gave their lives in the fight for Irish Freedom cast

aside and political expedencey [*sic*] take its place. You and I have seen all this happen under the Cosgrave and the De Valera regime, and you quit cold in 1922. Let us hope you have some respect left.[47]

These two letters may have been exceptional, the work of a couple of disaffected or bewildered elderly men. But whether they were simply more tempered than Swanton and Madden – who could not bear the thought of de Valera laying claim to the republican dead – is of little real importance. The committee had used the words 'republic' and 'republican' and there the problem begins. The committee never made matters clear to the people it appealed to. It made no distinction, perhaps astutely, perhaps naively, between types of republicanism. It appealed in the same fashion to Joseph McGrath, to Eamon de Valera, to Anti-Partition leagues, to the GAA as it did to the various groups who squabbled amongst themselves for the right to say they were the most republican of republicans in Cork, to 'the rule or ruin boys', to the men and women who still refused to recognise the state.[48] Some of these people who donated money felt that their pledge had been dishonoured when it was revealed that the traitorous de Valera was to come to Cork and talk of Terence MacSwiney and Thomas MacCurtain, men whom they felt he had betrayed by entering the Dáil and by interning and executing IRA men. MacSwiney's sister wrote to Seán T. O'Kelly in 1936:

> Do you and de Valera and Ruttledge think you are going to smash the IRA? Are you such fools as to think you can succeed where your predecessors failed? You are at the crossroads. Are you going to do what is right and just, or become a second murder-gang, like the Cosgrave-Mulcahy Ministry? On your heads be the responsibility! We do not recognise the people's right to surrender their independence. You did not once, but you have come to limit yourself by their mandate.[49]

To the IRA the thought of de Valera standing over the grave of John Joe Kavanagh may have given the answer to this set of questions. It had been all right for de Valera to stand over the graves of republicans in Tipperary in 1925, and countless other graveyards, before the founding of Fianna Fáil.[50] But that was long before he had been thought of in treacherous terms. Republicanism was more complicated than the committee allowed for, and Desmond Swanton went further than most to prove this point.

The episode in Cork, though marked apart by the extremity of Swanton's actions, was not unusual. Destroying British monuments was all very well. The great victories over George II in St Stephen's Green, over King William in Dame Street, and of course the less conclusive battle with Nelson in 1966, could be heralded from the highest rooftops, claimed as great symbolic victories for the IRA.[51] No one really cares to mention, because frankly it tarnishes the republican reputation, that republicans have destroyed as many, if not more, monuments erected to the men whose cause they claim to perpetuate. The monuments in question may not have been grand equestrian affairs or beloved familiar landmarks. In one case, at least, the small town may have welcomed the fervour that relieved it of the cheap piece of statuary, the eyesore that passed for commemoration because it was all the impoverished local committee could afford. At Emly a 17 foot statue of a Volunteer was mysteriously removed shortly after its unveiling in October 1955.[52] In Cork a cross to Jeremiah Herlihy was broken on three separate occasions.[53] And there were others. Although the dead were never referred to as anything but republican, after 1926, and especially after Fianna Fáil's entry to the Dáil, the struggle for ownership of the dead was intensified. It was no longer simply a question of which side was taken on the Treaty, of whether pro- or anti-Treatyites had the right to march to Bodenstown. An internal struggle, with rival claims to the republican dead, had begun. It was perhaps no coincidence that the National Graves Association was also founded in 1926. But while it may have been no coincidence, and although republicans may have destroyed republican monuments, it is too easy to assume that each movement was entirely separate from the other. Members or supporters of Fianna Fáil could join the National Graves Association; members or supporters of both could have been active, or at least sympathised, with the IRA. While continued government made the Fianna Fáil party increasingly and naturally wary of certain types of commemoration, the monuments were still used by the more extreme as an inspiration to complete the republican task. The people who often attended or participated – if Michael Kennedy is even remotely representative – cannot be categorised as conveniently as we may wish.

Local people turned out in their hundreds – and often thousands – to see a small monument unveiled. But celebrating the town's part in the struggle for Irish freedom did not necessarily make each man, woman and child in the crowd a card carrying member of Fianna Fáil, the National Graves Association or the IRA. In certain towns the prospect of a visiting dignitary and a marching band might have been more than enough to attract a crowd. In others that was never the case. A cross was unveiled in the republican plot in Kildare. Although there had been posters advertising the ceremony and promises of a marching band, the police report noted that 'no member of the general public attended . . . no local interest whatever was taken'[54], and that 'the bulk of those taking part will travel from other areas . . . locally these events have practically no support'.[55] While Kildare may not have been a traditional breeding ground for republicanism, the same could not be said of 'rebel Cork'. At Douglas Street, a plaque was unveiled to Captain Tadg O'Sullivan. This was in 1941, a year after the Kildare unveiling, and the police were now admittedly watching particularly closely. There may have been four hundred people in attendance, and although the reporting police officer might have been trying to reassure his superiors with the heartening news that 'very little public interest was taken in the ceremony', the report resembles too many from other areas for it to have been an isolated case.[56] That one of the orators, Seán O'Tuama, father of an IRA internee, took the opportunity to chastise what he called 'the successors of the RIC who . . . were doing the same things to the younger generation of republicans who were only trying to do the self same work for which Captain Tadg O'Sullivan was murdered' did little to help.[57] By the early 1940s, it was increasingly clear that the public wanted a tamer version of republicanism, one that called for little more than voting for 'the Republican Party' in general elections, that indulged in a more cosy reminiscence about 'being out in 1916' and doing our bit in the War of Independence. Commemorations that ended with calls to bless and protect the footsteps of the 'young soldiers of the Gael as they traverse the water-logged hills on the Cavan-Fermanagh border'[58] no longer had the same appeal when the said 'Republican Party' was interning these particularly zealous Gaels, when policemen reported on the ceremonies and Special Branch recorded the attendance for posterity. In some cases, such as the annual ceremonial return to the cross at Benbulben in Sligo, the police came to outnumber the participants.[59]

Granted there were more popular republican pageants. But Ballyseedy and Bodenstown are more the exception to the rule that has been less obviously set by these small, understated, monuments and crosses. In some places, the distinction between these different types of republicanism remained less defined. In Borris-on-Ossary, in County Laois, for example, a cross was unveiled in memory of Joseph Bergin, an IRA intelligence officer shot in Kildare in December 1923. Approximately 200 people attended the ceremony. The police report recorded the presence of one 'active IRA member' but noted that the rest of the attendance was largely composed of old IRA men wearing service medals, National Graves Association members and Fianna Fáil supporters.[60] Just like Michael Kennedy with his spade in Tyrellspass, the lines were never firmly drawn between one brand of republicanism and another.

During the 1950s Seán T. O'Kelly seemed to lose all track of where the lines were drawn. As president he unveiled many of the decade's sudden crop of republican statues and monuments. Bandon, Bruff, Soloheadbeg, Newcastlewest,[61] were all part of the sudden *statuomanie*, the sudden realisation of a generation of men and women who in their fifties, sixties and seventies wanted their stories told and their comrades remembered.[62] Age had brought an urgency, a familiar and almost desperate human response: the appeal to posterity before death. At each ceremony O'Kelly spoke of 'unity' and observed that 'the passage of time' had brought him to 'a different per-spective' from his civil war days.[63] He even conceded that 'the sufferings, sacrifices and bitterness of the Civil War could have been avoided'.[64] He did not seem to care that some of the statues he stood at depicted IRA volunteers with guns pointing purposefully North[65] and that there was a clear discrepancy between his speeches and the statues' symbolism. Newcastlewest's statue depicting Eire handing on the mantle from a dying volunteer to a boy soldier, was not the stuff that peace and reconciliation were made of, but it seemed to make little difference to O'Kelly.[66] At the foot of these monuments it was quite unclear what type of republicanism was being remembered and what type of republicanism they were intended to serve.

Indeed, the family of Joseph Bergin were left completely unsure. His relatives had already erected a monument to him on the family grave in Camross cemetery. William Bergin, the dead man's brother, had told the commemoration committee that his family did not want any monument, any ceremony, 'any display'.[67] No one took account of what the Bergin family wanted. Michael O'Kelly, a man who had spent five years in Crumlin Road Jail for making a seditious speech in Belfast,[68] was determined to come, determined to deliver his oration, and determined to claim the man in the name of the republic or at least his definition of it. In Michael O'Kelly's grand scheme of things, the wishes of the man's family were not even worth his consideration. In some respects, the experience of the Bergin family was not unusual. The republicans who threw leaflets in the air and cried 'Up the Republic' and 'Up Tom Barry' when Seán MacEntee began to speak in Tralee at an Easter commemoration in 1936 had little thought for the families of the republican dead who had come to watch a minister pay tribute to their relatives.[69] The families of the dead were only as useful as the last photograph of a mourning funeral march. Commemoration had more urgent and important purposes to serve.

Matters were not helped in the 1930s when opposition newspapers taunted Fianna Fáil their with headlines such as 'graveside brawl' and 'scrambles for the dead',[70] or when they criticised de Valera for not attending the unveiling of the Liam Lynch tower in April 1935. 'Neither Mr de Valera nor one of his Minister could be found to do Liam Lynch honour on the occasion of the unveiling of a memorial to him. Has de Valera, the constitutionalist, repudiated the Liam Lynch who gave his life for de Valera the President of the Republic? Or was it that Mr de Valera was not permitted to be present?'[71] This seemed sweet revenge for all the years when Fianna Fáil accused Cumann na nGaedheal of abandoning the principles of Collins and Griffith. But the opposition had possibly missed the point. The ten thousand people who climbed half way up the Knockmealdown mountains to listen to Moss Twomey, a man wanted by the police, a man who refused to recognise de Valera and his 'mongrel Free State', as he unveiled a monument to Liam Lynch, were not necessarily there as an act of defiance against de Valera and

Fianna Fáil.[72] They were there for a myriad of reasons that can not be explained by which party or movement they were members of. It may have been nothing more than that they wanted to see Moss Twomey for themselves. It may even have been because they were members of Fianna Fáil.

As time passed the confusion remained – and possibly remains. It is all very well to note the date when de Valera split from Sinn Féin, to record when *An Phoblacht* called him a traitor, when the leading republicans decided he was no better than the men who abandoned the republic in 1921. It is more difficult to demarcate the support for, and perception of, varieties of republicanism at a grassroots level. The relationship between Fianna Fáil and republicanism in its more vague and vivid shades may never be explained. But at these monuments, at these occasional commemorations, there is at least an opportunity to try. To examine these small, local, incidents of remembrance by people who came in cars, on the back of tractors or for miles on weary bicycles to Emly, Bruff and Ballylanders – who maybe came because this had never happened before or because there was nothing else to do – is to uncover something of what republicanism meant. The challenge is to look at how the public responded when they were faced with one of the few tangible representations of republicanism, when they were faced with it in the midst of their own small towns rather than the more predictable ceremonies in Bodenstown or the Republican Plot in Glasnevin cemetery where all who attended were well versed and rehearsed in republican ritual. At a small cross or an ugly statue in the middle of Limerick or Tipperary, even Kildare, there is a chance to see who is remembered, how they are commemorated and the numbers of men and women who attend. There is a chance also to catch a glimpse of what republicanism might mean to the people these honoured martyrs were supposed to have died for. These types of commemoration argue for a more subtle reappraisal of the divisions and variations of republicanism beyond the higher and more documented echelons. They reveal, in some cases, what being a republican entailed. For some, it required nothing more than defying an old colonel and digging a small hole in a village green in the middle of the night. For others, it demanded something more; it seemed worth dying for in a graveyard in the middle of Cork.

Notes

1 Report by Ceannphort P. O'Sullivan, 23 Apr. 1954 (National Archives of Ireland (NA), Dept. of Justice (DJ) 8/1018).

2 *Irish Press*, 23 Apr. 1954.

3 *Irish Independent*, 19 Apr. 1954.

4 Ibid.

5   Ibid. Boyd-Rochfort, a veteran of the Boer War, was awarded a Military Cross in 1917 (*Burke's Irish Family Records* (London, 1976 edn), p. 991).

6   *Irish Press*, 23 Apr. 1954.

7   Report by Ceannphort P. O'Sullivan, 23 Apr. 1954 (NA, DJ 8/1018).

8   Ibid.

9   The earliest correspondence relating to the committee dates from October 1960 (National Library of Ireland (NLI), Florence O'Donoghue papers, MS 31,455(1), MS 31,455(2) and MS 31,456).

10   O'Donoghue papers (NLI, MS 31,455(1)).

11   *The Irish Times*, 18 Mar. 1963.

12   'The President's oration at the unveiling of the memorial to Cork No. 1 Brigade, in St Finbar's Cemetery, Cork, St Patrick's Day, 1963' (NA, Office of Secretary to the President, p5898).

13   J. Bowyer Bell, *The Secret Army: A History of the IRA, 1916–1970* (London, 1972), p. 224.

14   D. Ó Conaill, 'Republican plot, Cork', in *An Cumann Cabhrach Testimonial Dinner* (1983), p. 6.

15   'The President's oration at the unveiling of the memorial to Cork No. 1 Brigade, in St Finbar's Cemetery, Cork, St Patrick's Day, 1963' (NAI, Office of Secretary to the President p5898).

16   *The Irish Times, Irish Press*, 18 Mar. 1963.

17   Bowyer Bell, *Secret Army*, 403.

18   National Graves Association, *The Last Post* (Dublin, 1985 [3rd edn]), p. 173.

19   See for example, D. Fitzpatrick, 'Commemoration in the Irish Free State: a chronicle of embarrassment', in I. McBride (ed.), *History and Memory in Modern Ireland* (Cambridge, 2001), pp. 188–9, 203.

20   Seán Lemass, *Dáil Éireann Official Report*, XXII, col. 1615, 21 Mar. 1928.

21   There is a monument to six IRA men killed in September 1922 by Free State forces on Benbulben mountain, Co. Sligo. There is a round tower commemorating Liam Lynch at Araglen, Co. Tipperary.

22   *An Phoblacht*, 3 July 1925.

23   See for example, Keith Jeffery, *Ireland and the Great War* (Cambridge, 2000).

24   *The Irish Times*, 18 Mar. 1963.

25   *Irish Independent*, 19 Apr. 1954.

26   *Sunday Tribune*, 21 Apr. 2002.

27   Con Coffey to Florence O'Donoghue, (n.d.) (O'Donoghue papers, MS 31,455(1)).

28   John J. O'Leary to Florence O'Donoghue, 22 Apr. 1961, ibid.

29   Dan Dooling to Florence O'Donoghue, 19 Apr. 1961, ibid.

30   Éamonn de Barra to Florence O'Donoghue, 11 Mar. 1961, ibid.

31   Edmund Burke to Florence O'Donoghue, 10 Apr. 1961, ibid.

32   Fr Donald M. O'Callaghan to Florence O'Donoghue, 6 Feb. 1961, ibid.

33   Florence O'Donoghue to Pa Murphy & Padraig Ó Caoimh, 15 Mar. 1961, ibid.

34   Connie Neenan to Florence O'Donoghue, 9 Feb. 1961, ibid.

35   Jim Whelan to Florence O'Donoghue, (n.d., received 13 May 1961), ibid.

36   Florence O'Donoghue to Jeremiah Hartnett, 10 Aug. 1961, ibid.

37   Florence O'Donoghue to C. O'Brien, 18 Nov. 1960, ibid.

38 Ibid.

39 Florence O'Donoghue to Concubhair Uas Ó Murchú, 23 Mar. 1961, ibid.

40 Tadhg Feehan to Florence O'Donoghue, 28 Mar. 1961, ibid.

41 Florence O'Donoghue to Connie Neenan, 30 Dec. 1960, ibid.

42 Florence O'Donoghue to Connie Neenan, 23 Mar. 1961, ibid.

43 Connie Neenan to Florence O'Donoghue, 29 Apr. 1961, ibid.

44 Note from Joseph McGrath, 24 Aug. 1961, ibid.

45 Florence O'Donoghue to Eamon de Valera, 21 Jan. 1963 (O'Donoghue papers, MS 31,456).

46 Jim Whelan to Florence O'Donoghue, 19 May 1961, ibid.

47 Jack Barry to Florence O'Donoghue, 27 July 1961, ibid.

48 Connie Neenan to Florence O'Donoghue, 28 Mar. 1961, ibid.

49 Mary MacSwiney to Seán T. O'Kelly, 11 May 1936 (University College Dublin Archives (UCDA), Mary MacSwiney papers, P48a/139).

50 See, for example, *The Irish Times*, 18 Mar. 1925.

51 George II was blown up in 1935, William III attacked and the head stolen in September 1928 (see p. 66)

52 Unveiled 16 Oct. 1955 (souvenir unveiling programme from private collection).

53 NA, DJ 8/81.

54 Report by Ceannphort J. S. Flynn, 21 Apr. 1940 (NA, DJ 8/881).

55 Report by Ceannphort J. S. Flynn, (n.d.), ibid.

56 Report by Ard Cheannphort V. Slavins, 28 Apr. 1941 (NA, DJ 8/881).

57 Ibid.

58 Quoted in *Irish Republican Bulletin* (Easter, 1961), p. 12 (NLI, Gerald Tighe papers, MS 28,894(B)1).

59 NA, DJ 8/865.

60 Report by Sergt. C. Sheehan, 20 Nov. 1945 (NA, DJ 8/881).

61 The Soloheadbeg monument, Co. Tipperary, was unveiled on 28 Jan. 1950. The Bruff memorial, Co. Limerick, was unveiled two years later, and those in Bandon, Co. Cork and Newcastlewest, Co. Limerick, in 1953 and 1955 respectively.

62 Maurice Agulhon, 'La statuomanie et l'histoire', in Maurice Agulhon, *Histoire vagabonde*, vol. 1 (Paris, 1988), pp. 137–85.

63 *Limerick Chronicle*, 18 Oct. 1952.

64 Speech by Seán T. O'Kelly at Cumann Tír Conaill, 1965, Seán Ó Lúing papers, (NLI, MS 23,516).

65 See particularly the monument at Bruff, Co. Limerick.

66 Letter to author from John Cussen, Newcastlewest, 22 July 1998.

67 NA, DJ 8/881.

68 Ibid.

69 Report by A/Capt. A. O'Meadhra, Tralee, 21 Mar. 1936 (NA, DJ 8/408).

70 *United Ireland*, 23 June, 14 July 1934.

71 Ibid., 20 Apr. 1935.

72 *Tipperary Star*, 13 Apr. 1935.

CHAPTER 9

A Nation Once Again

Towards an Epistemology of the Republican *Imaginaire*

* * *

Eugene O'Brien

'And Ireland long a province be
A nation once again.'

Perhaps the first things that need to be addressed, given the title of this chapter, are the terms 'republican' and *'imaginaire'*. The former term would seem to be self evident, in that it generically describes a political system in which power within a state is held by the people, through their represen-tatives. It also refers to a political system where there is a separation of power between the legislature and the judiciary. The two great republican examples are those of the American and French revolutions wherein a military overthrow of a political regime was accompanied by an intellectual and philosophical interrogation of notions of power and responsibility.

The genesis of the term 'republicanism', in a specifically Irish context, can be traced to the period antedating 1798. Republicanism has remained a potent signifier in subsequent Irish politics, and is still relevant today in the form of the Provisional Irish Republican Army, Sinn Féin, the Continuity IRA, the Real IRA and the 32 County Sovereignty Committee. Ironically, the motto of the Provisionals, 'tiocfaidh ár lá', translates as 'our day will come', and this is the exact phrase that is used by Davin in his conversation with Stephen in *A Portrait of the Artist as a Young Man*. As Stephen runs through the history of failed rebellions of the past, and states his refusal to join any such movement, Davin replies: they 'died for their ideals, Stevie . . . Our day will come yet, believe me'.[1] This verbal parallelism foregrounds the thematic and imagistic dimensions of Republican ideology as we have come to know it. Literary tropes are suasively used in order to reinforce a motivated connection between a particular group, a whole nation and notions of temporal closure: 'a nation *once* again'.

The *imaginaire*, on the other hand, is a term specific to the theory of the French psychoanalyst, Jacques Lacan. It is seen as the first order of development of the human ego, before progressing into the area of what he calls the symbolic, namely the register of language, symbols and agreed systems of meaning. In a ground-breaking essay entitled 'The mirror stage as formative of the function of the I',[2] Lacan sees one of the seminal stages of this 'construct' as the defining of the self in terms of a reflection. The self is defined in terms of a misrecognition (*méconaissance*) of an image of itself in the mirror, a process which he terms the 'mirror stage'. While initially seen as a moment which can be placed at a particular time in a child's life, between six and eighteen months, Lacan would later see this as a structural relationship vital to the formation of the ego.

This paper extrapolates this position into a societal and group matrix. The Lacanian imaginary is taken here as a model which can encompass the epistemological structure of republicanism in particular as a form or sub-set of nationalism. I shall explore the nature of Lacan's concept of the imaginary order before applying it to the construction of a republican idea of selfhood. I am aware that Lacan's theories are essentially based on the individual self, but would contend that there is theoretical justification in applying them to a more societal or group concept of identity. In Althusserian terms, society interpolates the next generation in its own image through socio-cultural and linguistic signifiers, and the epistemology of republican nationalism is suffused with such structures, and has successfully replicated itself in various individuals over a long period of time. Lacan's theories of the creation of the individual self through a form of reflection would certainly seem to have some place in such structures.

In this essay, Lacan pictures a child becoming aware of its own image in a mirror, and goes on to discuss the 'jubilant assumption of his specular image by the child' as it aspires to the totality of that image:[3]

> This . . . would seem to exhibit in an exemplary situation the symbolic matrix in which the *I* is precipitated in a primordial form, before it is objectified in the dialectic of identification with the other, and before language restores to it, in the universal, its function as subject. This form would have to be called the Ideal-I.[4]

The important point to note about this identification is that the image is ideal, it orients the 'agency of the ego' in a 'fictional direction'; it is something towards which the ego may aspire, but which it can never attain. It is also an identification that has no place for anything else outside its scopic field (the field where the visual dimension of desire is enacted). Lacan makes the point that the human ego is created as a result of identifying with one's own specular image, so what seems to be individual, internal and unique to the individual is, in fact, the result of an identification with a two-dimensional representation of that individual. The 'ideal-I' is both a fiction, and a fixed model which can never be more fully developed.

Samuel Weber comments astutely on one particular aspect of this theory. He notes that a human being is able, at a much earlier stage, 'to perceive the unity of an image than it is to produce this unity in its own body'.[5] The difficulty here is that the image is both that of the self, and also a form of alterity, in that it is clearly *not* the self. The recognition of the self is actually a misrecognition, but one which exerts a powerful hold on the ego, as it provides the comforting sense of wholeness which the ego desires. This prefigures an allied sense of alienation from the image, as feelings of narcissistic aggressivity arise in the tension between the specular image and the real body. In other words, through the agency of desire, the human child sees an image that is more coherent than the actuality of its own body and proceeds to identify with it. This is then taken as an image of our lifelong need to be better than we are. So, we see ourselves, ideally, as thinner, cleverer, more successful, more popular than we actually are.

Interestingly, Weber situates such conflicts in terms of temporality. He makes the point that for Lacan, the future anterior is of crucial importance in his discussion of the construction of identity, as it is through time that such notions are developed. Lacan himself stressed the importance of the future anterior in his own discussion on language and time:

> I identify myself in language, but only by losing myself in it like an object. What is realised in my history is not the past definite of what was, since it is no more, or even the present perfect of what has been in what I am, but the future anterior of what I shall have been for what I am in the process of becoming.[6]

Lacan, Weber notes, locates the time of the subject as an 'inconclusive futurity of what will-always-already-have-been . . . a "time" which can never be entirely remembered, since it will never have fully taken place'.[7] In other words, in the mirror stage, the identification of the subject with the imago[8] sets up a desire for imaginary wholeness in the future, a future towards which the subject strives, but which it will never reach. Hence, Lacan's vision of the imago as an 'alienating destination', which is reached by facing towards a 'fictional direction',[9] wherein the specular image 'traps the subject in an illusory ideal of completeness'.[10] This ongoing process of captation and mis-recognition is a performative through which the ego is created and defined. For Lacan, narcissistic aggressivity is the result of a desire that can never be fulfilled. Before desire can be mediated through language and the symbolic order, it: 'exists solely in the single plane of the imaginary relation of the specular stage, projected, alienated in the other'.[11]

What we see in Lacan's investigation of the mirror stage, then, is that he radically transformed a psychological experiment into a 'theory of the imaginary organisation of the human subject'.[12] This stress on the imaginary as a structural ordering of human relationships is important in our discussion of nationalism. It begins in the mirror stage, but continues into all aspects of our lives. Elizabeth Grosz provides a comprehensive overview of the imaginary:

> Imaginary relations are thus two-person relations, where the self sees itself reflected in the other. This dual imaginary relation . . . although structurally necessary, is an ultimately stifling and unproductive relation. The dual relationship between mother and child is a dyad [two individuals regarded as a pair], trapping both participants within a mutually defining structure. Each strives to have the other, and ultimately, to *be* the other in a vertiginous spiral from one term or identity to the other.[13]

Here, we see the symphysis between the Lacanian imaginary and the episte-mology of nationalism in general and republicanism in particular. At a basic level, this reflective captation of the subject by an image is what constitutes the imaginary order. Imaginary relationships are predominated by ambivalent emotions; a desire to become the image in the mirror, and, on realising the futility of this aim, a resultant aggressivity towards both the image, and anything which intervenes with, or blocks, the desired identification with that image. The image, as well as being a source of desire, is also, because it is fictional as well as external and can never be fully internalised, a source of hatred. The displacement of this hatred on all that is deemed to be outside this binary specular relationship is a possible explanation of the violence that seems to be inherent in practically all enunciations of nationalist ideology throughout history. The primary imaginary relationship for the ego is with the mother. Child and mother are seen as a unity, a biologically centred reaction as, of course, child and mother were a single entity during pregnancy

I shall contend that this captation of the self by a reflected, two-dimensional image of that self, is the *sine qua non* of the epistemology of nationalism and republicanism. An image of selfhood is set up as an ideal, an ideal which has a dual interaction with the temporal structures of history. The mirror in question here is one of language and time. This moment of ideal fusion between self and image is often postulated as a mythical alpha point, an ur-beginning, from which all ideas of the race or *Volk* derive. In an Irish republican context, for example, 1798 or 1916,[14] are such moments which seem to transcend time; from the unionist perspective, 1691, the date of the Battle of the Boyne, would be an analogous defining moment. Kevin Whelan makes the point that Daniel O'Connell's Catholic nationalism also appealed to selective notions of history, 'using an idealised past to destroy the decadent present'.[15] However, such moments of fusion are also postulated as a goal towards which the *ethnie*[16] should aim at some undefined time in the future. As we shall see, the discourse of nationalism abounds with variations of these two temporal imperatives, as peoples look to regain a lost prelapsarian past, or else to come into their kingdom in some golden futurity. In contemporary political discussion, this can be seen from a particular choice of descriptive locution.

Republican spokespeople constantly refer to 'the Dublin government' and 'the London government' in their comments. These terms have become a commonplace in the media, with both Irish and British broadcasters using them as norms. However, some conceptual unpacking will reveal that these terms are part of the predefined mirror image of the future that is central to republican epistemology. The term 'Dublin government' is used in preference to the term 'Irish government' because it is seen as an illegitimate state function which does not have jurisdiction over the '6 Occupied Counties' of Northern Ireland. The 32 County Sovereignty Committee makes this point explicit by declaring 'null and void any documents which usurp the sovereignty of our nation as declared in the 1919 Declaration of Independence'.[17] In this context, a two-dimensional image of Irishness from the past is seen as controlling all possible future developments of Irishness in the future, a temporal schemata which is very much in line with Lacan's conception of the imaginary. Similarly, the 'London government' lacks legitimacy in the imaginary scheme precisely because it is the occupying force in question in Northern Ireland, and will only be deemed 'British' when this occupation, a temporal hiccup, is ended and 'Ireland long a province' can become 'a nation once again'. Like the images of the reflected 'ideal-I', the 'Ideal-Ireland' is reified, or fixed, allowing for no deviation from the temporal path set out in the imaginary mindset. Only then will there be a legitimate 'Irish' government. The fact that republican ideology is suffused with personifications of Ireland as a mother figure is surely, in this context, no accident. The use of racial, religious and linguistic tropes that are rooted in the individual and group unconscious, gives nationalist ideology a strong hold on the minds of its audience.

In his study, 'The island of Ireland: a psychological contribution to political psychology', Ernest Jones analyses the dominant image of a female personification of Ireland in terms of how the signifier 'Ireland' has become particularly associated with an 'unconscious maternal complex'.[18] Jones made the point that for island peoples, the associations of their native land with the ideas of 'woman, virgin, mother and womb' are very strong and he went on to add that such phantasies tend to fuse 'in the central complex of the womb of a virgin mother'.[19]

The many different names that have been given to a personified Ireland – Erin, Cathleen Ni Houlihan, Banba, Mother Ireland, the Shan Van Vocht, the Poor Old Woman[20] – tend to demonstrate the accuracy of Jones's point, and I would largely agree with Cormac Gallagher's extrapolation from Jones's thesis that, in the case of Ireland, there is a strong connection between this personification and the 'repressed primary idea of Mother, the closest of all immediate blood relatives, to which powerful unconscious affective interests remain attached'.[21] What this means, in effect, is that the political has become mapped onto the familial, with the hugely affective and emotional aspects of family relationships mapped onto political structures. In *Defence of the Nation: Newsletter of the 32 County Sovereignty Committee*, for example, we find the following quotation in a section entitled 'Where We Stand', which enunciates that organisations's credo: 'the committee seeks to achieve broad unity among the republican family on the single issue of sovereignty'.[22] Here, the strong political and ideological differences among different strands of republicanism have been transposed into an internal family squabble, a rhetorical device which serves to naturalise republican ideology into a familial norm, with Ireland personified as a mother. Here the elements of choice, argument, debate and ideology are subsumed into a naturalised familial dialectic.

Gallagher's study points us in the direction of an answer to this complicated question. Developing his point about the connection between the idea of Ireland and that of a mother figure, he points out that, if nationalists unconsciously connect their actions with the 'primary idea' of the mother, 'their thoughts and actions will have such a compulsive force that no amount of reasoning or concessions will modify them'.[23] It is here, I would contend, that we approach the main epistemological dimension of the *imaginaire*. Lacan has identified desire as the most important human attribute, from the perspective of the development of the human ego. I shall argue that desire is precisely the compulsive force, unconsciously driven, and oriented towards primary images and ideas, which permeates and originates nationalist ideology. By an analysis of Lacan's paradigms of the mirror stage and the imaginary order, we can see, at an individual level, the effects and dimensions of this desire on identity; and we can then go on to develop this in terms of the group identity as predicated in the nationalist *imaginaire*. In the song 'A nation once again', this transposition from individual to group growth is framed within this imaginary notion of teleological nationhood. The song begins when 'boyhood's fire was in my blood', and proceeds through a process of political and religious development until manhood ('and so I grew from boy to man') is defined in terms of participation in the creation of the once and future nation.

In Lacan's account of the development of the ego, human identity is seen as emerging from the crossing of a frontier, from what he terms the 'imaginary order' (the dyadic world of mother and child), into that of the 'symbolic order', which is concerned with symbolic systems, language being the main one (though both stages continue to coexist within the individual afterwards). The imaginary is defined as the 'world, the register, the dimension of images, conscious or unconscious, perceived or imagined'.[24] Lacan's notion of the imaginary order is one wherein the human being becomes attached to an image, and attempts to find a wholeness and unity of meaning through a form of imitation or mimicry of this image.

It is the idea of the ego as being fascinated with, and ultimately fixated by its image that has such importance for our discussion of the modality of knowledge that is operative in, and through, nationalism. Lacan seems to see such mimicry as constitutive of our identity-generating process as humans, 'the field of phantasies and images', with its prototype being the 'infant before the mirror, fascinated with his image',[25] while Gary Leonard, in his Lacanian study of James Joyce's *Dubliners*, sees the imaginary in terms of a 'period of time in which individuals mistake their mirror images for themselves, that is, as proof that they are unified and autonomous beings'.[26] As Lacan himself puts it, the imaginary is, at its core, an erotic relationship: 'all seizing of the other in an image in a relationship of erotic captivation, occurs by way of the narcissistic relation'.[27] Here, he is pointing towards his theory of the importance of the image, or reflection, in the process of identificatory development of the ego, which he defines as a form of construct of self and image.

The important point to note about this identification is that the image is ideal, it orients the 'agency of the ego' in a 'fictional direction,' it is something towards which the ego may aspire, but which it can never attain. It is also an identification that has no place for anything else outside its scopic field. Lacan makes the point that the human ego is created as a result of identifying with one's own specular image, so what seems to be individual, internal and unique to the individual is, in fact, the result of an identification with a two-dimensional representation of that individual. Lacan's point here is that the ego is constituted 'by an identification with another whole object, an imaginary projection, an idealisation ("Ideal-I") which does not match the child's feebleness'. It is this 'alienated relationship of the self to its own image' that Lacan terms the imaginary.[28]

Nationalist narratives very often read as coherent and teleological, leading cohesively from past to future. In this sense, Lacan's notion of the future anterior is important as history, rather than being a record of events of the past, becomes a temporal mirror through which the nationalist imago is seen and reinforced: 'the future anterior of what I shall have been for what I am in the process of becoming'.[29] The wholeness of the reflected image of the self becomes the goal of the ego. In the narrative of history, this wholeness becomes the telos or goal. In a search for such wholeness and unity, as Bhabha notes, the subject assumes a 'discrete image which allows it to postulate a series of equivalences, samenesses, identities, between the objects of the surrounding world',[30] and this brings us to the third area of delimitation. The driving force behind these identities is what Bowie terms 'the false fixities of the imaginary order'.[31] The imaginary order attempts to hypostasise (to fix in terms of underlying substance) and hypertrophy (to enlarge in terms of one specific dimension) the specular image of itself, and to block any development of this position of fixity: it is 'tirelessly intent upon freezing a subjective process that cannot be frozen'.[32] This prioritisation of the static image, and the resultant imperative towards fixity in the viewing subject, necessitates relationships in nationalist discourse which are unchanging and foundational. In an attempt to remove itself from 'the flux of becoming',[33] the nationalist *imaginaire* insists on identifications that are as permanent as it can find, with the most obvious of these being the identification between a people and a place, between a language and a land, as we saw in the motivated description of the 'Dublin' as opposed to the 'Irish' government.

The lococentric[34] relationship between a people and a place, the archetypal nationalistic trope, is by its nature, imaginary because it is fictive. Stressing a monological and temporal essentialism, it cannot cope with aspects of real society which do not correspond to the ideal reflected image. The practices of cultural nationalism all serve to create this mirror, this delusory dyad in which nothing else exists except this specular definition of selfhood. The aggressivity that is a concomitant of narcissism, the child expelling that which upsets the specular symmetry, is an inherent aspect of the imaginary, and also, I would suggest, an inherent aspect of nationalism. All that is 'other' in terms of the imaginary selfhood must be expelled. Etymologically, the term 'territory' derives both from *terra* (earth) and *terrere* (to frighten) which leads, as Bhabha has astutely pointed out, to *territorium*: 'a place from which people are frightened off'.[35] If the people-place relationship is to enact the dyadic nature of the nationalist imaginary, then anything outside that dyadic scopic field must be elided.

In the establishment of the ego, as we have seen, the desire for some form of identity is paramount. From infancy, we seek to be desired and loved by the 'other', a term which, as Mark Bracher notes, alters as we develop. Initially, at the beginning of life, this designation refers to the 'mother, then both parents, later one's peers, and finally any number of bodies or figures of authority, including God, Society and nature'.[36] In many ways, it is the growth and development of our notion of the other that structures the type of identity which we develop. If the other is allowed to remain static, if it becomes hypostasised in an imaginary dyad, then this attenuation of the other will result in a concomitant attenuation of the development of the self. These master signifiers also form some of the *points de capiton* (anchoring points) which Lacan sees as necessary for normal interaction within discourse.

For example, a specific narrative of the past can also be used as a binding factor in this imaginary relationship, as witnessed by the rhetoric of the imaginary that is to be found in the *Green Book*, the training manual of the Provisional IRA. Here, the imaginary identification of a whole people with a minority movement is enacted through the creation of a temporal master signifier which anchors a particular reading of Irish history:

> Commitment to the Republican Movement is the firm belief that its struggle both military and political is morally justified, that war is morally justified and that the Army is the direct representatives [*sic*] of the 1918 [*sic*] Dáil Éireann parliament, and that as such they are the legal and lawful government of the Irish Republic, which has the moral right to pass laws for, and claim jurisdiction over, the whole geographical fragment of Ireland . . . and all of its people regardless of creed or loyalty.[37]

This is the discourse of nationalism par excellence, embodying its imaginary epistemology. Time is frozen in a specular identification with the 'Dáil of 1918' (actually convened in 1919) a term which is a *point de capiton* in Irish republican narrative.[38] All subsequent elections and democratic expressions of will are null and void; they do not correspond to the totalising image and must therefore be deemed invalid. All territory and people, 'regardless of loyalty or creed,' are claimed as part of the nationalist imaginary; the chilling question of exactly what is to be done with those whose loyalty is not to the Dáil of 1919 being left unasked and unanswered. Here, the master signifier sets limits to the development of the other in the discourse of Irish nationalism. The development of which Bracher spoke is stunted. Instead, the passive narcissistic desire (the desire to be the object of the other's love, idealisation or recognition)[39] of the addressees of this document (IRA members), is fixed on an other which defines itself in terms of the election in 1918. This is also the position of the 32 County Sovereignty Committee, whose whole *raison d'être* is predicated on this particular point in time: 'This committee solely stands to uphold the Declaration of Independence as proclaimed by Dáil Éireann on January 21st 1919'.[40]

Another master signifier in the above declaration is the term 'belief.' Here there is to be no rational debate, or attempt to win over opponents through force of argument. Instead, all that is necessary is that one should believe in the moral right of the IRA to carry out its political and military actions. As Renan has noted, nationality has a sentimental side to it: 'it is both soul and body at once; a Zollverein is not a patrie'.[41] In terms of the song 'A nation once again', this pattern of the language of belief and religion is a central trope. The chain of religious imagery, which I cite seriatim, functions as a narrative spine within the song:

And then I prayed I might yet see
Our fetters rent in twain . . .
Outshine that solemn starlight
It seemed to watch above my head
In forum, field and fane
Its angel voice sang round my bed . . .
. . . It whispered too that freedoms ark
And service high and holy . . .
. . . For, freedom comes from God's right hand
And needs a godly train
and righteous men must make our land
A nation once again . . .

Belief in the nation as an almost sacral manifestation is a central tenet. If one believes in the nation, in the cause, then all further action is legitimated by this belief – the epistemological structure operative here is that of a dyad, the 'I' of the song believes in the nation that is to come, and that nation, in turn, validates and legitimates the growth of the self in the song from 'boyhood' to adulthood: 'as I grew from boy to man'.

Here, then, is the epistemology of the republican *imaginaire*: a misrecognition, a *méconaissance*, in which self and image cohere to the exclusion of all others. According to Lacan, the ego is constructed as the child struggles to achieve the specular image of wholeness that is observed in the mirror; an image

> that is both accurate (since it is an inverted reflection, the presence of light rays emanating from the child: the image as icon); as well as delusory (since the image prefigures a unity and mastery that the child still lacks).[42]

For Lacan, this specular relationship initiates the imaginary order where the self is dominated by an image of the self, and it seeks definition through reflected relations with this image. The nationalistic *ethnie* is forever gazing towards a specular image that is fictional, optative (as in expressing a wish or desire) and, of necessity, a source of aggressive impulses when it cannot be internalised. In this specular dyad, there is no place for a developing, growing 'other', as outlined by Bracher. Instead, the specular image is fixed in a two-dimensional realm, and all three-dimensional changes which blur the purity of this image are alien, and must be purged.

This imaginary reflection is the driving force behind all nationalistic discursive formulations. Thus, the deistic sceptical Enlightenment thinker, Wolfe Tone, is captated[43] by the nationalist imaginary into a quasi-Catholic martyr, who died for his people in a salvific act of redemption. For the IRA, the ebb and flow of the signifying chain of Irish history is punctuated by a temporal master signifier – the first Dáil Éireann parliament – which renders insignificant and meaningless all prior and subsequent electoral contests and democratic processes. When these refuse to validate the imaginary nation-alistic vision of Ireland embodied in the 1919 Dáil, they are simply elided from the historical narrative structure. As Lacan tellingly put it: 'history is not the past. History is the past in so far as it is historicised in the present',[44] and the ideological and emotive elements which govern this historicisation are those of the nationalist *imaginaire*.

Hence, the image of a subject being captated by a reflection, which is both idealised and at the same time frozen, is a paradigm for the identificatory processes of nationalism. The captation of the child by his or her reflection is an analogue of the captation of a people by their nationalist mirror-image. The dual nature of the scopic field between an *ethnie* and the projection of its identity is central to nationalism. That there is no third party in this scopic bijection is another cogent factor. The identification is mutually fulfilling: there is no room for anything or anyone else. Such is the mindset of the IRA declaration which sees itself as having: 'the moral right to pass laws for, and claim jurisdiction over, the whole geographical fragment of Ireland'. Here we see a fusion of territory with a notion of religious warrant, as an essentially political movement expresses itself in terms that are profoundly religious in tenor: 'belief . . . moral right'. The specular imaginary deals with identities that exist outside its scopic field in an acquisitive way: the IRA here encom-passes 'all of its [Ireland's] people regardless of creed or loyalty'.[45] The choice for any other form of identity existing outside the nationalist imaginary is simple: leave the territory, or else be absorbed into the nationalist *mentalité*.

Lacan has made the point that: '[d]esidero is the Freudian cogito',[46] and has stressed the primacy of desire as a motive force in the construction of our humanity. Such desire is central to the creation of the nationalist and republican *imaginaire*. If there is to be a core definition of nationalism qua nationalism then surely it must focus on the mode of creation of the ethnic group, or on the methods used in imagining the identity of the community in question, or on the rhetorical and suasive strategies used in terms of creating nationalistic sentiment. The modality of these creations or inventions, what Anderson terms 'the style in which they are imagined',[47] is crucial if we are to come to any understanding of how nationalism utters and fashions itself. To quote Bennington: at 'the origin of the nation, we find a story of the nation's origin',[48] and there can be no doubting that this reflexive form of narrative is an important constituent of the epistemology of nationalism. Narratives create the myths of nationalism, and these are both protean and similar in that they feature a telling to the self of the self, a telling which, in the process, is performative in that it is creative of that self, at both conscious and unconscious levels.

Bennington's focus on narrative, I think, allows us to overcome the anti-nomies already observed in terms of the problematics of defining nationalism. Every culture defines itself through a process of narrative imagination, a re-telling of stories about its own past which reaffirms the ritual unities of the culture in question. For example, Irish people remember the 1916 Easter rebellion as a nodal or central point in the political and cultural reaffirmation of Irishness per se. Around this period, and for some time before, the major political parties, or their precursors, were founded, and the Gaelic, Celtic, Irish language and Irish literary revivals were set in motion. The Gaelic League and the Gaelic Athletic Association were set up, and the gradual adequation between the nationalist movement, both political and cultural, and the Catholic Church came into being. This period of colonial upheaval – with the almost standard attendant processes of nationalist consciousness-raising, independence movement, armed rebellion, war of independence/liberation and an ensuing civil war – became part of the process of a national imaginary, defining Irishness as it emerged from the colonial shadow of Britain. This whole period, or more correctly, the narrative enculturation of this period, became a nodal point, or *point de capiton* from which particular notions of Irishness were traced.

Such a process is necessary for cultural definition, but there is always a danger that such culturally sanctioned categories may become reified into some kind of epistemological orthodoxy which forms a hypostasised centre of identity. As Richard Kearney has noted, such a process of 'ideological recol-lection of sacred foundational acts often serves to integrate and legitimate a social order'.[49] However, he goes on to cite a warning note sounded by Paul Ricoeur, who points out that such a process of reaffirmation can be perverted 'into a mystificatory discourse which serves to uncritically vindicate or glorify the established political powers'. Ricoeur's point is essentially that in such instances the symbols of a community become fixed and fetishised; 'they serve as lies'.[50] Ricoeur has noted that imagination can function as two opposite poles. At one pole is the confusion of myth with reality brought about by a 'non-critical consciousness' which conflates the two into a societal 'given'. At the other end of the axis, where 'critical distance is fully conscious of itself', 'imagination is the very instrument of the critique of reality', because it enables 'consciousness to posit something at a distance from the real and thus produce the alterity at the very heart of existence'.[51]

I would argue that the narrative structure of nationalism is clearly allied to Ricoeur's initial pole, that of the confusion of myth with reality through a 'non-critical consciousness'. Such a narrative structure functions mainly at an unconscious level in culture and society, creating structural effects in terms of ethnic and racial stereotypes. Logic, reason and critical thinking allow us to discriminate between the value of stories as fictions, and their constative, or truth-telling status. However, by functioning at an unconscious level, through formal and informal apparatuses of communication, narratives and myths create a powerful drive, through which nationalist ideology can be disseminated. They create an imaginary selfhood which is reflected back into society as an ideal form of identity.

The stock example of such a process is Nazi Germany in the 1930s, but there are multifarious examples to be found of the unconscious effect of narratives that are uncritically equated with constative discourse. In an Irish context,[52] perhaps the *locus classicus* of this type of nationalist narrative operating at a pre-critical, unconscious level is Patrick Pearse's rewriting of the history of the United Irish rebellion of 1798. Pearse was a central figure in the Irish Republican Brotherhood, a sub-grouping within the Irish Volunteers, who organised a rebellion against the British Government in 1916.[53] In his efforts to create a narrative of nationalist resistance to British rule in Ireland, Pearse specifically set out to 'remember' the 1798 rebellion in highly specific terms.

The 1798 rebellion was led by Theobald Wolfe Tone.[54] Tone, a product of the French Enlightenment, had little time for religion, and saw the aim of his organisation, the United Irishmen, as the creation of a country where the terms Protestant, Catholic and Dissenter would be subsumed under the common name of Irishman.[55] Tone himself, as Marianne Elliott has observed, was a deist, 'who disliked institutionalised religion and sectarianism of any hue'. More importantly in the present context, she makes the point that, based on his writings, he had 'no time whatsoever for the romantic Gaelicism that has become part of Irish nationalism'.[56] Hence, if Pearse wished to create a seamless narrative wherein Tone was a historical nationalist avatar, and a Pearsean precursor, he would seem to have some factual historical difficulties with which to contend.

His response to these difficulties is a classic *exemplum* of what I have termed nationalist epistemology. In an oration given at the grave of Tone, in Bodenstown, County Kildare, in 1913, Pearse enfolded Tone in the following narrative structure:

> We have come to one of the holiest places in Ireland; holier even than the place where Patrick sleeps in Down.[57] Patrick brought us life, but this man died for us. He was the greatest of Irish Nationalists. . . . We have come to renew our adhesion to the faith of Tone: to express once more our full acceptance of the gospel of Irish Nationalism which he was the first to formulate in worldly terms. This man's soul was a burning flame, so ardent, so generous, so pure, that to come into communion with it is to come unto a new baptism, into a new regeneration and cleansing.[58]

Here there is no attempt to commemorate the historical Wolfe Tone, the 'child of the eighteenth-century Enlightenment' whose hope was that Enlightenment rationality would supplant what he regarded as 'superstitious beliefs'.[59] Instead, Tone is suasively captated into Pearse's own vision of Irish history. It is not accidental that Anderson has noted a 'strong affinity' between nationalist and religious imaginings.[60] Indeed, he has made the valid point that the dawn of the age of nationalism coincides with the dusk of religious thought,[61] as both tend to work with some form of 'sacred text'. The notion of a sacred text is important here, as the response to such a text is not that of close reading, or of some form of rational critical engagement; rather is it an acceptance, a belief, and a ready acknowledgement of the 'truth' that is revealed by this text.

His frame of reference is directed at an audience whose unconscious is saturated with Roman Catholic religiosity. The rhetorical device polyptoton[62] is used to cement the adequation of Tone with Saint Patrick in the opening line. This adequation transforms Tone from an historical figure, subject to the veridical discourse of history, into a mythico-religious one, comparable to the legendary Saint Patrick, about whom comparatively little is known, apart from his spectacular religious success. The connection between the two, the hinge upon which the whole rhetorical structure turns, is based on this loco-centric comparison in terms of the holiness of a specific place. This connection is then developed in the contradiction that while Patrick 'brought us life', a phrase which clearly implies religious life, Tone 'died for us'. By now, the adequation has done its work, and the unconscious religious background fills in any blanks in the narrative. In Catholic teaching, the notion of sacrifice, the one for the many, is a central tenet. The adequation between Tone and Saint Patrick is now elided and a stronger connection is set up. Given the religious frame of reference (reinforced by the lexical field of the paragraph: 'faith'; 'gospel'; 'soul'; 'communion'; 'baptism'; 'regeneration'; 'cleansing'), the notion of someone dying 'for us' implies an adequation between Tone and Christ, and at a broader level, between nationalism and religion.

For Pearse, and we must keep in mind his notion of Tone as the first to formulate in worldly terms the gospel of Irish nationalism, there is something quasi-sacred about the nation. Régis Debray, in an attempt to study the constituent factors of the historical nation state, has traced in nationalism the process whereby 'life itself is rendered untouchable or sacred. This sacred character constitutes the real national question.'[63] The teleology of Pearse's rhetorical transformation of the people into their own Messiah is to render them 'immortal and impassable'. Nationalistic selfhood creates a people, a Volk, which transcends time and death. The religious overtones of this message, allied to strong unconscious influences, combine to create a linguistic and suasive dimension to the epistemology of nationalism which can never be fully examined in any analysis which is not grounded in literary, linguistic, and psychoanalytic techniques. This, I would argue, is why the already discussed definitions will always fail to analyse the workings and imperatives of nationalism. It is only by looking at its modality of expression, and its epistemological status, that we can come to clearer perceptions about its nature.

Let us observe Pearse on the steps of the General Post Office in the centre of Dublin on Easter Monday 1916, when he inscribes his act of rebellion against the British under the rubric of a nationalistic, rhetorical reading of Irish history:

> Irishmen and Irishwomen: In the name of God and of the dead generations from which she receives her old tradition of nationhood, Ireland, through us, summons her children to her flag and strikes for her freedom.[64]

Through the use of a rhetorical structure largely underpinned by transcendental imagery, Pearse avoids the discourse of reason or of political debate, and instead appeals to the unconscious signification of the powerful images of 'God', the 'dead generations' and the notion of Ireland as a mother, calling her children to her flag.

The phantasy invoked here is telling. As Easthope has noted, phantasy turns ideas into narratives,[65] and the proclamation of a provisional government, while encapsulating a certain social doctrine (universal suffrage, and guarantees of 'religious and civil liberty, equal rites and equal opportunities to all its citizens'),[66] is largely premised on a narrative structure which creates and defines selfhood in its own terms. Keeping in mind his notion of the people as their own messiah, it is noteworthy that the proclamation concludes by stressing the sacrificial, and ultimately salvific, nature of this struggle. He concludes:

> We place the cause of the Irish Republic under the protection of the Most High God, Whose blessing we invoke upon our arms, and we pray that no one who serves that cause will dishonour it by cowardice, inhumanity, or rapine. In this supreme hour the Irish nation must, by its valour and discipline, and by the readiness of its children to sacrifice themselves for the common good, prove itself worthy of the august destiny to which it is called.[67]

The unconscious, pre-critical element that I maintain is a central tenet of the epistemology of nationalism, is evident here through close reading. The proclamation seems to come to a logical conclusion. Pearse's prayer is that the Irish nation must prove itself worthy of the 'august destiny' to which it is called, and this seems to make the act of rebellion almost preordained. Of course, on looking back to the beginning of the proclamation, we find that it is 'through us',[68] namely the splinter group within the Irish Volunteers, who defied their own command structure in order to undertake the Rising, that the personified notion of Ireland initially summoned 'her children to her flag' and struck 'for her freedom'.[69] Consequently, the seemingly impersonal 'august destiny' is, in fact, part of a suasive rhetorical device which exemplifies the circularity and reflexivity of nationalist epistemology. The 'we' who are called into service as the children of a personified Ireland are the very 'we' who have personified that notion of Ireland in the first place. In terms of an imaginary scene, which is altered in order to fulfil a wish for the subject, this whole exercise can be described as a locus classicus of phantasy, a phantasy which is constitutive in terms of defining the national subjectivity in question. This, in turn, produces an alteration from the communal and socially structured relationships of politics into the natural and organic relationships of the family: it is not a case of politically inspired revolutionaries deciding to fight for social or ideological aims, instead, it is children coming to the defence of their mother, an act which in itself requires neither explanation nor warrant.

The suasive and rhetorical effect of this process, when repeated, is to allow a linguistic performative to achieve a constative function. Here, myth and reality are fused in a nationalist *imaginaire*, and the mutual reflection of one in the other combines to create a narrative structure which is impervious to the conventions of political and veridical discourse. This narrative structure is also constitutive of what we might term nationalist identity, given that it reflects a particular type of subjectivity that is deemed to be Irish. No matter how much evidence of Wolfe Tone's attitude to religion is instantiated in biographies, he is still seen as part of a Catholic, Gaelic, nationalist pantheon, as narrated by Pearse, and it is to his grave in Bodenstown that the Provisional IRA have trooped in pilgrimage every year. The fact that their sectarian murder campaign over the past thirty years was the antithesis of everything that Tone stood for is not seen as any impediment to this process. What Pearse has been attempting is a narrative which will create trans-rational, unconscious, ethnic bonds between the past and the present. The facts of history are not part of such a discourse; they are only of value in selected instances, and if they reinforce the agenda of the narrative, they are creative of an identification, they are creative of an 'us'.

However, such valorisation or validation is actually defined relationally inasmuch as essentialist characteristics are actually predicated on a difference from otherness. For there to be an 'us', then there must be a 'them' who are by definition different from 'us'. This definition of the self promotes a desire for racial, linguistic, ideological, territorial and cultural purity which, at one end of the spectrum, validates a desire for socio-cultural identification and self-definition, and at the other posits a desire to differentiate one's own group from others and, by extension, a related desire to keep other groupings outside one's native territory, be that territory actual or psychic, and be that desire conscious or unconscious.

The Ulster loyalist, for example, believes that he or she is British, and that Ulster (comprising six counties since partition in 1922), as a political entity, is stable and viable. The Ulster republican, on the other hand, refuses to recognise the state of Northern Ireland, and instead sees Ulster (nine counties, part of the original quinary provincial divisions of Ireland) as part of the whole island of Ireland. The leader of the Orange march at Drumcree, during the summer of 1996, believed that even as these marchers defied the legal ban imposed by Sir Hugh Annesley, the Chief Constable of the Royal Ulster Constabulary, he was obeying some higher notion of 'Britishness', and was able to invoke the Queen in support of the actions of his followers and himself: 'we are the Queen's subjects, who wish to walk the Queen's highway'.[70]

If the Queen of England is the titular head of the British legislature, then, by extension, the Chief Constable of the Royal Ulster Constabulary is acting in her interests and at her behest through the British parliament at Westminster. From a logical or rational perspective, his enforcement of the law regarding the prohibition of parades from marching in a particular locality is validated by British legal and governmental writ. To claim that by breaking the Queen's law one is, in some way, demonstrating a higher form of loyalty to that Queen, is patently absurd. But of course, as we have seen in the case of Pearse, nationalist narrative is performative as opposed to constative, and this claim of a higher loyalty validates the Orange Order's sense of itself as some form of latter-day chosen people, who are proclaiming a '*true*' notion of 'Britishness' that only *they* can understand. Just as Pearse saw Tone as formulating the 'gospel of Irish Nationalism in worldly terms', so the Orange Order sees itself as revealing the 'truth' about notions of loyalism and Britishness in a similar manner.

The militant republicans who bombed Omagh in the summer of 1998 similarly believed that their action would in some way facilitate the coming into being of a united Ireland. While claiming that it is non-sectarian, the IRA, in all its manifestations, has pursued overtly sectarian policies, by targeting people and premises purely on the basis that they are Protestant, and by extension, unionist and loyalist in political persuasion.[71] Both traditions blend religion and politics, seeing their own creed as true and the other as heretical, and both traditions express their respective identities through a matrix of cultural signifiers: murals, graffiti, songs and icons, a matrix which is constitutive of powerful identificatory unconscious phantasies.[72]

If this type of politically motivated violence is to be removed from an Irish context, there is a need for a clear understanding of the nature of republicanism in a specifically Irish context. I would argue that Irish republicanism is very different from that of France or the United States in that it is a more essentialist political formulation, with none of the philosophical enquiry that underpinned the French and American revolutions. In terms of its mode of knowledge, of how it sees itself and its place in contemporary culture, Irish republicanism exemplifies all of the tenets of the Lacanian *imaginaire*, and only by progressing towards a more fluid definition of selfhood and alterity will it ever be able to acknowledge change and diversity as possible benefits to a changing dialectic. With the advent of Sinn Féin in the political spectrum of both Northern Ireland and the Republic of Ireland, an advent which offers de facto recognition of the legitimacy of both states, and by definition of the position of the Ulster Unionist population, some measure of progress has been achieved. If that is to be maintained, the idea of a nationhood that is temporally bound in the past and future anterior must give way to a more fluid concept, a concept that is enshrined in a different epistemology of Irishness, as enunciated by Daniel O'Connell: 'No man has the right to set a boundary to the onward march of a nation. No man has the right to say: 'Thus far shalt thou go, and no further.' This perspective on Irishness is one which the republican needs to embrace if it is ever to develop beyond the republican *imaginaire*.

A NATION ONCE AGAIN

I

When boyhood's fire was in my blood
I read of ancient freemen
For Greece and Rome who bravely stood
Three hundred men and three men
And then I prayed I might yet see
Our fetters rent in twain
And Ireland long a province be
A nation once again

Chorus
A nation once again
A nation once again
And Ireland long a province be
A nation once again

II

And from that time through wildest woe
That hope has shone a far light
Nor could love's brightest summer glow
Outshine that solemn starlight
It seemed to watch above my head
In forum, field and fane
Its angel voice sang round my bed
A nation once again

III

It whispered too that freedom's ark
And service high and holy
Would be profaned by feelings dark
And passions vain or lowly
For, freedom comes from God's right hand
And needs a godly train
And righteous men must make our land
A nation once again

IV

So, as I grew from boy to man
I bent me to that bidding
My spirit of each selfish plan
And cruel passion ridding
For, thus I hoped some day to aid
Oh, can such hope be vain
When my dear country shall be made
A nation once again.

Notes

1   J. Joyce, *A Portrait of the Artist as a Young Man* (Boston, 1993 edn), p. 177.

2   J. Lacan, *Écrits: A Selection* (London, 1977: A. Sheridan (trans.)), pp. 1–7.

3   The term 'specular image' is specific to the work of Jacques Lacan and refers to the image that the child sees of itself in the mirror. By definition, it will be a two-dimensional representation of a three-dimensional object.

4   Lacan, *Écrits*, p. 2.

5   S. Weber, *Return to Freud: Jacques Lacan's Dislocation of Psychoanalysis* (Cambridge, 1991: M. Levine (trans.)), p. 12.

6   Lacan, *Écrits*, p. 86.

7   Weber, *Return to Freud*, p. 9.

8   This term, introduced into psychoanalysis by Jung, is related to the notion of the image, but refers to the affective domain as well in that it stresses the subjectivity of the image by including feelings.

9   Lacan, *Écrits*, p. 2.

10 M. Sarup, *Jacques Lacan* (Hemel Hempstead, 1992), p. 66.

11 J. Lacan, *The Seminar of Jacques Lacan: Book I: Freud's Papers on Technique 1953–1954* (New York, 1988: J. Forrester (trans.)), p. 170.

12 E. Roudinesco, *Jacques Lacan* (Cambridge, 1997: B. Bray (trans.)), p. 143.

13 E. Grosz, *Jacques Lacan: A Feminist Introduction* (London, 1990), pp. 46–7.

14 1798 was the year in which the United Irishmen and the Defenders rebelled against British rule, under the leadership of Wolfe Tone. 1916 was the date of the Easter Rising, a rebellion carried out by the Irish Republican Brotherhood, the Irish Citizen Army and Cumann na mBan (the Women's Army), under the leadership of Patrick Pearse and James Connolly in Easter week of that year.

15 K. Whelan, *The Tree of Liberty: Radicalism, Catholicism and the Construction of Irish Identity 1760–1830* (Cork, 1996), p. 55.

16 See J. Armstrong, *Nations Before Nationalism* (Chapel-Hill, 1982); A. D Smith, *The Ethnic Origins of Nations* (Oxford, 1986) and F. Barth, *Introduction* in *Ethnic Groups and Boundaries* (London, 1969). Smith looks at the intrinsic meaning given to cultural practices, myths and symbols by ethnic communities which he terms *ethnies*. In both definitions, the *ethnie* is seen as an organic community, wherein social, cultural, religious and ideological practices cohere in a synthesis which promotes self-definition.

17 *Defence of the Nation: Newsletter of the 32 County Sovereignty Committee* 1, 3 (1998), p. 2.

18 Cormac Gallagher makes the point that this essay was first read at a particularly important time in Irish history. Jones's paper was delivered to the British Psychological Society on 21 June 1922, as the Irish War of Independence was gradually being transformed into the civil war. '"Ireland, Mother Ireland": an essay in psychoanalytic symbolism', *The Letter* 12 (Spring, 1998), pp. 1–14.

19 E. Jones, 'The island of Ireland: a psychological contribution to political psychology', in *Essays in Applied Psychoanalysis* (London, 1964), p. 196.

20 E. O'Brien, *The Question of Irish Identity in the Writings of William Butler Yeats and James Joyce* (Lampeter, 1998), p. 221.

21 Gallagher, *Mother Ireland*, pp. 4–5.

22 *Defence of the Nation* 1, 3 (1998), p. 2.

23 Gallagher, *Mother Ireland*, pp. 8–9.

24 Alan Sheridan, translator's note to J. Lacan, *Écrits – A Selection* (London, 1977), p. ix.

25 B. Benvenuto and R. Kennedy, *The Works of Jacques Lacan* (London, 1986), p. 81.

26 G. M. Leonard, *Reading Dubliners Again: A Lacanian Perspective* (New York, 1983), p. 188.

27 J. Lacan, *The Psychoses: The Seminar of Jacques Lacan, Book III, 1955–1956* (London, 1993: R. Grigg (trans.)), pp. 92–3.

28 Sarup, *Lacan*, p. 66.

29 Lacan, *Écrits*, p. 86.

30 H. K. Bhabha, *The Location of Culture* (London, 1994), p. 77.

31 M. Bowie, *Lacan* (London, 1991), p. 99.

32 Bowie, *Lacan*, p. 25.

33 Ibid., p. 92.

34 This term is a coinage drawing on Jacques Derrida's notion of logocentrism as an epistemology centred on a particular notion of language and reason. It attempts to give expression to a notion of identity that is focused in the centrality of very specific view of place.

35 Bhabha cites *The Compact Edition of the Oxford English Dictionary* for this definition. Bhabha, *Location of Culture*, pp. 94–5.

36 M. Bracher, *Lacan, Discourse and Social Change: A Psychoanalytic Cultural Criticism* (Ithaca, 1993), p. 24.

37 B. O'Brien, *The Long War: The IRA and Sinn Féin from Armed Struggle to Peace Talks* (Dublin, 1993), p. 350.

38 This term refers to certain anchoring points that are necessary for meaning to be generated, and these are what Lacan terms *points de capiton*, the 'minimal number of fundamental points of insertion between the signifier and the signified for a human being to be called normal' (Lacan, *Seminar, Book III*, pp. 268–9). These points are where the 'signifier stops the otherwise endless movement of signification' (Lacan, *Écrits*, p. 303).

39 Bracher, *Lacan*, p. 20.

40 *Defence of the Nation* 1, 4 (1998).

41 In his translator's notes, Martin Thom explains the term *Zollverein* as the German term for a customs union.

42 Grosz, *Lacan*, p. 39.

43 The term 'captate' is a neologism coined by the French psychoanalysts Édouard Pichon and Odile Codet. It derives from the French verb '*capter*' and has the double sense 'capture' and 'captivate': of the image as a captivating, seductive force as well as one which is capable of capturing and imprisoning the subject in a one-dimensional line of thought or ideology.

44 Lacan, *Seminar, Book I*, p. 12.

45 O'Brien, *IRA*, p. 350.

46 J. Lacan, *The Four Fundamental Concepts of Psycho-Analysis* (Harmondsworth, 1977: A. Sheridan (trans.)), p. 154.

47 B. Anderson, *Imagined Communities: Reflections on the Origins and Spread of Nationalism* (London, 1991), p. 6.

48 G. Bennington, 'Postal politics and the institution of the nation', in H. K. Bhabha (ed.), *Nation and Narration* (London, 1990), p. 121.

49 R. Kearney, *Poetics of Imagining: Modern to Post-modern* (Edinburgh, 1998), p. 166.

50 P. Ricoeur, *The Philosophy of Paul Ricoeur* (Boston, 1973), p. 29.

51 Kearney, *Poetics of Imagining*, p. 147. I have taken this quotation from Richard Kearney's translation of 'L'imagination dans le discours et dans l'action'. I can think of no better introduction to the work of Ricoeur than Kearney's *Modern Movements in European Philosophy* (Manchester, 1994). Two of Kearney's other books, *Poetics of Modernity* (New York, 1995) and *Poetics of Imagination* contain excellent discussions of Ricoeur's work, as well as contextual placements of that work in terms of contemporary critical debate.

52 Here, I would cite the *caveat* mentioned by Benedict Anderson in the acknowledgements to *Imagined Communities* (p. ix), where he notes that his own academic training, specialisation in Southeast Asia, accounts for 'some of the book's biases and choices of examples'. My own academic specialisation is in the area of Irish Studies, so this will, similarly, account for many of my own choices of examples, as well as for some of the biases in the book.

53 Perhaps the best available biography of Pearse is *The Triumph of Failure* (Dublin, 1990) by Ruth Dudley Edwards.

54   Marianne Elliott's *Wolfe Tone: Prophet of Irish Independence* (New Haven, 1989) is an excellent biography of Tone, and the monumental *Life of Theobald Wolfe Tone*, compiled by his son William T. W. Tone, and edited by Thomas Bartlett, was reissued by Lilliput Press in 1998.

55   O'Brien, *Irish Identity*, p. 66.

56   Elliot, *Wolfe Tone*, p. 1.

57   This reference is to Saint Patrick, the patron saint of Ireland.

58   P. Pearse, *Collected Works of Padraic H. Pearse: Political Writings and Speeches*, 5 vols (Dublin, 1917–22), II, p. 58.

59   C. Cruise O'Brien, *Ancestral Voices: Religion and Nationalism in Ireland* (Dublin, 1994), p. 100.

60   Anderson, *Imagined Communities*, p. 10.

61   Ibid., p. 11.

62   The repetition of a word with varying grammatical inflections.

63   R. Debray, 'Marxism and the national question', *New Left Review*, 105 (Sept.–Oct. 1977), pp. 25–41, p. 26.

64   Dudley Edwards, *Triumph of Failure*, p. 280.

65   A. Easthope, *Poetry and Phantasy* (Cambridge, 1989), p. 11.

66   Dudley Edwards, *Triumph of Failure*, p. 281.

67   Ibid.

68   It is possible that this construction, 'through us', is a conscious or unconscious homage to the Great Doxology for the Mass Liturgy: 'through Him, with Him, in Him, in the unity of the Holy Spirit, all glory and honour is yours, Almighty Father, for ever and ever'.

69   For a comprehensive bibliography of the 1916 Rising, and issues associated with it, see Dudley Edwards, *Triumph of Failure*, pp. 363–69.

70   This exchange was recorded on BBC1 news on 12 July 1996.

71   A record of the deaths in Northern Ireland, of those of all persuasions, has been published in Malcolm Sutton's *An Index of Deaths from the Conflict in Ireland 1969–1993* (Belfast, 1994).

72   In terms of the wall murals that have become something of an art form in Northern Ireland, there is an interesting website created by Rich Hitchens at the following web address: www.webgate.net/~rh/murals.html.

CHAPTER 10

The Rhetoric of Republican Legitimacy

* * *

Brian Hanley

Throughout the past century republican leaderships embarking on a new political direction have more often than not faced the accusation that they had 'sold out' their former principles. Naturally, republicans from Richard Mulcahy to Frank Aiken and, indeed, Gerry Adams today were sensitive to these criticisms, especially when they were accused not only of being traitors but agents of British rule in Ireland.[1] Republican leaderships have responded to such accusations in a number of ways. Paradoxically, republicans have often sought to justify a gradual retreat from militarism by reasserting their military and revolutionary credentials. In tandem with this, they have also attempted to undermine the physical force records of their opponents and argued that, whether by accident or design, it was the critics of change who were aiding the enemies of republicanism and Ireland.

The situation the new Irish government faced in 1922 was obviously very different from that facing Fianna Fáil in the mid-1930s, and vastly different from that of republican leaderships in 1970 or the present day. Moreover, the rhetoric of republican legitimacy was only one element among many in very complex political situations.[2] It is also difficult to judge just how effective it was. Most discussions of this nature occurred at rank-and-file level rather than in public. Many of the arguments presented were false, confused or contradictory but might still have been quite effective. However, there are notable similarities in at least *some* of the arguments employed by republican leaderships to defeat or marginalise their opponents.

The Irish civil war was accompanied by a propaganda as well as a military struggle. The standard republican view of that conflict has been that 'the Free State did Britain's bidding and crushed anti-Treaty dissent' and, as such, represented little more than tools of British imperialism.[3] Given the barrage of propaganda portraying them as British underlings and dependent on British military aid, the Treatyites were unsurprisingly forced to stress their nationalist credentials. The National Army, claimed one Treatyite publication in 1922, stood for 'Ireland for the Irish'.[4] The Treatyites saw themselves as coming from the ranks of the ordinary people of Ireland and claimed that many of their 'most violent' opponents were the 'most Anglicised' members of the Dáil. An Ireland which had defied 'Cromwell, Orange William, Pitt and Castlereagh' was not going to be ruined by unpatriotic 'Irregulars'.[5]

The anti-Treatyite political leadership was satirised as the mythical 'Clarence Edward Biggles'. English born, with a love for abstraction and metaphysics, Biggles (who had gaelicised his name to 'Cathal de Bigleas') deplored the 'rank materialism' of the Irish people in accepting the Treaty, which would only provide them with irrelevancies such as food, shelter and education. He attributed their weakness to the influence of the 'mere Irish' such as Collins, Mulcahy and MacNeill. Instead Biggles and the 'more Irish' wanted to fight on for a perfect 'Plato's republic'.[6]

The activities of Erskine Childers were characterised as altogether more sinister: he was openly referred to as a British agent intent on the destruction of Irish property in the interests of British business interests. The aim of 'Major Erskine Childers D.S.O.' was to make Ireland a 'mangled, bankrupt wreck'.[7] The anti-Treaty IRA's cutting of transatlantic cables at Valentia on County Kerry, allegedly directed by Childers, was designed to enable the service to be transferred to Cornwall.[8] Anti-Treaty propagandists, directed by Childers, were compared to England's 'paid liars' in the war against Germany. Childers's role in the crushing of the 'gallant Boer republics' was a mainstay of Treatyite propaganda.

The destruction by the anti-Treaty IRA of roads and railways was succeeding, where 'Cromwell and Elizabeth' and the Black and Tan terror had failed, in bringing about the economic ruin of Ireland. How could de Valera allow this in his 'adopted country', asked Desmond FitzGerald, one of the most prolific Treatyite propagandists?[9] Indeed it was suggested that the 'Irregulars' would not have been able to operate without the guidance of their 'English brains'.[10] The contrast with Michael Collins, an 'utterly authentic type' of Irishman, 'untouched by any alien tradition' could not have been greater.[11]

Of course, not all anti-Treatyites were portrayed as British agents but their activities provided the excuse needed for England to reoccupy Ireland. They were 'modern McMurroughs' and the toast of the Tory 'die hard clubs' of London who revelled in the destruction of Ireland. While Collins had successfully ended the rule of 'alien' government in Ireland, the anti-Treatyites' destructive activities were paving the way for its return.[12] It was also asserted that the Royal Navy had allowed arms shipments to reach the anti-Treaty IRA in order to justify British re-intervention.[13] Unionist hardliners were said to be jubilant as reunification with the six counties was being made impossible by the anti-Treaty IRA's activities.[14] The newspaper *Truth* argued that supporting the 'Irregulars' would bring the Black and Tans back to Ireland while standing with the National Army would keep them out. [15]

While occasionally accusing their opponents of communist sympathies, the Treatyites also appealed to social justice.[16] It was noted that while '21,000 families in Dublin lived in single rooms' and the children of the 'workers' still lived in slums, at last an *Irish* government could attempt to rectify these conditions. In contrast, 'linguisters and word twisters . . . and scholastic minds' contented themselves with arguments over words while their military allies destroyed the economic life of the country, making social reform impossible.[17]

Special attention was given to emphasising that while the Free State government retained the 'Fenian Faith', their opponents were opportunists and latecomers to the national struggle.[18] For Free State propagandists there was no connection between the 'patriotic minority of 1916' and the anti-Treaty IRA.[19] The men of 1916 had been drawn from the 'cream of the Irish-Ireland movement', from Sinn Féin, the Gaelic League and the GAA, while the 'Irregulars' were described as men who belonged to the 'disappointed, discontented and demoralised' who had never taken a real part in the national movement.[20] The IRA records of the men who led the attack on the Four Courts were emphasised to rebut the accusation that they had carried out British instructions. How could men like General Tom Ennis who had been 'out' in 1916 and Brigadier Paddy O'Daly formerly of Collins's 'Squad' be fighting for Britain?[21] The argument that the best of the IRA were represented in the National Army continued to be a major theme as did the suggestion that the anti-Treaty IRA was composed of persons who 'discovered there had been a war in progress shortly after July 11 1921'.[22] The 'noisiest' anti-Treatyites were those who were 'anywhere but' at the fighting of 1919–21.[23]

A satirical sketch of an allegedly typical 'Irregular' family claimed that the father would have been a Home Ruler who had laughed at the 1916 rebels, and who never made his opinions known during 1919–21 except by refusing to donate to Sinn Féin collections or the Dáil Loan. Indeed, at one stage, the IRA had even considered shooting him for spying. Following the truce, however, he had emerged as the leading local anti-Treaty diehard. His sons had become 'trucileers' and had made considerable sums of money through robbery and carving up neighbours' land.[24] The suggestion that much of the anti-Treaty IRA was composed of criminals was also used to explain their lack of fighting ability. They were characterised as either young inexperienced adventurers, who joined up with the promise of risk-free excitement or the possibility of meeting a 'pretty' Cumann na mBan girl, or more malevolent freebooters who practised sniping and mine laying but would not engage National Army troops in combat.[25] One writer complained in August 1922 that a 'lot of sob stuff' was being written about 'brother fighting brother.' Nothing of the sort was happening because while the National Army contained many with War of Independence records, few such men were 'Irregulars'.[26] One Treatyite writer even claimed that of 10,000 or so Irregulars fewer than 200 had actually fought the British.[27]

A list of anonymous anti-Treaty IRA men claimed that one commandant had been a railwayman who had refused to assist the IRA during the independence struggle while another was a student who had refused to hide arms for the IRA in 1920.[28] When two National Army officers were killed in July 1922 at Portlaoise, their War of Independence service was noted in contrast to that of the leader of the anti-Treaty forces who attacked them. It was alleged that he was a former British soldier who had been part of the guard on General Joe McGrath in Arbour Hill during 1920. At their funeral McGrath himself noted how two men who had fought for Ireland, had met their deaths at the 'hands of men who, when the fight with England was on, were not in the "Bearna Baoghal"'.[29] Tom Barry's past as a member of an ex-serviceman's organisation in Cork was similarly publicised.[30] When anti-Treaty leader Liam Deasy called for a truce in early 1923 it was noted that he had sounder instincts than many of his fellows because of his genuine record of service. [31]

Whenever possible the revolutionary credentials of leading anti-Treatyites were also questioned. Seán MacEntee was accused of informing his 1916 court martial that he had not known that he was taking part in a rebellion. It was noted also that he had expressed a desire to join the 16th Irish Division as an officer.[32] Paddy Ruttledge had allegedly praised Daniel O'Connell and the constitutional tradition as well as the British Empire at a solicitors' debating club some months after the Rising, while real republicans 'lay dead or in jail'.[33] However, anti-Treaty leaders were generally condemned for being inciters who left the fighting to their duped followers – as the 'fight to a finish people were never found on ramparts or in trenches'.[34] In this regard it was noted that as fighting raged in Dublin's O'Connell street, Robert Barton had been arrested while smoking cigars at Erskine Childers's home.[35]

The efficacy of this type of propaganda is difficult to judge but pro-Treaty propagandists were clearly anxious to present themselves as the authentic representatives of militant Irish nationalism. Elements of this would surface again, most dramatically in the heyday of the Blueshirt movement when Ernest Blythe hailed them as the successors of the men of 1916.[36] Of course, direct links did exist for this claim, as illustrated by the case of a Clare Blueshirt wanted in 1934 for the killing of a local IRA man. His father and brother had been killed by the Black and Tans in 1920 and his brother died in National Army service in 1922.[37]

II

The question of revolutionary legitimacy also concerned the Fianna Fáil party in power, particularly from 1934 to 1936 when confrontation erupted between the government and the IRA. Until then the party had maintained a complex and often uneasy relationship with the IRA. In the general elections of 1932 and 1933 the organisation had actively supported Fianna Fáil although there had been no formal alliance.[38] Contrary to perception, the IRA did not seize the opportunity of Fianna Fáil's accession to power to run amok but actually sought to restrain its followers while it awaited the outcome of Fianna Fáil's constitutional programme.[39] However, by late 1933 the emergence of the Blueshirts and increasing frustration among the IRA's membership brought it more and more into conflict with the state, a fact reflected in the numbers of IRA men being tried by Military Tribunal and the censorship of the organisation's newspaper, *An Phoblacht*.[40] By 1935 the IRA considered that there was no longer any difference between 'the new Free Staters and the old'.[41]

The problem for Fianna Fáil was that large elements of its rank and file remained susceptible to IRA calls for support, particularly on the prisoners' issue. Between late 1933 and 1935 numerous cumainn passed resolutions demanding political status for IRA prisoners in Arbour Hill and an end to the use of military courts.[42] A key battleground was Kerry, where despite IRA violence directed against supporters of their own party, Fianna Fáil members of Tralee Urban District Council and even TDs forwarded motions calling for inquiries into the treatment of IRA detainees.[43] The arguments used by Fianna Fáil to assert their right to republican legitimacy are remarkably similar in some ways, to those of the Treatyites a decade earlier. De Valera explained to a Kerry audience that the 'long pitiful list' of events in their county had only 'given courage to the enemies of our nation'. The critics of Irish republicanism abroad had said that a republican government would not be able to govern: were they not being proven correct by the activities of the IRA?[44] Frank Aiken alleged to a Fianna Fáil councillor in Tralee that the IRA's campaign against the Volunteer Reserve of the National Army was 'deliberately trying to prevent the Government from building up the National defences'.[45] The *Irish Press* noted how every IRA action was 'greeted eagerly by Ireland's enemies'.[46] In 1935 Fianna Fáil's County Kerry Executive noted that when the government had faced grave threats from Britain and from its right (the Blueshirts), the IRA had shamefully tried to undermine it from the left.[47] Seán MacEntee claimed that the IRA's 'bottle smashing' during the Boycott Bass campaign had almost goaded the British into putting extra tariffs on Irish beer.[48] However unwittingly, the IRA was weakening rather than strengthening republican Ireland.

Just as Treatyites had contrasted their military credentials to those of their enemies, Fianna Fáil reminded republicans that 'nearly all' its leadership possessed 1916 records.[49] From 1933 Fianna Fáil began to refer to the 'new IRA' which was sheltering behind the 'honoured name' of the older organisation.[50] In 1934 the *Irish Press* stated that in neither 'personnel' nor 'control' was the IRA of 1934 the same organisation as it had been between 1919 and 1923. Instead it had become a 'private army'. Condemning the IRA's intervention during the 1935 Dublin transport strike, de Valera claimed that the old IRA had been an 'army of the nation . . . of the whole people' while the new IRA were the instigators of 'sectional strife' who lent themselves out like some 'racketeering organisation'.[51] He warned youngsters not to be seduced by the 'glamour' attached to the IRA's name. [52] The youth and inexperience of the majority of IRA members became a potent weapon for Fianna Fáil. In Kerry it was noted that the party contained a much higher percentage of civil war veterans than the IRA. [53] Confronted by IRA supporters in Galway in 1936, Seán MacEntee reminded them that he had faced a death sentence when they were not 'even in the cradle'.[54]

Neither were those IRA leaders with military records spared. Jeered by IRA supporters shouting 'Up Tom Barry', Frank Aiken replied that while he and others had been fighting the Free Staters, Barry had been 'running around trying to make peace'.[55] Barry was also confronted with the accusation that he had wanted to disarm the IRA at the end of the civil war.[56] From 1933 Fianna Fáil organised its own Wolfe Tone commemoration at Bodenstown and in 1935 launched an 'Easter Torch – the symbol of a resurgent nation' to enable its supporters to 'honour the men of 1916' without contributing to the IRA through purchasing Easter lilies.[57] After reminding them of his participation in the 1916 Rising, the Black and Tan war and the civil war, MacEntee pointedly asked young IRA hecklers in Galway, 'can you tell me where you served?'[58] De Valera answered accusations that IRA prisoners were being ill treated by reminding a rally in Tralee that he knew that prison 'was never easy' because he 'had been there'. Moreover, both he and Kerry republican Austin Stack had endured far worse conditions in 1919 but 'we didn't grumble about it'.[59]

It would be ridiculous to claim that such rhetoric led to Fianna Fáil's victory over the IRA. The success of the party in broadening its own constituency, while satisfying at least some of the political and economic demands of its supporters, and the IRA's own counterproductive tactics are more important. But the effect of such rhetoric on those influenced by militarism should not be underestimated. Soon after de Valera came to power, the IRA's intelligence reports noted how elements within Fianna Fáil were spreading rumours that the IRA Army Council were a 'cowardly pack' who had shirked confrontation with the Cosgrave government.[60] Tom Hales TD told Cork farmers that while the old IRA had been a 'fine' organisation the current leadership were a 'harebrained lot'.[61] These attacks were undoubtedly repeated at cumann meetings and social gatherings across the Free State, reassuring Fianna Fáil members that they represented the truly republican force and helping them overcome what Seán Moylan called their 'inferiority complex' in the face of IRA criticism. Indeed at the IRA's General Army Convention in 1934 a leading republican, Mick Fitzpatrick, admitted that Fianna Fáil's claims that his organisation was not 'the army that fought the Black and Tans' were having some impact on republican support.[62]

III

The split in the republican movement during 1969–70 clearly occurred in very different circumstances from those of 1922. It involved much smaller numbers of people and was centred on issues both esoteric and obscure (recognition of the southern parliament and the ending of absententionism) against a background of rapidly escalating violence in Northern Ireland. However, those seeking a new direction (who eventually became the Officials) again found themselves not merely accused of betraying republican principles but also of abandoning the nationalist population of Belfast to pogroms. While the Officials would eventually publicly disavow armed violence, in 1970 they still claimed a role for a revolutionary army and sought not to lose ground to their aggressive new rival, the Provisional IRA.

In 1970 some reappraisal was undoubtedly taking place within the republican movement as a result of the last major armed campaign of the IRA, but the Officials could still claim that the 1957–62 border campaign had been 'well conceived, well organised and capably executed'.[63] There can be little doubt that the records of Cathal Goulding, Seán Garland, Seamus Costello, Eamon Smullen and others were used to point to the sound military background of the Official leadership. Moreover, the Officials rejected the claims that they had been found wanting in August 1969 as 'slanders' propagated by 'consistent enemies of republicanism' in the Irish and British establishments.[64] Without the IRA 'even more death and destruction' in Belfast would have occurred.[65] In contrast, the Officials alleged those now forming the Provisionals had 'refused to assist or help' the IRA during events of August 1969.[66] The new Provisional organisation in Belfast was described as the creation of 'ex-republicans' who had been out of the movement and inactive for many years, while some 80 per cent of the Belfast IRA had remained loyal to its Official leadership.[67]

As conflict between republicans and the British Army escalated during 1970 the Officials proudly claimed that their 'well trained and disciplined' volunteers were playing a major role in confronting the British Army, which they contrasted sharply with the Provisional's 'sectarian and destructive' bombing campaign. Were it not for the Official IRA, they claimed, 'the British Army would have run amok throughout Belfast'.[68] The Falls Road curfew of July 1970, a major turning point in the relationship between nationalists and the British Army, was depicted in heroic terms by the Officials. They claimed that their members had inflicted at least 18 casualties on British troops in the 'biggest military engagement between the IRA and Crown Forces since 1916'.[69] While their volunteers had fought to a standstill, the 'Provisional Alliance' had deliberately kept its members out of 'this historic battle'.[70] The introduction of internment in August 1971 saw at least 25 people killed across the north in three days of savage violence. The Officials again claimed that their members had borne the brunt of the fighting. While some Provisional leaders were 'found wanting' and 'deserted even their own men' the 'Army of the People' managed to kill at least six soldiers, with no losses of their own.[71] Its finest hour came in the 'Battle of the Markets' on 9 August when local Officials under Joe McCann engaged in a huge gun battle with far superior numbers of British troops. The image of McCann, M1 carbine in hand, silhouetted in the flames underneath a Starry Plough flag remained an iconic part of Official propaganda for many years after the armed struggle was abandoned.[72]

In retrospect, the bombing of the Parachute Regiment's base at Aldershot in February 1972, which resulted in the deaths of six civilians, can be seen as Official militarism's swan song. At the time, however, there was no public disavowal of the attack. It was claimed that at least twelve Parachute Regiment officers had been killed and their deaths covered up by the military establishment. The bravery and ingenuity of the Official volunteers who planted the bomb were praised and it was suggested that the British military elite would think twice about future Bloody Sundays now that there had been retaliation. The contrast between an attack on the British military and the Provo's 'sectarian' bombing campaign in Belfast was also noted.[73] The Officials declared a ceasefire in May 1972 (although attacks on British soldiers continued into 1975, as did other armed activities) but the myth of a clean, effective, non-sectarian military campaign remained part of the Official's self-image for many years.

As they vied for dominance with the Provisionals between 1970 and 1972, the Officials also questioned the agenda behind their rivals' tactics. The Provisionals were depicted as the creation of Fianna Fáil and southern businessmen who sought to undermine the leftward shift within the republican movement.[74] Later these elements were accused of pushing the Provisionals towards fomenting a civil war (which was in interests of the British and Irish establishments as it would eradicate any hope of revolutionary possibilities). With stability eventually restored, the country would then be brought into the greatest Official nightmare of the time, the European Economic Community.[75] There all elements within the 'Free State' would continue to 'lick the boots' of their 'British masters'.[76] Hence even the Provisionals, albeit in a very convoluted fashion, were doing Britain's bidding.

The attempts by the Treatyites to establish a state under conditions of civil war, Fianna Fáil's bid to establish itself in power and a section of the post-1969 republican movement's shift away from militarism are in many respects very different processes. However, it seems clear that in the battle to retain republican credentials – even when embarking on a path away from militarism – the glorification of your own past endeavours, the suggestion that your opponents have little or no 'active service' record, and that their opposition will play into the hands of the enemies of the republic has always played some part in the rhetoric of republican politics. In this regard Gerry Adams's dismissal of republican critics as 'ceasefire soldiers', and suggestion that British 'securocrats' are involved in facilitating dissident bombings and encouraging republican splinter groups have an all too familiar ring.[77]

Notes

1 *Saoirse* (RSF), July 2000; *The Sovereign Nation* (32 CSM), June 2000.

2 For various explanations see T. Garvin, *1922 The Birth of Irish Democracy* (Dublin, 1996); B. Kissane, *Explaining Irish Democracy* (Dublin, 2002) and J. M. Regan, *The Irish Counter Revolution, 1922–1936* (Dublin, 1999).

3 *An Phoblacht*, 21 Oct. 1999.

4 *Truth*, 22 Aug. 1922.

5 *Free State*, 4 Mar. 1922; *Eire Og*, 2 Sept. 1922.

6 Ibid., 18 Mar. 1922.

7 'The Sinister Activities of Major Erskine Childers D.S.O.' (University College Dublin Archives (UCDA), FitzGerald papers, P80/307 (1–2)).

8 *Free State*, 8 July 1922. See *Limerick War News*, 11 Aug. 1922, for a photograph of Childers in British Army uniform (Limerick City Museum).

9 'Ireland's Opportunity' (UCDA, FitzGerald papers, P80/318 (6)).

10 *Free State*, 12 Aug. 1922.

11 Ibid., 2 Sept. 1922.

12 Ibid., 19 Aug. 1922; *Limerick War News*, 11 Aug. 1922.

13 'A painful necessity' (UCDA, FitzGerald papers, P80/318 (3)).

14 'What might have been' (UCDA, FitzGerald papers, P80/320 (1)).

15 *Truth*, 5 July 1922.

16 *Eire Og*, 2 Sept. 1922.

17 'The cost' and 'The return to normality' (UCDA, FitzGerald papers, P80/318 (1) & (4)).

18 *Free State*, 18 Mar. 1922.

19 'A painful necessity'.

20 *Free State*, 29 July 1922.

21 *Truth,* 5 July 1922.

22 *Free State,* 25 Mar. 1922.

23 Ibid., 5 Aug. 1922.

24 Ibid., 4 Nov. 1922.

25 Ibid., 13 Aug. 1922.

26 Ibid., 5 Aug. 1922.

27 Ibid., 28 Oct. 1922.

28 Ibid., 5 Aug. 1922.

29 'The ambushers' (UCDA, FitzGerald papers, P80/315).

30 *Free State,* 5 Aug. 1922.

31 'The return to normality'.

32 'The court martial of Sean MacEntee' (UCDA, FitzGerald papers, P80/327 (1)). Both allegations against MacEntee were accurate. See Declan Kiberd (ed.) *1916 Rebellion Handbook* (Dublin, 1998), pp. 117–18.

33 'Ruttledge and the Empire' (UCDA, FitzGerald papers, P80/318 (9)).

34 'Republican leaders efforts to end the struggle' (UCDA, FitzGerald papers, P80/317 (1)).

35 UCDA, FitzGerald papers, P80/298 (22).

36 *Irish Press,* 19 Nov. 1934.

37 *Clare Champion,* 29 Sept. 1934.

38 IRA Army Council to Clan na Gael, 7 May 1932 (UCDA, Twomey papers, P69/185 (298–302)); *An Phoblacht,* 14 Jan. 1933.

39 B. Hanley, *The IRA, 1926–1936* (Dublin, 2002), pp. 126–39.

40 'Departmental notes on events, 1931–1940' (UCDA, MacEntee papers, P67/534, pp. 17–21).

41 *Kerry Champion,* 16 Feb. 1935.

42 See, for example, the motion from South East Cork comhairle ceanntair, Fianna Fáil, Oct. 1933 (National Archives (NA), Department of Justice H306/31) and motions from Tipperary cumann, Jan. 1935 (UCDA, Aiken papers, P104/2801 (85–103)).

43 Tralee UDC to Department of Justice, 10 Jan 1935 (UCDA, Aiken papers, P104/2801 (100)) and motions forwarded by Tom McEllistrim, Eamon Kissane and Denis Daly, Feb. 1935 (UCDA, Aiken papers, P104/2801 (77–83)).

44 *Kerry Champion,* 23 Dec. 1933.

45 Aiken to D. Curran, 10 Jan. 1935 (UCDA, Aiken papers, P104/2801 (113)).

46 *Irish Press,* 5 Apr. 1935.

47 *Kerry Champion,* 23 Feb. 1935.

48 *Irish Press,* 22 June 1936.

49 Ibid., 6 Apr. 1935.

50 *Kerry Champion,* 26 Jan. 1935.

51 *Irish Press,* 8 Feb. 1934; de Valera to National Executive of Fianna Fáil, 28 March 1935 (NA, Department of Taoiseach S7495).

52 Eamon de Valera, *National Discipline and Majority Rule* (Dublin, 1936) p. 11.

53 *Kerry Champion,* 9 Feb. 1935.

54 *Northern Standard,* 27 July 1936.

55 *Irish Independent*, 4 June 1935.

56 Barry initially left the IRA following its rejection of his proposals to destroy its arms at the conclusion of the civil war. Report, 9 Aug. 1924 (UCDA, Twomey papers, P69/179 (126–9)). Copies of the Aiken/Barry debates from 1935 are contained in UCDA, Aiken papers, P104/1283 (1–5).

57 *Irish Independent*, 5 Dec. 1935. Although Fianna Fáil won the political battle with the IRA its 'Torch' never replaced the Easter Lily as a republican symbol.

58 *Irish Press*, 22 June 1936.

59 *Kerry Champion*, 23 Dec. 1933.

60 IRA intelligence report, 28 July 1932 (UCDA, Twomey papers, P69/199 (102)).

61 Tom Barry to Moss Twomey, 3 Apr. 1933 (UCDA, Twomey papers, P69/53 (212)).

62 *Irish Press*, 9 Nov. 1933; 'Notes of 1934 General Army Convention' (UCDA, MacEntee papers, P67/525).

63 *United Irishman*, Jan. 1970.

64 IRA Easter statement, *United Irishman*, Apr. 1970.

65 *United Irishman*, Dec. 1970.

66 Ibid., June 1971.

67 Ibid., July 1970.

68 Ibid., Oct. 1971.

69 Ibid., Aug. 1970.

70 Ibid., July 1971.

71 Ibid., Sept., Oct. 1971.

72 The photograph appeared on the cover of *United Irishman* in September 1971. For many years it was a popular poster among Official republicans. See Jack Holland and Henry McDonald, *INLA: Deadly Divisions* (Dublin, 1994), pp. 10–15, 29. McCann was shot dead by British troops in 1972. See D. McKittrick, S. Kelters, B. Feeney and C. Thornton, *Lost Lives* (Edinburgh, 1999), pp. 175–6.

73 *United Irishman*, Mar. 1972.

74 Anonymous, *Fianna Fáil and the IRA* (Dublin, n.d.); *Fianna Fáil: The IRA Connection* (Dublin, n.d.). For contemporary support for that analysis see R. Sweetman, *On Our Knees: Ireland, 1972* (Dublin, 1972) pp. 138–9, 149, 202–3.

75 *United Irishman*, June 1972

76 Ibid., Oct. 1971.

77 *An Phoblacht*, 19 Feb. 1998; Danny Morrison, 'The dirty war', *Andersontown News*, 16 Dec. 2001.

CHAPTER 11

Provisional Republicanism

Internal Politics, Inequities and Modes of Repression

* * *

Anthony McIntyre

'Among those who dislike oppression are many who like to oppress.'
Napoleon I

THE PEACE PROCESS IS WATCHING YOU

In most cases, studies of Provisional republicanism have been guided by a desire to understand strategy, dynamics, personalities or ideology. This is also true for those accounts where the focus is largely on its internal workings. Seemingly absent from the relevant body of literature is any substantive appraisal of the internal repressive measures that Provisional republicanism has exercised in order to maintain discipline and leadership dominance. References to the deaths of informers notwithstanding, there have been many other mechanisms of control applied to members or supporters who, for one reason or another, have stepped out of line on issues unrelated to breaches of military security. In recent years these have been most pronounced in the area of policing dissent.

Mechanisms employed in the earlier years of the conflict included suspension from active IRA service; alcohol bans; locking Volunteers in the cupboard below the stairs in someone's home; having Volunteers scrub a back yard with a toothbrush;[1] or dropping Volunteers many miles from home with a large signed stone or breeze block and ordering them to walk back to their local unit carrying the weighty object.[2] These were mundane punishments for trivial offences. But more ominously, as the 'long war' kicked in, a sterner approach was employed against those who were perceived to have the potential to threaten the authority of the leadership in a more structured manner. Ruairí Ó Brádaigh (president of Sinn Féin between 1970 and 1983) and some of his key allies were told in 1986 that they would be executed if they considered forming a military alternative to the Provisional IRA.[3] A year earlier the former chief of staff, Ivor Bell, and his colleagues were told likewise.[4]

Despite the Good Friday Agreement (GFA), and contrary to the frequent assertions that IRA guns are silent, that the ceasefire has not been breached, and that the IRA poses no threat to the peace process, these repressive mechanisms of control have not disappeared. In one case, Real IRA member Joseph O'Connor was assassinated in West Belfast by the Provisional IRA in what I felt was a bid to ensure that sufficient hostility existed between both IRAs, so that in the event of the decommissioning of Provisional IRA weaponry or acceptance by the Provisionals of the Police Service of Northern Ireland, no significant crossover from the Provisional IRA to the Real IRA would occur if resignations took place.[5]

The range of internal policing activity which the IRA has engaged in over the years has generated sufficient subject matter to form the basis of a PhD. But this chapter, utilising both written material and interviews with former IRA Volunteers, ex-internees and ex-prisoners, will restrict itself to flagging an area of republicanism that has been considerably under-researched. There is work that touches on the IRA's policing of its own community; for example the compilation edited by Liam Kennedy on crime and punishment in West Belfast.[6] However, 'community policing' – including expulsion, kneecapping, punishment attacks and, to a lesser extent, killings – has resulted for the most part from community pressure rather than any desire on the part of the IRA leadership to 'shoot or beat hoods'. The focus here is more specific, dealing only with the body of active republicans that make up the movement either through membership or close affiliation to the IRA and Sinn Féin, and who are policed by the leadership, not as a result of community pressure, but out of a perceived need to maintain its own dominance through internal control and the suppression of dissent. Like other bureaucratic organisations, the structure of Provisionalism cannot function 'without the routinised exercise of structural power'.[7]

Because we inhabit an environment where the 'Peace Process is watching you' from some Bentham-type panoptican interminably seeking out those the journalist Jack Holland terms 'enemies of the peace process' and others 'not helpful to the peace process', there seems to be a reluctance amongst those whose responsibility it is not to be reluctant to pose the awkward question or arrive at the unpopular conclusion.[8] Speaking on New York's Radio Free Éireann, Ed Moloney was recently scathing of this type of presentation, pointing out that one journalist actually referred to some of his colleagues as JAPPs – Journalists Against the Peace Process.[9] Jane Gow, the widow of IRA assassination victim Ian Gow, has also noted that 'any criticism of the peace process has become a form of blasphemy'.[10]

The peace process has developed into such a powerful and invasive discursive formation, with its own regime of truth, that those supposedly from competing ideological perspectives find little difficulty in miming from the one discursive hymn sheet when violations of peace take place.[11] Media, politicians, governments and security agencies all to varying degrees become silent subjects in the application of the technology of control – a discursive practice embedded in the peace process. For this reason, the subject under scrutiny here will be regarded in certain established quarters as one to be tiptoed around with plenty of 'creative fudge' and reams of 'constructive ambiguity'. In these domains the prevalent view may amount to: 'why should "responsible" people care if the "irresponsible" are policed by the increasingly "responsible" republican movement?' Consequently, there seems to be an institutional cataract that allows officialdom to avoid seeing IRA activity below its very nose if the matters are restricted to what is euphemistically described as 'housekeeping'. Hence, I recently felt prompted to write an article titled 'Bertie Talking Bollix' having read the Taoiseach Bertie Ahern's comment that when the IRA say something they are generally to be believed given their record for honesty.[12] Apparently, one of Kevin Myers's observations is held with revered esteem by the Irish Taoiseach: 'facts, and even abundant literature, will not obstruct the power of myth when it is politically endorsed'.[13]

A more critical engagement with the subject matter might show that while conceptually and discursively there is a wide gap separating those termed 'oppressed' from those called 'oppressor', the actual mechanisms of internal control wielded within the ranks of the 'oppressed' suggest that the gap is in practice not so great. In a sense this may amount to nothing more than a reaffirmation of the anarchist belief that quite often the methods that revolutionaries claim to be fighting against are those they themselves employ to maintain internal dominance: a case of 'why vote – sure, the government always gets in?' While such a suggestion is not a recommendation for conservative approaches to an existing political or social malaise, it does allow us to think that the more we behave like those we fought to replace, the less we were ever justified in fighting them to begin with. Institutional power seems so insidious, and resistance to it so porous, that the former even moulds many of those who ostensibly oppose it into its own image. Patsy McGarry has a point in claiming that 'totalitarianism breeds its mirror-image in opponents'.[14]

Irish republicanism is hardly unique among political ideologies by internally employing the methods of repression that it ostensibly protests against externally. As Justin O'Brien observed:

> South Africa may have required truth but it was a politically self-serving truth designed to smooth the transfer from one elite to another, placing the blame for communal violence on the past regime and minimising the scale of the abuse that

undoubtedly occurred within the black community itself . . . Truth and justice are conditioned by political realities.[15]

Likewise, Robert Fisk could write of Palestinian leader Yasser Arafat:

I always regarded him during his time in Lebanon as being a very cynical and a very despotic man. Even before he got a chance to run his own state, he was running 13 different secret police forces. Torture was employed in his police station.[16]

Even Robert Mugabe, before he stopped listening to himself, warned that 'our majority rule . . . could easily turn into inhuman rule if we oppressed, persecuted or harassed those of us who do not look or think like the majority of us'.[17] These are but three examples from a mere glance at newspapers. A modicum of serious research would reveal the phenomenon to be considerably wider.

A PERSONAL ACCOUNT

The idea for this paper developed much less as a result of any academic interest than as a consequence of personal experience. Relating such experience is perhaps not the established way of engaging in an academic pursuit. However, I tend to see myself as neither established nor academic, but rather as a dissident Provisional republican with, among other things, a certain if not absorbing interest in academia. Nevertheless, if academia is serious about broadening the parameters of existing knowledge, it can ill afford to be epistemologically haughty or chauvinistic about knowledge that is not 'academically' produced. Leaving aside its somewhat self-serving function who, for example, would dispute the value of the book on the IRA by the now deceased Eamonn Collins based on his personal involvement in the organisation?[18] In the pursuit of knowledge it is worth risking the charge of 'journalism' levelled at Gitta Sereny for academic work that is written in the first person.[19]

That said, however, I do not intend to restrict myself to personal experience and shall call on it insofar as it may serve to convey to the readership the nature of events that can lead to a certain fundamental rupturing of an outlook leading to a radical reappraisal of the nature of republicanism and the purpose of its armed campaign without 'going over to the other side' as has seemingly been the case with Vincent McKenna before he went under lock and key. Such reappraisal is not motivated by 'academic' ambitions, as it has put me in a position considerably at odds with the authoritarian forces that hegemonise Provisional republicanism.

Shortly after my release from prison I submitted a paper for a conference organised by the Irish Political Studies Association. It quickly brought me into conflict with my old comrades in the republican movement. Within days I found myself in Connolly House being carpeted by the Sinn Féin leadership. The outcome amounted to an edict being directed my way: I could neither deliver academic papers nor teach anything at university which contravened party policy. Shades of Stalinism. Was I to bring *An Phoblacht/Republican News* to Queen's University to teach the students? I refrained from asking at Connolly House in case it was considered a good idea.

And so began a prolonged period of public and private conflict with the dominant forces within republicanism which has lasted to this day. My experience in Connolly House was to be repeated on numerous occasions over the years. By way of example, in March 1996 I had barely sat down at home after delivering a paper on the peace process in London when a senior leadership figure called to admonish me with the advice: 'you cannot question the leadership in public'. When Sinn Féin did not arrive to read out the riot act, the visitation came in the form of the IRA. I was initially reminded that I was a member of 'the Republican Movement' and would be subject to party discipline. Unlike those de Tocqueville referred to, I was more afraid of accepting what I knew to be wrong than I was of facing isolation. The leadership's reminders fell on deaf ears.

Upon leaving the movement after it settled for the Good Friday Agreement, any further appeals to allegiance the leadership felt I might have owed it based on my membership were rendered null and void. In a period of five years I had travelled from a position of receiving what *The Irish Times* described as the loudest applause of the day at an internal Sinn Féin conference in Dublin's Royal Dublin Society – having made an address which was highly critical of the leadership's strategy – to a position of extreme marginalisation.[20] I found myself subjected to intimidation, being shunned, ostracised, marginalised, demonised, assaulted, my house picketed, my pregnant partner threatened, visited in my home by leadership figures in the IRA doubling up as thought police, and at one point written about by Mr Adams, whose nose was as long as his pen by the time he had completed his article, in an American newspaper.[21] Small wonder that I should wax ironical while reading Danny Morrison's reflections on the recent 'dirty' election campaign waged by the establishment parties against Sinn Féin in the Republic in which he referred to 'the black propaganda, the slurs cast, the moral blackmailing, the lies and scaremongering'. I surmised that it was a cap that would easily fit the head of Sinn Féin.[22]

To paraphrase a Leonard Cohen song, it had all come 'a long way down'. What previous delusions I had about a Chinese wall separating a radical grassroots party from a conservative leadership intent on monopolising power were shattered. Both leadership and led were prepared to sit atop that wall and kick anybody off it who threatened the power structure. The republican movement was replete with what the anthropologist Gayle Ruben identified elsewhere as characterising sexuality: 'internal politics, inequities, and modes of oppression'.[23]

The anomaly was that the IRA was now on ceasefire. It was supposedly a new era in which the army and its strict centralised discipline could have been expected to take a back seat and allow republicanism to become more democratic by pushing the party to the front. As John Bruton argued in 1999: 'war requires such strong controls. Peace means giving up power and allowing people freedom.'[24] Indeed, the former hunger-striker Lawrence McKeown stated at a local Sinn Féin meeting shortly after the 1994 ceasefire that the problem with the peace process was that republicans possessed only a structure that was capable of fighting the war and were devoid of one that could strategise for peace.[25] There seemed no reason why all the clandestine activity, tight secrecy and whispering in dark corners should not be replaced with a culture of open discussion where the free flow of ideas rather than clipped militaristic commands would become the norm.

In practice it was not to be. One serious attempt to promote discussion in a post-ceasefire atmosphere was quickly closed down by the leadership. The Bobby Sands Discussion Group was sabotaged and those of its members who were IRA volunteers or Sinn Féin activists were prohibited from speaking publicly in a manner which might cause people to think something the leadership did not want them to think. At what were termed 'republican family' gatherings, those at the heart of republicanism – army Volunteers and party activists – were prohibited from asking questions that might trouble the leadership or cause others to think that republican leaders did not always speak *ex cathedra*. Army Volunteers and party activists were reminded that they had alternative forums where they could raise their views.

The IRA definitely had not gone away. Rather, the party was to be ruled with the ethos of the army. Small wonder that the journalist Anne Cadwallader, by no means hostile to Sinn Féin, continues to describe the party as 'the political wing of the Irish Republican Army'.[26] As Minette Marrin observed: 'it is quite impossible to run an army without hierarchy and the authority of hierarchy . . . civilian ideals of equality and full democratic rights have no place in the Army'.[27] In what at first glance appeared a strange quirk, the army was to become the extension of Sinn Féin policy. But rather than republicanism democratising itself, the IRA has remained as much internally – as externally – what Fergal Keane terms 'an anti-democratic, ultra-nationalist militia'.[28] Those in charge of the army who thought in terms of a predominantly Sinn Féin future would manipulate the situation to their advantage by promulgating the line that if Sinn Féin policy were challenged, those responsible were being disloyal to the army. Given the existence of a culture that had for years viewed Sinn Féin as wasters – a hiding place for those who wanted to be republicans without the baggage of suffering that went with being members of the IRA – it was easier to mobilise support and manufacture consent, not to mention bias, if the request was seen to emanate from the army rather than the party.

REPRESSION OF REPUBLICAN PRISONERS

Standard accounts of the IRA tend not to deal with the above. The best of the 'testimony of the touts' – such as the accounts by Sean O'Callaghan and Eamonn Collins – which might reasonably be expected to deal with internal matters, refer to instances of informers being killed by the IRA but do not purposefully address other internal policing methods.[29] While two recent works – one by Lawrence McKeown and the other co-authored by Ruth Jamieson and Adrian Grounds – give a feel for internal repression (albeit restricted to the prisons) the issues raised function as mere still shots in what is a considerably wider and more fluid arena.[30]

Throughout its history the IRA has engaged in authoritarian methods of internal control. As noted above, the question of how informers are dealt with is public knowledge. Like other control mechanisms utilised by the Provisionals, the execution of informers has always been intended to deter others as much as to punish the unfortunate victim. For this reason there has long been wonderment in some IRA quarters at the Belfast Brigade's policy of 'disappearing' alleged informers in the early 1970s. Disposal and denial were hardly a visible deterrent. Although the present Taoiseach may not agree, the disappearance of the truth has long been a malaise afflicting the IRA. This has become so pronounced within both the IRA and Sinn Féin in recent years that it is credible to claim that, at one level, republicanism under its present leadership functions as a corporate lie.

A disappearing truth, less widely known than that of the actual dis-appeared, is that in spite of its much vaunted respect for its members or supporters who happen to be prisoners, the organisation has at times behaved with a ruthlessness that most in the republican community would contend was the exclusive property of their enemies. Small wonder that the then republican prisoner and INLA member, Willie Gallagher, could comment on the republican H-Blocks in 1992 that 'the place is full of bastards and the screws are nearly as bad'.[31] Chris Ryder in his work on the Maze Prison refers to the death during internment of Patrick Crawford in June 1973.[32] Ryder quotes then republican internee Phil McCullough as saying there was a weekly Sunday republican parade after which:

The body of young Pat Crawford was found hanging from one of the huts. The emotion felt by one and all was undescribale [*sic*]. The tension was so thick one could almost see it. As Pat's body was carried out on a stretcher and placed into the grey prison wagon we all once more formed up and came to attention as a final mark of respect for a comrade.[33]

The following day the IRA's Belfast Brigade released a statement warning the prison service that if brutality against prisoners was not halted 'male and female prison officers in Northern Ireland would now be regarded as legitimate targets'.[34] Whatever the prison service were involved in at the time, there was no change in their behaviour. Yet the first prison officer to die did not meet his fate until April 1976 and then not at the hands of the Belfast Brigade. His killing was related to the wider question of the denial of political status rather than brutality within the prisons.[35]

The IRA did not act against prison staff in 1973 because the organisation, despite its statement in the wake of the Crawford death, did not hold the prison service responsible. According to two former IRA Volunteers with knowledge of the affair, Patrick Crawford was killed by his fellow internees after the Belfast Brigade sent a directive into the prison. The regular Sunday parade served to clear the hut where Patrick Crawford died of any potential witnesses. This particular sanction, however, remained the exception rather than the rule, occurring only once and occupying a lonely space at the extreme end of the continuum.[36]

Throughout internment, ostracism was an effective weapon applied in every cage against those who broke the code of conduct. In one case

Most in the camp disagreed with it. But it was organised by the camp staff. The situation was despicable. The guy was not allowed to speak with us and we were not allowed to speak to him. He lived his life day by day cocooned within his own silent little world. Due to the lack of space there was nowhere for him to go so he could not avoid us. He slept beside us, ate beside us but was never permitted to be part of us. It was really horrendous for him. Such was the extent of this ostracism policy that the camp leadership deemed it necessary to use a full cage – the infamous Cage 8 – to house all those who were ostracised. We were not allowed to even acknowledge them when we saw them on visits. And the stigma attached to anyone in that cage was akin to an informer.[37]

Other instances of brutality against prisoners included what one former IRA Volunteer termed 'Japanese style torture' employed by the IRA in both Crumlin Road Prison and Long Kesh in 1974 when it felt it had been extensively penetrated by the British Military Reconnaissance Force. A combination of comments by two former Volunteers convey something of what it was like during the dark days of 1974. At that time, a public image was manufactured which sought to depict a republican population united against the administration in an idealistic campaign to improve prison conditions which ultimately ended in the burning of Long Kesh. Concealed beneath it was a very different aspect of prison life:

> It was an atmosphere of absolute terror. The thing that was most sad about it was that we who were in charge of the jails either oversaw it all, took part in it or turned a blind eye to it. People, the bulk of them innocent and whose names were given by some other poor tortured fucker, were subjected to nothing less than Japanese style torture . . . They were beaten, held over heaters until they fainted, had their nipples locked in cigarette lighters and then twisted, made to turn round and round until they were sick and nauseous. They were forced to stand against walls in the search position for ages and were denied sleep. In one hut in Cage 10 some were allegedly made to drink from the slops bucket while others were thrown to their fellow prisoners, the latter enraged upon being told by the leaders that the unfortunates had blown up Catholic children on behalf of the MRF . . . All the tricks the Brits and Special Branch used against us in Palace Barracks we used. The mail, both outgoing and incoming, was not only read by the prison authorities but by the IRA as well. It is a sorry episode in our history and it needs to come out. The sanitised version of how we behaved in jails just does not tell the story. For fuck's sake men, republican prisoners, were cutting their fucking wrists to get away from us.[38]

Harassment of republicans by the leadership was at times so severe that one ex-prisoner said of one of his tormentors: 'Such a powerful figure that I would have shot him dead if I had met him on the outside'.[39]

As Ó Brádaigh and Bell learned, the IRA always feared any alternative to itself. Within the prison it was continuously at pains to undermine the INLA (Irish National Liberation Army) and later – although not to so great an extent – the IPLO (Irish People's Liberation Organisation). Always sensitive to the INLA, prisoners' claims to have every right to political status given that three of the ten dead hunger-strikers were members of the organisation, the Provisionals could never actually force them off the wings but did everything to undermine them. This ranged from poaching the group's members to restricting its policy-making input in the jail. A former INLA prisoner put it as follows:

> And we had the IRA day and daily coming out with what was like a big baton putting you down every time you opened your mouth. And at that time I had people who were sitting trying to get an education and the Provisional IRA were putting obstacles in your way to stop you educating yourself or throwing different wee things in your way.[40]

Some prisoners sought to attribute this to one power-hungry right-wing IRA leader who was central to running the prison for many years and functioned as a sort of kingmaker – reserving a particular hatred for prominent republican socialist prisoners Dominic McGlinchey and Gerard Steenson, presumably in case their high public profile and sense of notoriety threatened his authority. But the attempt to undermine the organisation was more structural in character and requires a deeper explanation than the appetite of any one power-monger. Essentially, it fitted into a much wider pattern of suppressing alternatives.

The League of Communist Republicans, founded by Tommy McKearney in 1986, which for the most part emerged from the ranks of the Provisionals claims to have feared for the safety of their members, arguing that they ultimately left the prison to escape the potential threat. McKearney, a life-sentence prisoner and member of the 1980 hunger strike team, spoke of an environment in which the leadership within the prison encouraged hostility and isolation in order to stamp out opposition to the line of the outside leadership in the wake of the decision to sit in the parliament of the Irish republic. This decision was reached both within the IRA and Sinn Féin without any consultation with the republican prisoner population. McKearney recalled:

> A few even talked of beating prisoners who disagreed with bed-ends. Critique was not viewed as comradely dissent but as hostility from disloyal or anti-republican elements. While no actual violence was used against us, it was rapidly becoming an environment where safety from attack from fellow republicans could no longer be taken for granted.[41]

The intolerant atmosphere that increased the likelihood of such attacks was enhanced when 'a message issued under full IRA authority was circulated in the prison describing those who formed the league as "counter-revolutionaries" and "people offering assistance to the enemy"'.[42] The term 'Contra' also became part of an official discourse of alienation exclusively employed by the IRA leadership within the prison against those who questioned the leadership. In the H-Blocks of Long Kesh the IRA leadership established a formidable network of 'spies' who would monitor the wings, report on what their fellow colleagues were doing and, in some cases, open personal communications between republican prisoners. In the view of one prisoner who spent more than a decade behind bars under the command of the IRA, the jail system 'was very repressive'.[43]

While in Magilligan prison in the mid-1970s, I became aware that escapes were available only to 'cleared' Volunteers. As the republican camp staff ensured that very few Volunteers had such clearance, this meant they determined who would escape if the opportunity arose. Those most opposed to the staff invariably populated the ranks of 'suspended' Volunteers. In the remand section of Crumlin Road prison, after the withdrawal of political status in 1976, an apartheid regime known as the 'back table' was instituted. IRA prisoners who broke under RUC interrogation – which the IRA at the time characterised as torture – were segregated by the IRA leadership from the so-called 'sound men' and were compelled to sit at tables at the back of the canteen. Lawrence McKeown described the measure:

> Those who had given information under interrogation such as names of others in the IRA or had revealed the whereabouts of arms dumps were made to sit at the back table in the canteen. Suddenly familiar faces who had sat beside me or across from me at meal times and whose backgrounds or cases I knew little or nothing about were physically positioned so as to let us all know that we should be wary of them. We were encouraged not to associate with them although that wasn't exactly an order. I felt totally confused at the time but my overriding thought was that I was very glad that I was not one to be put at the back table.[44]

Given the treatment meted out to IRA Volunteers by the prison leadership, one is forced to reflect on the psychological rather than the political reasons behind the decision by some prisoners to go on the arduous blanket protest. One former protester made the following point:

> I was personally broke by Castlereagh. And as well as being broken by the Special Branch and police you were broken again to a certain extent in the prison . . . because there is a very definite hierarchy in the prison . . . I felt myself I was in the very bottom league . . . and your own estimation of yourself is completely gone at that stage . . . the fact of going on the blanket protest was an attempt to prove to yourself again and to try to get your self-esteem back.[45]

Over the years the nature of repression within the prisons was refined from the overt and brutal to more subtle measures of control. Leo Green, while O/C of the republican prisoners in the H-Blocks, observed that the prison leadership should, like the government, govern through a mixture of consent and coercion but with the emphasis placed greatly on consent.[46] Manufacturing such consent became the dominant feature of control in prison life. But according to one former prisoner 'consent' was a very self-serving concept as far as the IRA leadership in the prison was concerned.

> The IRA leadership of the prison had too much interference in the personal lives of those under its control. The purpose was to mould a consensus within the prison that would only work to the benefit of a power clique, the staff. Opinion formers within republican wings would not tolerate any view contrary to their own. This related not only to wider political concerns but also to the way in which the prison was managed by the republican staff. People were accepted or rejected on

the basis of whether they agreed or disagreed with the people of influence in the prison. It was not coincidental that those with least influence and who were not on the camp staff were also those that were in disagreement with the staff on a range of issues. The staff used patronage as a means of winning support for their line or perspective. The end result was that the staff successfully used the consensus that they had established to marginalise detractors.[47]

POST-GOOD FRIDAY AGREEMENT REPUBLICANISM

The preceding narrative insists that the story needs to be told rather than claims to tell the full story. Control technologies were undoubtedly employed outside the prison in the years prior to the signing of the Good Friday Agreement. Ó Brádaigh, for example, refers to low-level harassment in Donegal, Cavan and Kerry where Republican Sinn Féin meetings were disrupted in a bid to prevent a new republican alternative emerging.[48] Moreover, there has been no discussion here of the Provisional purges against the Official republican movement or the IPLO which resulted in fatalities.

But it is instructive to look at the post-GFA period for two reasons. Firstly, it shows a link between republican technologies of control in the jails and those on the outside, permitting some insight into the manner in which a discourse of leadership can develop and establish for itself a regime of truth. Secondly, it facilitates a tentative exploration of the reasons behind the development of an internal totalitarian trend at a time when the externally directed discourse is democratic and postmodernist. While more contingent than causal, the two are, nevertheless, conjoined.

Outright coercion no longer forms such a key part of Provisional internal management, yet it has remained to the point where, as in other bodies, 'the *structure* of coercion and socialisation was so formidable that defiance could not simply be contemplated'.[49] There are other powerful ways to punish dissent. John Cleary said of Argentina: 'that's the trouble with a police state. You are trained to feel guilty, that it is wrong to speak out against the government.'[50] Brendan Hughes identified a similar phenomenon within republicanism, pointing to how the leadership played the loyalty card to make people feel guilty for waging critique.[51] He, too, would be subject to a whispering campaign and marginalisation by the republican movement. Despite having commanded the IRA's Belfast Brigade, escaped from Long Kesh and led the blanket protest and 1980 hunger strike, he was to find himself – along with three other former blanket prisoners – denied the right to speak at a meeting of students in Queen's University in 2000. A Sinn Féin councillor instructed the organisers to cancel the meeting rather than give a platform to people opposed to the party line.[52] As a result, Hughes argues that GFA stands for 'Got Feck All'.[53]

In spite of the GFA, the Provisional IRA leadership continue to police republicans who have difficulty accepting the very structures that they had fought and killed to destroy. In the words of Jack Holland:

> As a category, Enemy of the Peace Process goes back a few years. In October 2000, after the murder in West Belfast of Joe O'Connor, a member of the Real IRA, some people who dared to claim that the Provisional IRA was involved were denounced as Enemies of the Peace Process. They were also threatened. The Provisionals issued a statement which said: 'The malicious accusations suggesting IRA involvement are designed to promote the agenda of those opposed to the current IRA strategy' – the 'current strategy' being the Provisionals' commitment to the peace process . . . for the IRA to call them 'malicious' is to suggest that it is the allegations, not the murder, which are the danger.[54]

In the wake of the O'Connor killing, houses were picketed by Sinn Féin-led mobs and intimidation by the IRA occurred. Carrie Twomey, who managed an independent republican bulletin board, was visited by republican 'internet police' who informed her that her board had been under surveillance for almost two months and that she would be held to account for its contents. Heavily pregnant, and fearing for her safety, she closed the board.[55] O'Connor's extended family circle was subjected to a marginalisation campaign characterised by organised and systematic vilification.[56]

Elsewhere Marian Price, who served a life sentence for her part in the 1973 London bombings, was visited by the Provisional IRA leadership and told to keep her views on the GFA to herself.[57] The mechanisms of control and repression were geographically diffuse. After the Omagh bomb, the homes of Real IRA members or their supporters in the 32 County Sovereignty Committee were visited. They were given two weeks to disband under threat of violence if they refused.[58] After leaving a hotel in Monaghan, Tyrone republican Paddy Fox was kidnapped, beaten and held by the Provisional IRA. Fox's parents had previously been murdered by loyalists and he had served several years in prison as a member of the Provisional IRA.[59] A former Tyrone IRA Volunteer stated that a 'reign of terror' was exercised in the county to ensure that republicans took the leadership line and desisted from dissent.[60] Micky Donnelly, chairperson of Republican Sinn Féin's Ulster executive and a former internee, had his leg broken by the Derry Provisional IRA after he ignored warnings to desist from public criticism of the group.[61] The sole INLA representative on the 1980 hunger strike was confronted by the IRA in Armagh City after he stated his intention to contest local council elections. He was informed that if he stood for election the organisation would leave him without legs to stand on.[62]

Central to applying the technologies of control have been the many former prisoners who became key apparatchiks in the centralised republican bureaucracy after their release. According to one ex-prisoner: 'it is no coincidence that many of those involved in the process of control in the jail are now in positions of middle to upper leadership on the outside'.[63] The authoritarian traits they display in outside life 'as far as IRA structures and ways of controlling people go' were nurtured in the prison. He argues:

> Outside was a carbon copy of inside. I think Mo Mowlam's description of the way in which the British Labour Party is managed would fit as easily to the Republican Movement. A small group of people sit like a business consortium, never consult the workers and then send a directive down which they tell everyone is the consensus. And ultimately, as a lesson the leadership will always take out someone like Jo Jo O'Connor to let people know it is still in charge. And many former prisoners, secure in their new positions of authority, defend and promote anything the leadership regards as necessary.[64]

Within their communities these ex-prisoners occupy key roles as opinion formers and would, with the aid of the leadership, gravitate to the centres of community power. Quite often they can be found staffing the salaried bureaucracies at the heart of the community worker network, where they act as a powerful brake on the development of alternative ideas. Many who do not accept the leadership's version of events will testify to the nepotism and favouritism that is utilised in the selection process that leads to employment in the community group network. In one case, the former Maidstone escapee Tommy Gorman had his employment in an ex-prisoner group terminated because a leading member of the Sinn Féin backed ex-prisoners' group, Coisde na hIarr Cime, informed his manager that Gorman wrote articles critical of the peace process – the insinuation being that he was somehow aligned to the Real IRA.[65] This resonates heavily with John Waters's observation that 'the nomination of cronies to positions involving influence and fat salaries is an integral part of the political process'.[66] They find themselves in a situation like that of the Tunisian judges who, despite widespread abuses, 'were forced to be compliant for the sake of their careers'.[67]

Almost eight years since the beginning of the first IRA cessation in 1994 it seems that, rather than having gone away, the IRA sits as heavily in poorer nationalist areas as it did during the armed struggle. Henry Patterson has argued that 'the IRA continues as a para-state structure ruling over tens of thousands of Northern Irish nationalists'.[68] And since Mo Mowlam's ruling on the death of Charles Bennett in 1999 – that while he was legally dead he was somehow politically alive (merely to ensure that no determination could be made pronouncing the IRA ceasefire breached) – it is clear that the British government is prepared to allow para-state control to continue so long as its only victims are those who are subject to it.[69] Dublin has behaved likewise.

Both governments turn a self-interested blind eye to the violent policing of political dissent within nationalist areas in an act of obeisance to the peace process.

The real question is of course why republicanism – with its discourse of democracy, equality, liberation and anti-censorship – has regressed to such a reactionary point where, in the words of a Dublin politician, 'they hate those who disagree with them'?[70] According to Piven and Cloward, 'organisations endure by abandoning their oppositional politics'.[71] McAdam argues that within them a process of oligarchisation occurs which can lead to the creation of 'a certain class of individuals who come to value the maintenance of that organisation over the realisation of movement goals'.[72] And within Provisional republicanism those goals have been reduced to mere discursive objectives. The leadership of Provisional republicanism – realising that its demands were impossibilist – opted to accept an outcome that included republicans but excluded republicanism. This has translated itself in terms of acquiring the maximum amount of institutional bureaucratic and political power, north and south, rather than the goals the movement fought to attain.

Prior to the emergence of the Adams hegemony, the Provisional leadership could not impose rigid centralised control on the movement because of the looser structure of organised republicanism. This was largely due to the spontaneity that characterised much of earlier nationalist protest politics. The Provisional IRA did not create the northern conflict: the conflict created it. The old engine of pre-1969 republicanism found itself at the front of many new carriages. Apart from the old objectives of republican ideology, it was bereft of ideas where to bring them, seemingly opting to 'charge up the line as far as we get and see what is there when we stop'. But the leadership was in effect pushed by the insurrectionary groundswell that threw up the carriages in its trail: the command from the back was one of 'follow us we are right behind you'. Due to the existence of decentralised spontaneous insurrection rather than centrally controlled strategic force, republicanism of the early 1970s was relatively fragmented and localised. This allowed local figures to gain a form of national prominence without ever having to be part of the national leadership. Republican activists like Martin Meehan, Kevin Mallon, Martin McGuinness, Gerry Adams, Billy McKee, and Jim Bryson illustrate the point. At times they had greater public prominence than key national leaders such as O'Conaill, Ó Brádaigh and MacStiofain. In such circumstances it was difficult for centralised command to make its authority felt. This was nowhere more pronounced than in the circumstances surrounding the ending of the 1972 truce which the Belfast IRA agreed to terminate before they left London, despite MacStiofain, the chief of staff, wanting it to continue.[73]

It was not until the insurrectionary era had passed that centralisation became more pronounced and tighter measures of control implemented. This resulted from the development of a controlled 'long war' strategy and the ascendancy to national leadership of those most likely responsible for devising it – Gerry Adams and his coterie.[74] According to Tommy McKearney:

> In the early 1970s areas like Tyrone, South Armagh and Derry City had a measure of autonomy. The IRA was almost like a federation of local armies. It was never so localised that the Brigade O/C could go to Twomey, the chief of staff and tell him to 'get lost'. But the leadership was never so centralised that Seamus Twomey could afford to go to the local brigade O/C and tell him to get lost. Subsequently, there was no real mechanism that could completely stifle critique. Debate and dissent did exist along with local initiative and responsibility. In the past fifteen to twenty years we have witnessed a move away from that and very much to the centre. People are virtually afraid to speak out of place.[75]

There are those who are inclined to think that republicans merely operate within an authoritarian culture that is as old as the philosophy itself: what Giddens once termed 'the sedimented power of tradition'.[76] This is not only insensitive to the many ways in which Provisional republicanism was not a product of pre-1969 republicanism but rather a departure from it, but also ignores the ease with which other vestiges of the republican tradition have been unceremoniously usurped by new discourses which bear little resemblance to the traditional ideology. What is the psychological lure of maintaining, for the sake of tradition, authoritarianism in circumstances where tradition has been booted into touch unless that authoritarianism serves a specific and conjunctural function? And that function involves utilising the energy and sacrifice of a different struggle in pursuit of an entirely new project. The republican movement has, as Tommy Gorman observed, 'become much more internally repressive the further it moves away from traditional republicanism and supposedly towards democratic values'.[77] In order to internally blur the shift, the leadership has come to increasingly rely on what the American writer Tammy Bruce once described as a 'strategy for enforcing silence'.[78]

Many in the present Provisional leadership seem bereft of any moral compass, content to exist in an ideological vacuum, doing what is necessary to maximise the vote and increase power. Like the Fianna Fáil that Chubb described, an attitude of unquestioning support has 'led to an almost complete separation of roles between a few top leaders charged with policy making and their . . . followers, who have little or no part in policy making and have expected none'.[79] This point has been underlined by Sinn Féin councillor Tom Hartley, who – while complaining that Irish Protestants were democrats 'to their arse' – claimed that Adams could, 'like an archbishop', secretly negotiate the Good Friday Agreement assured that his party would support him without even knowing what it contained.[80] The unquestioning support, or 'loyalty' referred to by Brendan Hughes, is in the words of Chubb (who was describing Fianna Fáil), 'a loyalty to institutions and especially persons rather than ideas'.[81]

The discursive device employed to usurp the hegemony of ideas and replace them with people is a deified concept of leadership which in many ways has become the cult of leadership or a modern day 'Fuhrerprinzip'. It has been meticulously interwoven into a leadership discourse that seeks to rationalise, through an elitist prism, the exclusive right of leadership to make important decisions without reference to the grassroots. And it has been predicated on the totalitarian principle of refusing to accept that events might be outside leadership control. For a leadership 'obsessed with control' it was logical to deny the grassroots any effective forum to discuss strategic shifts.[82] The structures of communication were vertical rather than horizontal. Censorship, coupled with no small measure of self-censorship, ensured that there was not even the existence of a samizdat. This constituted a deliberate attempt on the part of leadership to atomise the grassroots so that the person with a differing view on the ground could be isolated all the easier. Or alternatively, in a Foucauldian sense, 'the web of discipline aims at generalising the homo docilus'.[83] Leadership has become a site of domination. Hence, it was essential to reject any Foucauldian notion whereby

> It is important to show people that they are much freer than they feel, that people accept as truth, as evidence, some themes which have been built up at a certain moment in history, and that this so called evidence can be criticised and destroyed.[84]

In its place was an appeal for the type of solidarity of which Adorno said 'can call on us to subordinate not only individual interests but even our better insight'.[85] Such total leadership control was illustrated in the 1994 ceasefire decision which was taken without any consultation with IRA Volunteers. The same happened with decommissioning. At one point Gerry Adams moved to claim that he felt the leadership had 'put itself dangerously far in front of its grassroots base'.[86] However, just prior to the Republic's general election he told *The Irish Times* that if Sinn Féin could win concessions on better housing, healthcare and social welfare it would 'go into a coalition'.[87] Yet, as far as we are aware, the special conference of the party has not yet sat which would decide on such matters

CONCLUSION

Commenting on the organised left in the USA, Tammy Bruce claimed that having attained cultural power 'it turned into a monster that found perpetual victimhood, combined with thought and speech control the most convenient way to hold onto that power'.[88] Likewise the Provisional leadership operating along similar lines enjoys the autonomy its strategy of enforced silence has created for it. Neither left nor right but increasingly authoritarian populist, it will take republicanism wherever the vote is. Like other protest groups that have become heavily dependent on outside 'elite' sponsorship it is a 'virtual chameleon changing tactics and programs to suit the whims of their sponsors and, in many cases, functioning as a cooptative mechanism for siphoning off movement leadership into more moderate, less disruptive reform efforts'.[89] It increasingly behaves like the Irish in America who, Chris McNickle said, 'understood politics as the means one group used to secure power for itself, to hold on to it and exploit it. Morality had nothing to do with it, nor did any grand ideology'.[90] There is no internal brake that can be applied to a leadership intent on securing more power and willing to dispense with every principle to facilitate its access to such power. On its journey it has forged a cohesive group out of relatively disparate forces and trampled dissent and critique underfoot.

Writers such as Ronan Bennett, uncomfortable with this type of analysis, have attempted to deflect criticism of the Adams leadership which would seek to depict it as fascist.[91] While correct in this, he falls short by failing to identify the authoritarian attitudes and activities that the Adams leadership has so assiduously cultivated. And, in a world increasingly susceptible to postmodernist influences where meaning is positional rather than fixed, if fascism is viewed not only as a historically and conjuncturally specific phenomenon the distinction becomes rather more meaningless. By straddling Raymond Aron's concept of 'peace impossible, war improbable', that leadership has crafted the freedom to manoeuvre its way forward in a manner which is both authoritarian and abusive.[92] From an internal perspective this is perhaps best illustrated by a comment from Erich Fromm:

> For all irrational and exploitative forms of authority, self-assertion – the pursuit by another of his real goals – is the arch sin because it is a threat to the power of the authority; the person subject to it is indoctrinated to believe that the aims of the authority are also his, and that obedience offers the optimal chance for fulfilling oneself.[93]

And, as Bruce reminds us, 'group dynamics and the decision to sacrifice the individual for the group are the first steps in the march down the road to . . . totalitarianism'.[94] And, at that point, the fascist/non-fascist argument of writers like Bennett becomes mere semantics.

Notes

1 Author's interview with former IRA Volunteer, South Belfast, Apr. 2002.

2 Author's interview with Tommy Gorman, Apr. 2002.

3 Author's interview with Ruairí Ó Brádaigh, May 2002.

4 L. Clarke, *Broadening The Battlefield* (Dublin, 1987), p. 229.

5 *The Scotsman*, 3 Nov. 2000.

6 L. Kennedy, *Crime and Punishment in West Belfast* (Belfast, 1995).

7 Michael Schwartz, quoted in D. McAdam (ed.), *Political Process and the Development of Black Insurgency, 1930–1970* (Chicago, London, 1985), p. 37.

8 *Newshound* (www.nuzhound.com), 2 May 2002.

9 Radio Free Éireann broadcast, 4 May 2002.

10 *The Irish Times*, 3 Aug. 2000.

11 Jack Holland, *Newshound*, 9 May 2002.

12 *The Blanket* (lark.phoblacht.net), 23 Apr. 2002.

13 *The Irish Times*, 13 Nov. 2001.

14 *The Irish Times*, 14 Feb. 2001.

15 *The Irish Times*, 12 Apr. 2002.

16 *Los Angeles Weekly*, 19–25 April 2002.

17 *The Irish Times*, 26 Apr. 2000.

18 E. Collins and M. McGovern, *Killing Rage* (London, 1997).

19 R. Eaglestone, *Postmodernism and Holocaust Denial* (Cambridge, 2001), p. 49

20 *The Irish Times*, 2 Oct. 1995.

21 *Irish Voice*, 25 Oct. 2000.

22 *Andersonstown News*, 22 May 2002.

23 Gayle Ruben, quoted in T. Spargo, *Foucault and Queer Theory* (Cambridge, 1999), pp. 5–6.

24 *The Irish Times*, 26 Aug. 1999.

25 A. McIntyre, 'A Structural Analysis of Modern Irish Republicanism 1969–1973', unpublished PhD thesis, Queen's University of Belfast, 1999, p. 42.

26 *Christian Science Monitor*, 17 May 2002.

27 *Daily Telegraph*, 3 Mar. 2000.

28 *The Independent*, 18 May 2002.

29 S. O'Callaghan, *The Informer* (London, 1998); Collins and McGovern, *Killing Rage*.

30 L. McKeown, *Out of Time* (Belfast, 2001); R. Jamieson and A. Grounds, *No Sense of an Ending* (Monaghan, 2002).

31 Author's conversation with Willie Gallagher.

32 C. Ryder, *Inside The Maze* (London, 2000), p. 127.

33 Ibid.

34 Ibid.

35 D. McKittrick, S. Kelters, B. Feeney and C. Thornton, *Lost Lives* (Edinburgh, 1999), p. 639.

36 Author's interview with former IRA Volunteer A, West Belfast, Apr. 2002; Author's interview with former IRA Volunteer B, West Belfast, Apr. 2002.

37 Author's interview with former republican internee, West Belfast, May 2002.

38 Author's interview with former republican remand prisoner, West Belfast, Feb. 2002; Author's interview with former republican remand prisoner, South Belfast, Mar. 2002.

39 Quoted in Jamieson, *No Sense*, p. 20.

40 Ibid.

41 Author's interview with Tommy McKearney, May 2002.

42 L. O'Ruairc, 'The League of Communist Republicans 1986–1991', MA thesis, Department of Politics, Queen's University of Belfast (2001), p. 5.

43 Author's interview with former republican sentenced prisoner, West Belfast, May 2002.

44 McKeown, *Out of Time*, p. 50.

45 Quoted in Jamieson, *No Sense*, p. 20.

46 Author's conversation with Leo Green.

47 Author's interview with former republican sentenced prisoner, West Belfast.

48 Author's interview with Ruairí Ó Brádaigh.

49 F. F. Piven and R. A. Cloward, *Poor People's Movements: Why They Succeed, How They Fail* (New York, 1979), p. 189 (my italics).

50 Quoted in T. P. Coogan, *Wherever Green is Worn* (London, 2000), p. 617.

51 *Fourthwrite*, Spring 2000.

52 Author's interview with Brendan Hughes, March 2002; *Sunday Business Post*, 21 May 2000.

53 *Other View*, Spring 2001.

54 *Newshound*, 2 May 2002.

55 Author's interview with Carrie Twomey, May 2002.

56 Author's interview with Charlotte Notarantonio, June 2002.

57 Author's interview with Marian Price, Apr. 2002.

58 *Parliamentary Brief*, Nov. 1998.

59 *Sunday Tribune*, 7 Feb. 1999.

60 Author's interview with former IRA volunteer, Tyrone, Apr. 2002.

61 *Saoirse*, Feb. 1999.

62 Author's interview with John Nixon, May 2002.

63 Author's interview with former republican sentenced prisoner, West Belfast.

64 Ibid.

65 Author's interview with Tommy Gorman.

66 *The Irish Times*, 11 Sept. 2000.

67 *The Irish Times*, 4 May 2002.

68 *Daily Telegraph*, 3 Sept. 1999.

69 *The Observer*, 2 Sept. 2001. Charles Bennett was killed by the IRA in 1999. Labelled by the republican grapevine as a low informer, his death posed problems for both Sinn Féin and the British Government as a result of unionist accusations that the IRA were breaking their ceasefire. Mowlam ultimately concluded that, while the IRA were responsible their ceasefire had not been broken, as a means to keep the negotiations on track and prevent the collapse of the peace process.

70 *The Irish Times*, 4 Apr. 2000.

71 Piven, *Poor People's Movements*, p. xxi.

72 McAdam, *Political Process*, p. 55.

73 McIntyre, 'Modern Irish Republicanism', p. 307

74 C. Keena, *A Biography of Gerry Adams* (Dublin, 1990), p. 77.

75 Author's interview with Tommy McKearney.

76 *The Observer*, 2 May 1999.

77 Author's interview with Tommy Gorman.

78 T. Bruce, *The New Thought Police* (California, 2001), p. 9.

79 B. Chubb, *The Government and Politics of Ireland* (Oxford, 1974), p. 56.

80 Tom Hartley, quoted in M. Juergensmeyer, *Terrorismo religioso. El auge global de la violencia religiosa* (Madrid, 2001), p. 43 (transl. Rogelio Alonso).

81 Chubb, *Government and Politics*, pp. 55–6.

82 L. Shriver, 'The Irish connection', *Jerusalem Post* (www.jpost.com), 9 May 2000.

83 J. Mequoir, *Foucault* (London, 1991), p. 94

84 P. Dews, 'The return of the subject in late Foucault', *Radical Philosophy* 51 (Spring 1989), pp. 37–41.

85 T. W. Adorno, 'Messages in a bottle', in Slavoj Zizek (ed.), *Mapping Ideology* (London, 1994), p. 43.

86 *Reuters Ltd*, 29 Nov. 2001.

87 *The Irish Times*, 30 Apr. 2002.

88 Bruce, *Thought Police*, p. xii.

89 J. C. Jenkins, quoted in McAdam, *Political Process*, p. 28.

90 Quoted in Coogan, *Wherever Green*, p. 275.

91 R. Bennett, 'Divided by the same language', *Index On Censorship* 3 (1997), pp. 25–9.

92 *The Sunday Times*, 6 May 2001.

93 E. Fromm, *The Anatomy of Human Destructiveness* (Middlesex, 1977), p. 264.

94 T. Bruce, *Thought Police*, p. 46.

Index

* * *